THE SPLENDOUR THAT WAS EGYPT

Gold and jewelled coffin of Tut-ankh-Amon,
Dynasty xviii

From a painting by Winifred M. Brunton

The
Splendour that was
EGYPT

MARGARET A. MURRAY

New and Revised Edition

SIDGWICK AND JACKSON LIMITED
LONDON

First published 1949
Second Impression 1949
Third Impression 1950
Fourth Impression 1951
Fifth Impression 1954
Sixth Impression 1957
Seventh Impression 1959
Eighth Impression 1961
Revised (and reset) Edition 1964

PRINTED IN GREAT BRITAIN BY THE WHITEFRIARS PRESS LTD.
LONDON AND TONBRIDGE

TO THE MEMORY OF
FLINDERS PETRIE
WHO OUT OF THE HOBBY OF ANTIQUARIANISM
CREATED THE SCIENCE OF
ARCHÆOLOGY

CONTENTS

LIST OF ILLUSTRATIONS

Gold Coffin of Tut-ankh-Amon   *frontispiece*

LINE DRAWINGS IN THE TEXT

PREFACE

The difficulty of writing a book of this kind is the mass of available material which confronts the author. Each section could have been amplified so as to fill several volumes; therefore my sins of omission must inevitably loom very large. I have, however, been guided in my choice by experience of what I have found to interest my students and my general audiences to whom this book is chiefly addressed.

Another difficulty which arises is the spelling of Egyptian names. I have followed the line of least resistance in spelling the names in the conventional way, with the one exception of Setekhy. The name of the god, which is usually spelt Set or Seth, should be pronounced as two syllables with a guttural at the end. As the spelling Seth does not express this to English readers, I have called the god Setekh; and the derivative names are therefore Setekhy and Setekh-nekht, instead of Sethy and Seth-nekht.

My grateful thanks are due to Mrs. Winifred Brunton for the painting of the gold coffin of Tut-ankh-Amon, to Mrs. Violet Pritchard for the painting of the jewellery, to Dr. Stephen Pritchard and to Captain M. M. Barker for photographs, to Miss Myrtle Broome for the drawings of the hieroglyphs on pp. 8 and 197, to Lt.-Col. J. S. Yule for reading the proofs, and to the authorities and staffs of the Fitzwilliam Museum and of the Museum of Archæology and Ethnology in Cambridge for the facilities and help so kindly and cordially given.

M. A. MURRAY

INTRODUCTION

Egypt is the one country that has been most carefully explored by modern expert archæologists. In this survey I have tried to give to the general reader some account of the achievement of that great civilisation and to help him to realise the importance of Egyptology in that study of the Past which is now called Archæology, and which, when viewed as a whole, is seen as the study of the Advance of Man, mentally and therefore spiritually. The aim of the true Archæologist is expressed in the well-known lines, "The noblest work of God is Man", and "The proper study of mankind is Man". Human life is too short for a serious study of more than one small portion of world archæology. But one can study one small nation and trace it through the vicissitudes of its advance in civilisation until it is overwhelmed by a higher culture or obliterated by an invasion of barbarism. Every part of the habitable world, every tribe or nation, however small or poor, may produce more important evidence of this Advance of the human mind than any of the great finds of gold and precious stones which serve only to show the wealth of the country at the time, and to dazzle the eyes of visitors to Museums. But a blast-furnace for the smelting of metal dated to the ii-nd dynasty has had more effect on the advance of civilisation than all the wealth of the Treasures of Lahun or of Tut-ankh-Amon. For the principle on which this primitive blast-furnace was founded is the same on which every blast-furnace ever since is founded. Though used at first for smelting copper, the mixture of metals now called "bronze" soon came into such common use that its name has been given to a definite archæological period. When iron superseded copper in the use of tools and weapons, there was a great advance in material culture and the standard of living showing the advance in mental capacity.

As the mental capacity increases religion must keep pace with the developing mind, though the material representing the Deity may remain the theory of the Divine Power must change. This is seen in the inscription so ably translated by the well-known American Egyptologist J. H. Breasted.★ This one inscription is a landmark in the development of religion, for though the date of the inscription is about eleven hundred years before Christ, it has affected every sect and

★ *Development of Religion and Thought.*

form of Christianity. No one else appears to have attempted to study the deep underlying meaning of the religious inscriptions and writings of the ancient Egyptians and their contemporaries. For these religions show the soul of the people as clearly as the excavated objects show the material culture. Modern scholars are apparently concerned only with exact word-for-word translation; the results are that even hymns and prayers are terrifyingly bald and soulless but "scholarly".

For every student of our modern civilisation Egypt is the great storehouse from which to obtain information, for within the narrow limits of that country are preserved the origins of most (perhaps all) of our knowledge. In Egypt are found the first beginnings of material culture—building, agriculture, horticulture, clothing (even cooking as an art); the beginnings of the sciences—physics, astronomy, medicine, engineering; the beginnings of the imponderables—law, government, religion. In every aspect of life Egypt has influenced Europe, and though the centuries may have modified the custom or idea, the origin is clearly visible. Centuries before Ptolemy Philadelphus founded his great temple of the Muses at Alexandria, Egypt was to the Greek the embodiment of all wisdom and knowledge. In their generous enthusiasm the Greeks continually recorded that opinion; and by their writings they passed on to later generations that wisdom of the Egyptians which they had learnt orally from the learned men of the Nile Valley.

Egypt always held a unique position among the ancient civilisations of the world. Geographically she was in touch with three continents, Europe and Asia were on her threshold, and she herself was situated in Africa. Contact with so many peoples, differing from one another in culture and mentality, had great effect on her own civilisation and was part of the secret of her own greatness.

The Nile Valley appears to have been unfit for human habitation during the Stone Ages; it was only when the Nile had ceased to be a raging torrent and had deposited sufficient alluvium to allow of agriculture that settlers from the Libyan steppe drifted in. These brought with them the knowledge of pottery and agriculture, showing that though not necessarily far advanced they had already possessed the rudiments of civilisation. There is proof also that they were in contact with foreign countries, for they were importing metal and other products not obtainable in the Valley of the Nile.

It is to her dry climate and her dry soil that Egypt owes the preservation of the material that makes it possible to trace the course of her development from the barbarism of the remote past to the full flower of civilisation and then to its decay. No other country has given so rich a harvest to the archæologist, nor can any other country show such splendour of material, such beauty of technical skill, and such power of artistic expression, extended over so long a period.

Egypt was the supreme power in the Mediterranean area during the whole of the Bronze Age and a great part of the Iron Age; and as our present culture is directly due to the Mediterranean civilisation of the Bronze Age it follows that it has its roots in ancient Egypt. It is to Egypt that we owe our divisions of time; the twelve months and the three hundred and sixty-five days of the year; the twelve hours of the day and the twelve hours of the night are due to the work of the Egyptian astronomers. The earliest clocks, the clepsydræ, were the invention of Egyptian physicists. The earliest known intelligible writing is the Egyptian, so also are the earliest recorded historical events. It is due to the passion of the Egyptians for making records that so much has been preserved of their history and their literature, of their religious beliefs and their religious ritual. This passion for writing made them invent the first actual writing materials —pens, ink, paper—materials which could be packed in a small compass, were light to carry, and easy to use.

The splendour of Egypt was not a mere mushroom growth lasting but a few hundred years. Where Greece and Rome can count their supremacy by the century Egypt counts hers by the millennium, and the remains of that splendour can even now eclipse the remains of any other country in the world. According to the Greeks there were Seven Wonders of the World; these were the Pyramids of Egypt, the Hanging Gardens of Babylon, the statue of Zeus at Olympia, the Temple of Diana at Ephesus, the Tomb of Mausolus, the Colossus of Rhodes, and the Lighthouse of Alexandria. Of all these great and splendid works, what remains to the present day? Babylon and its gardens are a heap of rubble, as ruined as a bombed city; the statue of Zeus was destroyed long ago; the Temple of Diana is utterly demolished, leaving only a few foundations; fragments of the Mausoleum are preserved in museums where they are a source of interest to experts only; the Colossus of Rhodes survives only in legend, so completely has it disappeared; the Lighthouse of Alexandria has perished almost without trace. Of the Seven Wonders the Pyramids of Egypt alone remain almost intact, they still tower above the desert sands, dominating the scene, defying the destroying hand of Time and the still more destructive hand of Man. They line the western shore of the Nile for more than a hundred miles, and are the most stupendous and impressive as they are the most ancient of all the great buildings in the world.

The temples of Egypt still stand as a witness to that firm belief in God which can be traced back to the most primitive inhabitants of the

Nile Valley. At Luxor the worship of the Almighty Creator has continued without a break for thirty-five centuries on the same spot. The name by which the Deity was known has changed with the passing of time; but whether known as Amon, Christ, or Allah, the feeling that prompts the worship of God is unchanged and the place is as sacred now as it was fifteen hundred years before Christ.

Though the outward aspects of human life may alter with the passage of the centuries, the essentials remain the same. It is only the outward life that varies, for the human being still requires food and shelter for his material needs, affection and beliefs for his spiritual cravings. The family is still the unit, the mating of the sexes still continues and children are brought into the world, life and death still walk hand-in-hand, the changes and chances of this mortal life are still as uncertain as ever they were. And "while the earth remains, seed-time and harvest, cold and heat, summer and winter, day and night, shall not cease".

The past is understandable only by realising how closely it resembles the present, for then it is possible to differentiate the essential factors from the non-essential, the permanent from the transitory, and to mark the effect of climate and natural conditions on customs and beliefs. The form which religion takes is largely influenced by the climate of the country in which the ritual is performed. In Egypt, where agriculture does not depend on rain and the water supply comes from one source only—the river—there is but one Water-god, the Nile itself. Setekh is certainly a storm-god, but it is in his aspect as the controller of the thunder that he was regarded, not as the giver of rain. This is very different from those countries where rain is an essential for the production of food. Even in Palestine, the nearest land geographically to Egypt, the deity was the rain-giver, who "doeth marvellous things without number, who giveth rain upon the earth, and sendeth water upon the fields".* And in time of drought he could be induced to send rain by calling his attention to the magnificent temple which Solomon had built in his honour.† In Egypt the sun is a destructive agent, in northern climates it is the beneficent giver of food and warmth. Yet the feeling which prompted the worship, the utter dependence of Man for the barest necessities of life on powers that he could not control, was the same, whether he prayed to the Water-god or to the Sun-god. But the ritual of the worship will be different, and in many cases the ritual will often effect a change in the legend which

---

* Job v. 10.

† "When heaven is shut up and there is no rain, because they sinned against thee; if they pray toward this place . . . then hear thou in heaven, and forgive the sin of thy servants, and give rain upon thy land." (1 Kings viii. 35, 36.)

originally explained the rite. This is one of the most interesting fields of study.

In those elements of the mind and spirit which constitute civilisation the Egyptians were in advance of their contemporaries. Their ethical standards were high; and though like all other nations on the face of the earth they did not always attain to the standard set, at least their actions showed that they lived up to their ideal more consistently than their neighbours and contemporaries, and even those peoples who came after them whom one would therefore expect to be more civilised. It is only necessary to compare the behaviour of the Egyptians to the tribes whom they conquered in Palestine with the action of the invading Israelites to the same peoples; or with the savagery of the Assyrians who, like the Israelites, spared neither age nor sex in their conquests.

In certain aspects of knowledge the Egyptians surpassed most of the nations of ancient times. They were famous for their medical knowledge, for their skill in divination and the interpretation of dreams by which they could declare the will of God; their acquaintance with geography makes the Greeks look like ignorant barbarians; they were "the first who introduced the names of the twelve gods, and the Greeks borrowed their names from them; they were the first to assign altars, images, and temples to the gods, and to carve the figures of animals on stone".* They were the first to undertake large engineering works, and the first to erect large buildings in stone. In almost every aspect of human life Egypt is found to have made the earliest advance towards civilisation and to have reached a high standard in that subject. The wisdom of the Egyptians became proverbial both in ancient and in modern times.

Even with our present limited knowledge of the ancient world it can be seen that every country bordering on the Mediterranean owes a debt to Egypt; but as our knowledge increases it will be found that countries farther field, such as Russia, Persia, Arabia, and perhaps even India and China, were in contact with the greatest civilisation of the ancient world. Trade relations were certainly continuous from the earliest times, for foreign goods are among the remains of the prehistoric inhabitants of the Nile Valley as well as in every period throughout the whole of the long history of Egypt. One of the most important, as it is one of the most fascinating, pieces of research in an almost untouched field is to trace the sources of the foreign objects found in the town-sites and tombs of Egypt. With this must also go the research into the trade-routes by which those objects were brought

* Herodotus, ii. 4.

to Egypt. The mysterious Land of Punt,* or Land of God as it was sometimes called, is usually dismissed as being vaguely "somewhere on the Red Sea"; but if, as I suppose, Punt was a generic word for "trading station", then the field of inquiry is greatly enlarged and may extend to all the ports of the Indian Ocean, not only to the Red Sea. If Punt merely means a trading port no matter where situated, the variety of costumes worn by the Puntites and the very miscellaneous objects which are said to have come from Punt are explained. The type of the men of Punt, as depicted by Hatshepsut's artists, suggests an Asiatic rather than an African race; and the sweet-smelling woods point to India as the land of their origin. A voyage from Egypt to India by coasting vessels would be quite feasible, and undoubtedly ports for the Indian trade existed along the south coast of Arabia.   Coastwise trade has been in use ever since Man ventured on the water in a boat, and the Arabs have always been daring and accomplished sailors.

For the archæologist Egypt is a vast treasure-house. The dry climate and the sand have preserved objects and materials which have perished long since in moister climates.   In Egypt are found organic materials, such as cloth, wood, leather, rope, and even flowers, from the remotest past.

The greater part of our knowledge is due to the custom of burying objects of daily life with the dead. This was a common custom in all countries, including our own; yet we know less of the daily life of our pagan ancestors of fifteen hundred years ago than we do of the Egyptians who lived fifteen hundred years before Christ. An excavation in Egypt scientifically conducted will often yield a complete picture of the lives of the people of that period. To the archæologist the objects which he finds in the course of his excavations or which he studies in museums are of little value in themselves, they are merely the means by which he arrives at a knowledge of the past. Statues of bronze or marble, treasures of gold and precious stones, pompous inscriptions of the deeds of kings, conventional hymns or prayers to the gods, are not necessarily important in understanding the soul of a people.   Over and over again some small object from an artisan's dwelling, a child's toy (pl. xxix. 1), a piece of work from a woman's hand, will illuminate the past with a vividness denied to a statue, a jewel, or an inscription.

No archæologist is well equipped for his work unless he has some knowledge of the modern science of Anthropology, for both

* The root of the word is Pwn, the T being the usual feminine ending for a foreign country. Is this a word of some primitive language meaning "sea-shore, littoral", and is it the origin of "Phœnician", the coast people of Palestine, and "Punic" the littoral of North Africa?

Archæology and Anthropology are the study of Man. The only difference is that the anthropologist studies Man in the present, the archæologist studies Man in the past. But no anthropologist can afford to ignore the past, for tradition plays a large part in the culture of every country, and every archæologist should know and understand the people of the country where he works or he will fail to interpret his finds. Both should know the field in which they work in all seasons, in heat or cold, in wet or dry, for then only will they be saved from making egregious mistakes. How can anyone understand Egypt who has seen it only in the tourist season, when the fields are green with clover or yellow with ripe grain? But let such a person stay through the summer, and see those same fields parched and burnt under a pitiless sun, with dust-devils driving across the arid surface and the muddy yellow river giving an almost sinister aspect to the scene; then see the country again with water across the whole land making vast lakes, and the dark-red river running bank-high; then the sinking of the flood and the sudden and almost incredibly swift burst of verdure. When one has experienced the summer's heat in upper Egypt where the thermometer never falls below 105° during the twenty-four hours, and the first rays of the rising sun strike like the flame from a furnace, then and then only can one understand that the sun was to the populace of Egypt an inimical power, that "the evil days of summer" was not merely a picturesque phrase, that "the sweet breezes of the North Wind" should have been desired with so ardent a longing, and that to give water to the thirsty was accounted among the most charitable of all actions.

I have divided my subject into seven sections. The Prehistory is perhaps more important in Egypt than elsewhere, for the social structure and much of the religion can be seen there only a little less clearly than in the historic periods. The History of Egypt, *i.e.* the period for which there is documentary evidence, can be traced to a more remote era than in any other country which has yet been excavated. The details of certain periods are often so fully and precisely recorded that a consecutive history can be worked out with more exactness than the history of the Heptarchy. The Social Conditions are peculiarly interesting, for Egypt made many experiments which have been repeated in later times and other lands, with varying success and failure. The Ptolemaic experiment of complete control by the State has a special topical interest. So much has been written on the Religion of Egypt that the subject has become somewhat stale. So many volumes have been published on the gods, on the burial customs, on mummification, on the beliefs of the Hereafter, on the temple ritual, on Sun worship, that the general idea of the ancient Egyptians

is of a people engrossed in religion, spending half their lives in worshipping their very queer gods and the other half in preparing for death.
Yet it is not impossible that five thousand years hence all that will
survive of our own material civilisation will be the stone buildings and
stone objects, churches and tombstones, which will give to the exca-
vators of that remote future the same erroneous idea of us as people
that we have of the ancient Egyptians. I have tried, however, to show
the Egyptian religion as it must have appeared to those who believed
and practised it, and have recorded, as far as I can, any survivals of
those ancient practices and beliefs. The Art of Egypt has also attracted
great attention, for statues, and especially bronzes, have always been
regarded by the "antiquarian" collector as being the only objects of
the Past worth studying. That phase is passing, but there are still
people who think that a figure must necessarily be regarded as Art
if it is cast in bronze. Museums and private collections of Egyptian
objects are full of bronze statuettes, of which ninety per cent have no
artistic merit whatever though interesting archæologically. The Art
of Egypt should not be judged by the bronze figures only, for it is
certain that the austere lines and the dignity of Egyptian statues has
had great effect on the Art of the West. The days are past when Byron
could write to a friend that he had been sitting for an hour gazing at the
Venus de Medici and had come away "drunk with beauty". Egypt
was the Home-land of Science as we know it; it was passed on to the
Greeks who recorded it in writing and so gave it to the world. The
monumental script* of the ancient Egyptians was a source of amaze-
ment to the Greeks, who saw in it something mystic and awe-
inspiring; they named the figures *Hieroglyphs*, "sacred signs". It is
the most decorative script ever invented, even the ornamental Arabic
cannot compare with it. Hieratic, which was the running hand, can
also be effective, but it was for use and not ornament. It was in
hieratic that most of the literature was written. The Literature has
suffered, as all literature does, from translation. Most translators are
desirous of giving the exactly equivalent words and keeping as much
as possible to the alien construction of sentences, whereby the translation becomes stiff and often uninteresting. I have perhaps erred in
the opposite direction by translating Egyptian poems into English
verse. But I claim that it is the only way in which ancient poems can
be made understandable to the modern reader.

* See pp. 196-198 for transliteration of the signs.

THE SPLENDOUR THAT WAS EGYPT

I

PREHISTORY

THE prehistory of Egypt is divided into five periods, known as (1) Tasian, (2) Badarian, (3) Amratean, (4) Gerzean, (5) Semainian; the names being taken from the villages near which the principal finds were first identified.

The sequence of the periods was first worked out by Flinders Petrie from the Amratean and Gerzean pottery, which at that time was the only prehistoric Egyptian pottery known. He evolved a system of "Sequence-dating", which has now become one of the recognised methods of archæology. By using an arbitrary system of numbers, beginning at 30 and ending at 80, he was able to place the different shapes of pottery in their correct sequences; the earlier vessels having the lower numbers. Thus a pot of Sequence-dating 35 is earlier than one of s.d. 38, one of s.d. 52 is later than one of s.d. 47. For this early period dating by years is impossible, the sequence only can be indicated.* With the pottery once in order the other objects found in the excavations could also be placed in their right sequence. It then became clear that there was a marked division at about s.d. 40, when new types of vases in pottery and stone were rapidly ousting the old types, and by s.d. 42 the old types had disappeared. The complete change suggests an armed invasion with practical extermination or enslavement of the indigenous population.

The position of the *Tasian* culture is still uncertain. It may be of an earlier period than the Badarian, or it may be a different culture contemporary with the Badarian. Until further evidence is found, no definite pronouncement as to its position with regard to the Badarian can be made. The pottery of the Tasian people shows that they were already well advanced in the art of pottery-making, though it was not so fine and sophisticated as that of the Badarians. No metal has been found on Tasian sites. It would seem from this fact that this culture belongs to the Neolithic Age. But as "negative evidence is no evidence", the Tasian has—in our present state of knowledge—to give way to the Badarian, which takes pride of place as the earliest known culture in Egypt.

When the *Badarian* culture was discovered, it was found to precede the Amratean. There was, however, no break between the two

* For the full dexcription of the method of Sequence-dating, see Petrie, *Diospolis Parva*, pp. 4–12.

cultures; the Amratean followed the Badarian smoothly. This shows a peaceful change, due partly to increasing knowledge, partly to foreign contacts, and partly possibly to peaceful penetration by a more highly civilised people. The rather stocky Badarian (pl. iv. 1, 2) was replaced by the tall and slender Amratean (pl. i. 2); the shapes of the pottery altered, owing perhaps to different methods of cooking or keeping food; foreign contacts were more frequent, and foreign imports were not only larger in quantity but more varied in kind.

The most important of these foreign materials was metal. The Badarians already knew copper, but the use they made of it was very slight, though their tiny crucibles show that they understood how to melt the metal, but the Amrateans were able to make tools, notably chisels, of copper. This was a great advance, and shows that the Amrateans had reached a higher state of civilisation than their predecessors in the Nile Valley.*

Another interesting foreign import was the foreign pottery which occurs in both periods. This pottery is made of a clay totally unknown in Egypt; the shapes and the decoration are also un-Egyptian both in the prehistoric and historic periods. Pottery is always the last thing to be carried in trade, for by its nature it is bulky, heavy, and fragile, and therefore not easily transported. This suggests that it was carried by water, and would indicate a sea-borne trade of sufficient volume to make it worth while to risk the danger of breakage and loss of the contents of the pots. It would appear then that even at this early period there were other civilisations as advanced as the Badarian and Amratean with whom the inhabitants of the Nile Valley were in contact.

So much work has been done on the Badarians that is possible to have a clear view of their culture. They were in the Chalcolithic Age, when metal was known but tools were still made of stone; they were farmers, growing wheat and barley, and keeping domestic animals. Their food consisted of bread or porridge, varied by fish caught in nets and traps (no fish-hooks have been found), with an occasional feast of meat after a sacrifice. They dressed in woven linen with an outer garment of fur or leather in cold weather. Their dwelling-places were probably mere huts with walls of wattle and daub and roofs of thatch; sufficient in a rainless country as a shelter against sun and wind. Their artistic sense was not highly developed, but their technical skill, as shown in their ivory carvings and glazed stone, was surprisingly great. Their burial customs indicate a belief in a survival after death for objects of use and ornament were placed in the graves, and the

* The earliest known blast-furnace for smelting metals was found far south in the Nile Valley. It is dated to the ii-nd dynasty.

corpse was laid facing the west. This, as the cemetery lay to the east of the village, suggests the belief that the dead could watch the living and take part in, or at least know of, all happenings there. In short, the Badarians of prehistoric Egypt were little, if at all, removed in civilisation from many tribes now to be found in Africa and the Pacific Islands.

The *Amratean* culture, though derived from the Badarian, shows a great advance. Not only had the use of metal increased, but the artistic sense was more highly developed and the standard of living was higher.

The Amratean pottery was the direct outcome of the Badarian. As pottery it was not so good as the Badarian, but the shapes were no longer the squat, rather clumsy forms which the Badarian potter produced. On the contrary, the beautiful proportions, fine curves, and careful finish show how much the Amratean had advanced in artistic feeling beyond his predecessor. The pottery also shows that there was a certain amount of luxury trade, for the potters produced many fancy forms; double vases, square vases, vases in the form of birds and fish (pl. iv. 5, 8), vases with long necks, and so on. In the decoration of the pottery the Amratean differed from the Badarian. Instead of rippling the surface of the vessel like the Badarian, the Amratean preferred a smooth surface on which he applied a slip decoration. The chief motifs were geometrical forms, usually triangles, filled in with criss-cross lines suggesting a basket-work origin; but figures of animals were also popular (pl. iv. 12).

Throughout the whole of the prehistoric period slate palettes were in common use (pls. i. 1; iv. 4, 6). These were used for grinding malachite to powder; the power was then mixed with water and applied to the eyes as a protection against the glare of the sun and as a preventive of eye-diseases. In Badarian times the slates were roughly made, but the Amratean with his keen artistic sense made them in the form of birds, hippopotami, fish, and antelopes. These slates with traces of malachite on them are found in the tombs, and with them are often small bags of roughly crushed malachite and the smooth pebbles with which the grinding was done.

The ivory, of which there is a surprising amount in the Amratean period, is often hippopotamus tusk, but there is a considerable quantity of elephant ivory as well. This last must have been imported as the elephant does not seem to have ventured farther north than the first cataract. The ivory statuettes show that there were two races; one is a tall slender figure, usually nude, the other is short with a pointed beard and wrapped in a cloak (pl. iv. 3). Short tusks carved to represent an object wrapped in a strip of cloth are common; these seem to have had some kind of magical meaning, for when found *in situ* they were stitched on leather and attached to the forearm (pl. iv. 7). Throughout this period ivory was in great request for personal objects, such as combs and hairpins; these were carved with figures of birds and animals. The combs had long teeth, and were clearly for holding up long hair, not for combing it.

In flint-working the Amrateans excelled all the flint-workers of the world. The Badarians had also been flint-workers, but theirs was a core-industry produced from rough nodules picked up on the surface. The Amrateans obtained their flint from the beds in the cliffs which border the Nile Valley, and they used that beautiful material with unsurpassed skill. The ripple-chipped knives were too fragile for ordinary use; they have a rounded butt and the point turns backwards in a fine curve. The blade was first bevelled on both edges and ground quite smooth on both faces; at that stage it was a serviceable tool for the use for which it was required. The rippling was done on one face only and was purely for ornament; it consists of evenly spaced parallel grooves running diagonally across the face of the blade; the triangular spaces between the grooves at the edges of the blade are filled in with minute chipping (pl. lxxxvi. 1). Such a knife could have been intended for some special purpose only, such as cutting the throat of a sacrificial victim or performing the ritual ceremony of circumcision.★ The fish-tail lance with delicately serrated edge has a curious history. This also was a ritual implement. It survived into historic times, but when metal displaced flint the shape was gradually altered and it became an instrument of such magical power that in the highly developed and sophisticated burial ritual of the New Kingdom it was, under the name of *peshes-kaf*, the chief implement in the ceremony of the *Opening of the Mouth*.

It is a curious fact that while the Amratean potters produced shapes which are a delight to the eye, and the makers of slate palettes succeeded in giving a sense of life and vivacity to flat pieces of slate, and the flint-workers are still unrivalled, the Amratean makers of stone vases were failures. The shapes of the stone vases are coarse and clumsy, the walls of the vases surprisingly thick, and the workmanship is poor (pls. ii. 3, 4; iv. 13). The stones were all local; basalt, limestone, and alabaster. The basalt and limestone vases often end in a foot, which, in the early forms, was large enough to support the long, narrow and rather top-heavy vase. The gradual degradation of the foot to a vestigial button-like excrescence with a convex surface gives an indication of the position of any vase in the sequence.

★ Flint was still the correct material for circumcising as late as the times of Moses and Joshua. (Exod. iv. 25; Joshua v. 2, 3.)

In viewing the Amratean period as a whole, it is seen that there was an influx of a new and virile culture entering the Nile Valley, a culture not necessarily hostile to the earlier peoples, for much of the old Badarian culture survived. The best period of the Amratean culture was from S.D. 31 to S.D. 34. At this time the art and technical skill were at their highest, but towards the end of the period there were many signs of decadence.

Amratean houses have not survived, but as sun-dried bricks have been found it seems that some of the houses were brick-built and not mere reed-and-thatch hovels. Trade was carried on vigorously, and the Amrateans developed a system of owners' marks which were continued into the Gerzean period, and were perhaps the precursors of the hieroglyphic system of writing.

The Amrateans were apparently a peaceful people, for their weapons were few and inadequate. Arrows are found but no bows; their most powerful weapon was a stone mace head which, being disc-shaped, depended for its efficacy on its cutting edge and not on its weight (pls. ii. 1; iv. 10). Judged by the size the harpoons could have been used only for spearing fish.

In appearance the Amratean was tall and slender, long-haired and clean-shaven. The women wore linen or woven grass skirts and were freely tatooed. Both sexes painted the eyes with green malachite; their personal ornaments were tortoiseshell or ivory bracelets and finger-rings, and they wore strings of stone and shell beads and amulets round their necks.

A belief in a future life is shown by the objects of use and ornament which were laid in the grave with the dead; but at the same time there appears to have been some form of ceremonial cannibalism. Nothing is known with any certainty as to the deities, but it would seem that the bull, the hippopotamus, and the crocodile were worshipped, for amulets in the form of these animals are found, and in historic times all the three animals were regarded as divine.

I have already pointed out that at S.D. 40 a great change is found in almost all the objects, showing the introduction of a new type of civilisation. I have suggested that the change was due to a hostile invasion, and this suggestion becomes a certainty when the change in the type of weapons is seen. In all warfare there is but one main idea, so to strike your enemy as to prevent his striking you. In primitive hand-to-hand fighting the man who had the heavier weapon could kill or at least stun his enemy with one blow would be the victor over a more lightly armed man. This was certainly the case with the Gerzean. The Amratean mace (see pl. ii. 1) was quite effective if the blow fell exactly in the right place, breaking the skull or cutting an artery, but the Gerzean was armed with a greatly superior weapon. Instead of being disc-shaped with a cutting edge, it was a solid pear-shaped object, hafted like the Amratean on horn or hippopotamus hide (pls. ii. 2; iv. 11), and by one blow could kill the enemy or stun him or break his arm and so render him helpless. The Gerzean mace head is a truly formidable weapon. When the two weapons are compared it will be seen that the Amratean, however brave, could never make any real resistance against the Gerzean. The Gerzean mace head was so invariably made of white limestone that the picture of it, hafted and with a leather loop for securing it to the owner's wrist, became in historic times the hieroglyph for the word *white*, and then with a transferred meaning for the words *light* or *bright* (pl. xcvi. 6).

Besides introducing new shapes (pl. iv. 9) the *Gerzean* invader appears to have revolutionised the making of pottery, especially in the matter of firing. Fuel has always been a difficulty in Egypt, which perhaps accounts for the bad firing of Badarian and Amratean pottery. It is possible, therefore, that the Gerzean had an improved type of kiln, which could produce a higher temperature and retain it longer than the Amratean, which was probably made in a hole in the ground. The Gerzean kiln may well have been an open-air affair so built as to give a draught through the furnace. The picture of such a kiln became a hieroglyph in historic times (pl. xcvi. 8). Gerzean pottery is perhaps the finest of all the prehistoric Egyptian pottery in material, texture, form, manufacture, and colour. The clay is well levigated, the firing is perfect, there is not a trace of black in the substance of the clay, the colour being buff right through. The decoration was by painting in manganese on the surface of the vessel before firing. The brush used was undoubtedly a slip of reed with the fibres teased out at the end, such as Egyptian scribes used in the Pharaonic periods. Not only are the brush-marks visible, but it is possible to see where the painter has started with a full brush and continued a line till the paint gave out and he was obliged to dip his brush again. This is best seen in the spirals.

The designs are numerous. Besides spirals, there is an attempt to represent scenes, with boats, hills, plants, animals, birds, and human beings (fig. 1). The boats are invariably rowing boats (the rowing galley was essentially the boat of the early Mediterranean peoples); in some cases the great steering oars are shown at the stern. At the prow is the killick and also an overhanging branch of a tree. In the centre are two cabins; from the back of the after cabin rises a tall pole on which is set an emblem, the fetish of the port from which the boat hailed. That these boats were dealing with foreign ports is clear from the emblems on the poles and also from the shapes of the hills near which the boats are passing. These hills are invariably pointed or conical, whereas in Egypt what hills there are are flat-topped, being merely isolated remains of the limestone plateau through which the Nile cut its way in geologic times. Pointed hills form the hieroglyphic determinative for a foreign country, and the detailed hieroglyph shows that below the group of hills is an expanse of blue or green representing water (pl. xcvi. 4). The nearest place to Egypt to be reached by water where there are pointed hills rising above the sea is

Fig. 1

Crete, an island so closely connected with primitive Egypt that it has even been suggested by Sir Arthur Evans that the Cretans were a colony from Egypt. The group of pointed hills, three, four, or even five in number, are among the most common of the emblems on poles of the Gerzean ships. As the pole with its two streamers becomes the hieroglyphic sign for God, it is not too much to suppose that the emblem which surmounted it was the object of worship at the port from which the boat came; that is to say, the boats which carried the hill emblem came from a place where a hill-god was worshipped. There is no indigenous hill-god in Egypt, but occasionally in historic times a hill-god is mentioned who is written with the sign of the hills set on the emblem of divinity followed by the figure of a god. The reading of the name is known in the xxvi-th dynasty, where the letters when transliterated read Yhw or Yahwe (fig. 2).

Fig. 2

The painted decoration of the Gerzeans is at its best between s.d. 40 and s.d. 50; after this, the designs are lost and become meaningless scrawls and squiggles, finally dying out altogether by s.d. 60.

The Gerzean was as much superior to the Amratean in making stone vases as in pottery. He delighted not only in beautiful form but in beautiful stone. Besides the usual limestone, basalt, and alabaster, the Gerzean used porphyry, red breccia, marble, diorite, granite, syenite, and serpentine. The variety of form and the variety of material show a high degree of technical skill and artistic ability (pls. iii. 1; iv. 9). The size of some of the vessels is remarkable. The diorite vase found at Hierakonpolis* has a diameter at the widest part of 61·5 cm., and the walls have been worked so thin that the stone is translucent.

In metal-working the Gerzean had advanced beyond the Amratean. His tools had increased in number, variety, and efficiency. Among the most interesting are copper needles, suggesting that clothes were now being made by sewing and were not mere strips of cloth or leather wrapped round the body. Other metals besides copper were in use. Gold first appears at this period; it was not melted or cast, but was beaten out into sheets, then cut into strips of the required width, and applied as a covering to the object to be decorated. The country of its origin is unknown, but it must have been imported for no metal occurs in the Valley of the Nile between the First Cataract and the sea. Silver, though rarer than gold, occurs occasionally. The rarest of all metals to be used at this period was iron, but a few beads of meteoric iron were found in a tomb of the Gerzean period; they were evidently regarded as of the utmost value for they were threaded on the same strings as gold beads.†

Glass was not made in Egypt so early, but a small pendant of dark-blue glass in imitation of lapis lazuli was found in a Gerzean tomb. But though glass was not made, glazing of stone was practised as early as the Badarian period. The Badarians glazed steatite beads with a

---

* Now in the University Museum, Manchester.   † Wainwright, *Labyrinth*, p. 15.

blue glaze to imitate turquoise; the Gerzeans did the same, but they also glazed quartz, and produced beads of the colour and translucency of zircon. They were capable also of producing objects in glazed quartz on a larger scale; the best example is a boat of glazed quartz, which when complete must have been over two feet in length. It was made in sections, which were held together by copper or gold wire passing through holes drilled in the sides of the sections, the junctions being covered with gold bands.

It is in this period that the human side of a prehistoric people begins to be revealed. The miniature pieces for a game of ninepins show that indoor games formed part of the daily life of the people. Judging by the number of little stone balls which are found, it is evident that marbles were popular for some kind of game. There was also a game played on a kind of chessboard, where the moves were governed by the throw of something which took the place of our dice. Such games could be played with primitive pieces, bits of wood and pebbles, so that though only the examples in precious materials have survived, there is no doubt that such games were played in all classes and among all ranks.

The Gerzeans had as strong a belief in a future life as their predecessors, and provided food and other necessaries, and even luxuries, for the use of the dead in the next world. They appear to have had more fear of evil during life than the Amrateans, for the number and variety of amulets are very great. Beliefs and ritual can be conjectured, partly from the amulets and partly from ritual objects which have survived. Amulets in the form of heads of hippopotamus and bull, beautifully carved in hard stone, show that these animals were regarded as sacred, possibly as incarnations of the deity. Small spoons of ivory or silver are found; the precious material shows that they were not for ordinary household use, but were probably for ritual sprinkling of some sacred liquid. Double-spouted vessels also suggest a religious ritual, when a libation had to be made to two deities at once.

The Gerzean culture is of extreme importance in the study of ancient Egypt, for it is the direct ancestor of that great civilisation.

The *Semainian* period, though in some ways merely a continuation of the Gerzean, has certain characteristics which differentiate it from its forerunners. The painted pottery continued but the style of decoration had changed. Instead of definite representations of objects the painter preferred comma-like twists and unmeaning lines. The type of vessels was also altered. In the Gerzean period there were few large pots but the Semainian needed a great many of a size which shows that they were storage pots, and indicates that owing to greater facilities for keeping food the standard of living was steadily rising.

B 2

Another indication of the increasing comfort of Semainian times was the presence of furniture. Low stools made of stone with the legs carved in one piece with the seat were clearly for people of some wealth; so also were beds made of a framework of wood with legs fitted in, the mattress being formed of soft linen cord plaited and lashed to the frame. Small boxes to hold a lady's possessions were made of ivory or of wood inlaid with ivory.

The burial customs were practically the same as among the Gerzeans, the body being contracted and laid on the left side. But the rule as to the orientation of the body was not so strict.

Artistically the Semainians produced statuettes in copper, ivory, and clay. These are the immediate precursors of the fine work which distinguishes the i-st dynasty.

HISTORY

See p. 234 for dates and list of kings

Note. The references in this section are given to the publications of the originals in hieroglyphs or hieratic. For translations of these see Breasted's *Ancient Records*.

EGYPTIAN dating is most conveniently expressed by reference to the dynasties. The division into numbered dynasties is due to the historian Manetho, High-priest of Sebennytus, who at the command of Ptolemy Philadelphus (*c.* 270 B.C.) wrote a history of Egypt from the records then remaining. The manuscript was deposited in the great Library of Alexandria and presumably perished when the building and its contents were destroyed by the Moslem conquerors in A.D. 642. Large extracts from it had, however, been copied by various ancient authors, and some of these are still extant. Manetho's method is to give the number of the dynasty, the number of kings which compose it, the name of each king, and the chief events and length of each reign, and sums up the duration of the dynasty at the end. The sequence of dynasties and of events is thus easy to follow. Herodotus and other late authors also give summaries of Egyptian history. One of the earliest historical documents is the Palermo Stone, which was engraved with the record of the kings of the first five dynasties. The record is in the form which Manetho followed, giving the name of the king with the chief event of each year of the reign recorded in a separate division.

	Division into periods	*Dynasties*
Proto-dynastic	*c.* 4777–3998 B.C.	i–iii
Old Kingdom	*c.* 3998–3335 B.C.	iv–vi
First Intermediate Period	*c.* 3335–3005 B.C.	vii–x
Middle Kingdom	*c.* 3005–2112 B.C.	xi–xiii
Second Intermediate Period	*c.* 2112–1738 B.C.	xiv–xvi
New Kingdom	*c.* 1738–1102 B.C.	xvii–xx
Late Period	*c.* 1102–525 B.C.	xxi–xxvi
Persian Period	*c.* 525–332 B.C.	xxvii–xxx
Ptolemaic Period	*c.* 332–30 B.C.	
Roman Occupation	*c.* 30 B.C.–A.D. 641	
Arab Conquest	A.D. 641	

One of the chief difficulties in the dating is the fact that the Egyptians dated from the regnal year of each king, and not from a fixed point.

The dating by regnal years only is too inexact to be of real use unless the record is complete, which is not the case in Egypt. Therefore any early dating can be only approximate. The most accurate check on the dating is by astronomy. The division of time in Egypt was by the year of 365 days, whereby the calendar lost a day every four years. Consequently two calendars were in use; the *official* calendar which began on the first of the month Thoth, and took no account of leap-year, and the *solar* calendar which was based on the rising of the Dog-star at dawn, and therefore was accurate astronomically. The two calendars originally started together on the first of the month Thoth; after four years the official calendar had lost a day and the heliacal rising of Sirius then took place on the second of Thoth; in twenty-eight years the calendar had lost a week, in 120 years it had lost a month; and in 1460 solar years or 1461 official years the wheel came full circle and the two calendars coincided again. Such an event is known to have taken place in A.D. 139, and it is from this date that modern calculations of the Sothic cycle are made. At irregular intervals the heliacal rising of Sirius is mentioned in Egyptian inscriptions; when the record gives the day and the month of the occurrence the date within a known Sothic cycle can be calculated. The earliest date which has been calculated by this method is in the reign of Thothmes III of the xviii-th dynasty.*

Manetho begins his history with dynasties of gods and demi-gods who reigned for a fabulous length of time. The copies of his history by Syncellus and Eusebius give 36,525 years as the duration of Egyptian history from the beginning of the first dynasty of the gods till the end of the thirtieth historic dynasty; "which number of years, resolved and divided into its constituent parts, that is to say, 25 times 1461 years, shows that it is related to the fabled periodical revolution of the Zodiac among the Egyptians and Greeks; that is, its revolution from a particular point to the same again, which point is the first minute of the first degree of that equinoctial sign which they call the Ram, as it is explained in the Genesis of Hermes and in the Cyrannian Books". Though the length of the reigns and the dynasties is fantastic, they show that there was a tradition of a long period of settled government before the historic records began. It is also possible that the division into dynasties of gods and demi-gods may record the cleavage between the Amratean and Gerzean cultures.

Ten kings of Thinis (Abydos) follow the demi-gods, and of these some scanty remains were found in the royal tombs in that place.

* Meyer, "Aegyptische Chronologie", in *Abhandlungen der Königlichen Preussischen Akademie*, 1905. See also Sidney Smith, *Alalakh*. The modern method of dating each object by the C14 process has revolutionised, though not entirely replaced, the astronomical method.

The Palermo stone* also records that there were kings in the Delta, but neither at Abydos nor in the Delta has any real information been obtained of these pre-dynastic Pharaohs.

PROTO-DYNASTIC

One of the most important monuments of the i-st dynasty is the slate palette of Narmer (pl. lxviii).† On the obverse is the king wearing the crown of Upper Egypt. He is represented as of gigantic size, and is in the act of killing an enemy whom he has seized by the hair. The enemy's title is above his head, "Chief of the Waters", perhaps meaning Chief of the Fayum.‡ Above this again is a symbolic group; a falcon, the totem of the king, stretches out a human hand and arm, and holds a rope which passes through the upper lip of a human head. The head emerges from a pool of water from which spring seven papyrus plants, symbolising the Delta. The papyrus blossom in early hieroglyphs stands for the numeral 1000; the group therefore means that the king, in the form of his totem, had captured seven thousand Northerners. On the reverse of the palette is a scene of the king, wearing the crown of Lower Egypt, apparently taking possession of the conquered country and celebrating the occasion by the sacrifice of ten victims, whose decapitated bodies with the arms bound are laid out in two rows. The hieroglyphs above the scene read "The Great Port", which suggests that the sacrifice took place when Narmer reached the sea, the ultimate limit of his conquest.

Narmer (pl. v) has been identified with Menes who, according to both Herodotus and Manetho, was the first mortal King of Egypt. Herodotus records a great engineering feat which Menes accomplished, the turning of the course of the Nile: "Menes, the first ruler over Egypt, in the first place protected Memphis by a mound. . . . Beginning about a hundred stades above Memphis, he filled in the elbow towards the south, dried up the old channel, and conducted the river by a canal so as to make it flow between the mountains: this bend of the Nile which flows excluded from its ancient course, is still carefully upheld by the Persians. . . .When the part cut off had been made firm by this Menes, who was the first King, he in the first place built on it the city that is now called Memphis; for Memphis is situated in the narrow part of Egypt; and outside it he excavated a lake from the river towards the

* Schaefer, "Ein Bruchstück altaegyptischer Königsannalen" (Anhang zu den *Abandlungen der Königlichen Preussischen Akademie*, 1902).
† Quibell, *Hierakonpolis*, i. pl. xxix.
‡ More probably "Chief of the Sea", *i.e.* "Chief of the sea-going ships".

north and west; for the Nile itself bounds it towards the east."* To
alter the course of a river the size of the Nile shows that the dynastic
people were already well advanced in the science of engineering.

The kings of the i-st dynasty appear to have sent trading expeditions
under military escort to Sinai to obtain copper. A sculptured scene on
a rock near the copper mines shows King Semerkhet† smiting a
Bedawy chief, signifying that the military escort had been obliged to
fight for possession of the mines. Beyond this there is practically no
historical information until the ii-nd dynasty. There was then a
successful nationalist rising under a Pharaoh named Perabsen. There
are indications that during his reign there was trade with the north as
far as the Black Sea, a fact which shows that peaceful conditions must
have prevailed during the greater part of his time. On his death the
country was reunited under one king, who with his successor claimed
to have fought great battles and to have killed thousands of the enemy.
If the record is true it suggests a frustrated invasion with the massacre
of all the invaders to the number of 47,209.‡

The iii-rd dynasty is one of the landmarks of Egyptian history, for
it was then that a new form of religion was introduced. This was sun
worship, which though never the religion of the people became after
many centuries the religion of the upper classes. With sun worship
came also the custom of mummification, the preservation of the
body by spices and other means, and with these two new ideas
of religion came also the still unexplained custom of building
pyramids. How far these three ideas are connected is still a matter for
investigation, and it is not yet known from which country they were
introduced.

The kings of the iii-rd dynasty, who have left monuments which
still survive to show what manner of men lived and worked in that
period, are Zoser and Snefru. Both these Pharaohs built pyramids
which are still the finest in Egypt; not even the Great Pyramid of
Khufu can be compared with them.

Zoser is probably the Tosorthros who according to Manetho was
"called Asclepius by the Egyptians for his medical knowledge. He
built a house of hewn stones, and greatly patronised literature." His
"house", i.e. his pyramid and its adjoining temples, still stands at
Saqqara (pl. xlv. 1, 2). He must have been a very remarkable man
that his reputation for learning and his love of literature should have
remained in the memory of his people for more than three thousand
years.

* Herodotus, ii. 99.   † Petrie, *Researches in Sinai*, pl. xlvii.
‡ Quibell, *Hierakonpolis*, i, pls. xxix, xl.

خط يده و رسمه ... بابه ريس

Snefru* built his magnificent pyramid about forty miles south of Cairo in his own private estate, now known as Medum but originally called Ded-Snefru (pl. xlvi). His second pyramid was at Dahshur. Officials of his pyramids are known, and the worship of this king was maintained by endowed priests as late as the Ptolemaic period. The Palermo Stone records Snefru's ship-building achievements. "Building of 100-cubit† *dua-tauy* ships of *meru*-wood, and of 60 sixteen-barges‡ of the King." Egypt could not have produced so much timber, and the wood was imported, for the record goes on: "The bringing of 40 ships filled with cedar-wood", and a little later, "The building of a 100-cubit *dua-tauy* ship of cedar-wood and 2 100-cubit ships of *meru*-wood". The fleet seems to have been for trading purposes, both in the Mediterranean and the Red Sea, for there was already a considerable amount of trade with the East in spices, sweet-scented woods, and fragrant gums. It would be possible for vessels of 167 feet in length to navigate not only the Red Sea but the Indian Ocean as well at certain seasons of the year.

OLD KINGDOM

The iv-th dynasty is one of the most splendid periods of the whole of Egyptian history. There had been no wars since the civil war under Perabsen of the ii-nd dynasty and the country had had time to develop the arts of peace and to amass wealth by trade. Already in the iii-rd dynasty the Pharaohs had begun to build enduring monuments and to enrich them with various decorative devices. But on the other hand, the priesthood had risen to power and were obtaining a stranglehold on the country. Endowed "chantries" for the worship of dead kings and for ensuring offerings to dead nobles had increased to a surprising extent. Land for these endowments was rapidly becoming the property of royal and private priesthoods and the cost of providing for the sacrifices to the gods had become a burden. Then there came to the throne a man who had courage and determination, a realist who understood the condition of the country. This was Khufu (the Cheops of Herodotus) (pl. xlviii. 1). As the priests were also the recorders and as they hated Khufu he is described as "having plunged into all kinds of wickedness"; but the reason for the priestly hatred is given in the words, that "having shut up all the temples he forbade the sacrifices".§ As the priests' living depended on the sacrifices, their consternation at Khufu's action must have been extreme. Khufu's monument, the

---

* This should read more correctly Snefer-fu, as there is an F written after the R.
† A hundred cubits = 167 feet.
‡ This perhaps means a sixteen-oared barge.   § Herodotus, ii. 124.

Great Pyramid of Gizeh, gave the priests another opportunity of vilifying their enemy. Herodotus records what they told him about the workmen employed by Khufu: "They worked to the number of a hundred thousand men at a time, each party during three months. The time during which they were thus harassed by toil, lasted ten years on the road which they constructed. . . . Twenty years were spent in erecting the pyramid itself." It is now known that Herodotus must have misunderstood or have been purposely misled in this account, for it is clear, to anyone who knows Egypt and is not a tourist like Herodotus, that the three months during which the hundred thousand men worked was the time of the inundation when all agricultural work is at a standstill. The peasantry were therefore idle, and having little means of storing food were liable to be half-starved. The King employed them on the building and fed them during the worst period of the year; the remains of their barracks round Khafra's pyramid show that they were housed as well. Herodotus records that the workmen were well fed: "On the Pyramid is shown an inscription, in Egyptian characters, how much was expended in radishes, onions, and garlic, for the workmen; which the interpreter, as well as I remember, reading the inscription, told me amounted to one thousand six hundred talents of silver. And if this be truly the case, how much more was probably expended in iron tools, in bread, and in clothes, for the labourers."* Khufu was kindly remembered by his people for he figures in folk-tales some centuries later.

Khufu's successor, Khafra (pls. vi; xlviii. 2; liv. 1), is known by his buildings and by the fine statues of himself. He was as much hated as Khufu by the priests, who told Herodotus that during those two reigns "the Egyptians suffered all kinds of calamities, and for this length of time the temples were closed and never opened". Herodotus carries on this notion of the extreme tyranny of Khufu and Khafra when he gives an account of their successor, Men-kau-Rê (Mycerinus) (pl. xlix. 2). He records that "Mycerinus, the son of Cheops, reigned over Egypt: that he opened the temples and permitted the people, who were worn down to the last extremity, to return to their employments and to sacrifices; and that he made the most just decisions of all their kings". From the fact that there were no wars, no threats of invasion, no skirmishes on the frontiers, nothing but the routine picture of the Pharaoh smiting a Bedawy chief in Sinai, it seems safe to conclude that the whole of the period covered by the iv-th dynasty was an era of peace. The magnificence of the buildings and of the art also shows that the country was sufficiently prosperous to cultivate art in its highest forms.

* This inscription disappeared long ago,

The iii-rd and iv-th dynasties are said by Manetho to have come from Memphis, and the v-th from Elephantine. As the succession appears to have been peaceful, the old line must have died out and the new kings were descendants of a collateral branch. The v-th dynasty is as barren of historical events as the iv-th but the inscriptions are fuller of detail and it is possible to obtain some idea of the character of a Pharaoh. The chief physician of King Sahu-Rê was evidently devoted to his master: "I praised the King greatly and lauded every god for Sahu-Rê's sake, for he knows the desire of all his retinue. When any command goes forth from the mouth of his Majesty, it comes to pass at once, for God has given to him knowledge of what is in the heart, because he is more noble than any god. If ye love Rê, then praise ye every god for Sahu-Rê's sake."*

The v-th dynasty saw an immense increase in travel and trade, and insteady of recitals of war and battle the inscriptions are full of accounts of journeys in foreign countries. Egypt was steadily increasing in wealth, for it was not only the king who had large stone buildings, but the nobles and officials, great and small, had sculptured tomb-chapels and made large endowments for the annual offerings to the dead. There was a spread of luxury among the lesser people such as had not appeared in earlier times. There was also a spread of education; letters to and from the king are frequently mentioned, and papyrus began to be used for correspondence and for accounts. At the same time there was a great rise of priestly power, for endowment of tombs meant the endowment of mortuary priests. So great was the importance of maintaining the offerings in perpetuity that warnings against the infringement of the endowment were sometimes inscribed on the wall of a tomb-chapel: "As for any people who shall enter into this tomb as their mortuary property, or shall do any evil thing to it, judgment shall be had with them before the great God."† It may be noted that the curse is directed against the disturber of the financial arrangements, not against the disturber of the bones of the dead.

The vi-th dynasty is remarkable for the records of trading expeditions with armed escorts, and for punitive campaigns against tribes who interfered with those expeditions. Autobiographic inscriptions begin to be made, and of these the best-known is that of Uni. He had a successful legal career, for when only a Nekhen-judge he heard cases "in the name of the King, being alone with the chief-judge-and-vizier,‡ in every private matter of the royal harem and of the Six Courts of Justice. When legal proceedings were instituted against

* Sethe, *Urkunden*, i. 38–40. † Sethe, op. cit., i. 49–51.
‡ This title belonged to the highest official in the State.

the King's Great Wife, Yntes, his Majesty caused me to enter, in order to hear [the case] alone. No chief-judge-and-vizier at all, no prince at all was there, but only I alone, because I was trustworthy, because I was pleasing to the heart of his Majesty, because his Majesty loved me. I alone was the one who put it in writing, together with a single Nekhen-judge. Never before had one like me heard the secrets of the royal harem, it was only the King who caused me to hear them."* He was then sent in command of a punitive expedition against the Bedawin, with a heterogeneous collection of nobles and officials as his assistants. He was not only successful in the campaign but so handled his officers and men that "not one thereof quarrelled with his neighbour, not one thereof plundered food or sandals from the wayfarer, not one thereof took away bread from any town, not one thereof took away a goat from any person". He proved himself so good a military commander that he was sent five times on campaigns of the kind, on one occasion outflanking and utterly defeating the enemy. His Triumph-Song on this victory is the first of this type of poetry (see p. 207).

The chief of the travellers of this period was Harkhuf who appears to have been a professional leader of caravans, like his father before him. He made several journeys to the South, of which the third and fourth are the most interesting. "His Majesty sent me a third time to Yam. I found the chief of Yam had gone to the land of Temeh, to smite Temeh as far as the western corner of heaven. I went after him to the land of Temeh and I pacified him." Harkhuf then went all round the land of Irthet before returning to Egypt: "I went down with 100 asses laden with incense, ebony, *heknu*, grain, panthers, ivory, throw-sticks, and every good product. When the chief of Irthet, Sethu, and Wawat saw how strong and numerous was the troop of Yam, who were going down with me to the Court together with the soldiers who had been sent with me, he brought and gave to me bulls and small cattle, and conducted me along the roads of the High-lands Irthet, because I was more excellent and more vigilant than any chief or caravan-conductor who had been sent to Yam before."

But Harkhufs fourth journey gave him the most pleasure and his account of it is perhaps the most interesting and human of all the inscriptions of this period. The Pharaoh was Pepy II, a small boy of about nine years old. Harkhuf had written to his royal master that he had obtained a dancing dwarf, whom he was bringing to the Court. The excitement of the little king at this news is amusingly shown in the letter which he wrote to Harkhuf, an excitement which keeps on

* Sethe, op. cit. i. 98–110.

breaking through the stilted phraseology then considered correct for
a letter from the Pharaoh to a subject:

Royal seal, year 2, third month of Yakhet, day 15.

Royal decree: O privy counsellor, lector-priest, and caravan-leader,
Karkhuf. I have noted the matter of this thy letter, which thou hast sent to
the King, to the palace, in order that it might be known that thou hast
come down in safety from Yam with the army which was with thee. Thou
hast said in this thy letter that thou hast brought all great and beautiful
gifts which Hathor, Lady of Yamu, has given to the King of Upper and
Lower Egypt, Neter-ka-Rê, who lives for ever and ever. Thou hast said in
this thy letter that thou hast brought a dwarf of divine dances from the land
of spirits, like the dwarf whom the Treasurer of the God, Ba-ur-dad, brought
from Punt in the time of King Ysesy. Thou hast said to my Majesty, Never
before has one like him been brought by any other who has visited Yam.
Each year shows thee doing what thy lord desires and praises; thou spendest
day and night with the caravan doing what thy lord desires, praises, and
commands. His Majesty will make thy many excellent honours to be an
ornament for the son of thy son for ever, so that all people will say when
they hear what my Majesty does for thee: "Is there anything like this which
was done for the privy counsellor Harkhuf, when he came down from Yam,
because of the alertness he showed to do what his lord desired, praised, and
commanded." Come northward at once to the Court. And thou must
bring with thee this dwarf, alive, sound and well, from the land of spirits,
for the dance of the god, and to rejoice and gladden the heart of the King of
Upper and Lower Egypt, Neter-ka-Rê, living for ever. When he comes
down with thee into the vessel, appoint trustworthy people who shall be
beside him on each side of the vessel; take care lest he should fall into the
water. When he sleeps at night, appoint trustworthy people who shall
sleep beside him in his tent; inspect ten times a night. For my Majesty
desires to see this dwarf more than the products of Sinai and Punt. If thou
arrivest at the Court and the dwarf is with thee, alive, sound and well, my
Majesty will do for thee a greater thing than was done for the Treasurer
of the god, Ba-ur-dad, in the time of King Ysesy, according to the heart's
desire of my Majesty to see this dwarf. Commands have been sent to the
Governor of the New Towns to command that provisions are to be taken
by him in every store-city and every temple without stint.*

There were many other caravan-leaders who travelled to the south
and to Punt, for at the beginning of Pepy II's reign trade was flourishing.
But it is clear that the Pharaoh as he grew up did not fulfil the promise
of his youth. He was a weak ruler and the country seems to have
gradually lost all initiative. Pepy II lived to be nearly a hundred years
old, having reigned more than ninety years.

* Sethe, op. cit., i. 120–31.

FIRST INTERMEDIATE PERIOD

The prosperity of Egypt had declined during this immensely long reign. This was largely due to the method of government. As the Pharaoh was the mainspring of the whole administration the country always suffered when the monarch was too indolent or too decrepit to take an active and personal part in the government. Egypt therefore had sunk low when the aged Pharaoh died. There are indications that foreigners, probably Syrians, took possession, though there were titular Pharaohs who carried on the succession. Of these there remain little more than the names. From the vii-th to the x-th dynasty history is almost silent. What little record survives is chiefly of the fighting in Middle Egypt when the princes of the south were attempting to invade the north and were resisted by the princes of Siut. Civil war and lesser risings distracted the greater part of the country, so that, according to the record, "the land trembled, Middle Egypt feared, all the people were in terror, the villages were in panic, fear entered into their limbs". Still there were districts which were well governed by the local prince, where "every official was at his post, there was no fighting, nor did anyone shoot an arrow. The child was not smitten at the side of his mother, nor the citizen at the side of his wife. There was no evil-doer in the land, nor anyone who did violence against another's house."*

MIDDLE KINGDOM

In spite of the efforts of the princes of Siut the southerners prevailed in the end, and the princes of Hermonthis became the Pharaohs of Egypt. The earliest of these kings, Yntef the Great, boasted that "I enlarged my northern boundary as far as the nome of Aphroditopolis, I drove in the mooring-peg [*i.e.* I landed] in the sacred valley, I captured the whole of the Thinite nome, I opened all its fortresses, I made it the Door of the North."† There is a little touch of human nature about this warrior of ancient times, for he is represented on his funerary stela with his five dogs, from whom he apparently did not wish to be parted even in death. The early part of this period appears to have been spent in battles and fighting until the xi-th dynasty was firmly established; then, when peace was restored, trade began to revive. Under Mentu-hotep III trade had increased so much that it was considered worth while to send a ship far afield to the Land of Punt, which was famous for spices and incense, for gold and ivory.

---

* Griffith, *Inscriptions of Siut and Der Rifeh*, iv. 75.
† Mariette, *Monuments Divers*, Texte 15.

To reach Punt, however, a ship had to be built, and Henu, the governor of the southern district, was commanded to do so. As Punt lay to the east, Henu had to go to the Red Sea to build the ship, and his way led through the Wady Hammamat, five days' journey without water. "His Majesty sent me to dispatch a ship to Punt to bring to him fresh myrrh from the chiefs of the Red Land. Then I went forth from Koptos upon the road which his Majesty commanded me. There was with me an army of the South, I went forth with an army of 3000 men. I made the road a river, and the Red Land [*i.e.* the desert] a stretch of water, for I gave a leather bottle, a carrying pole, 2 jars of water and 20 loaves to each one of the army. I made wells in the defile, two wells in Yda-het, 20 square cubits in one, and 31 square cubits in the other; I made another in Ya-heteb, 20 cubits by 20 cubits on each side. Then I reached the Sea; then I made the ship, and I dispatched it with everything after I had made for it a great sacrifice of cattle, bulls, and ibexes. After I returned from the Sea I executed the commands of his Majesty, and brought to him all the products that I had found in the Land of God."*

Mentu-hotep III built his mortuary temple and pyramid on the west side of the Nile at Deir el Bahri. Centuries later Queen Hatshepsut took his temple as her model for the magnificent building which she erected to the glory of Amon. His memory was kept alive by later kings, for Senusert III of the xii-th dynasty increased the endowments of the temple.

Mentu-hotep IV's reign was so uneventful that nothing is recorded officially except some miraculous happenings. On one occasion he sent the Chief of Works, Amonemhat, to the Wady Hammamat to bring a block of a special kind of stone for the lid of the royal sarcophagus. Amonemhat recorded the marvel: "This wonder happened for his Majesty, that the beasts of the High-land came down for him. For behold, there came a gazelle, great with young; she went with her face towards the people before her while her eyes looked backward. She did not turn back until she reached this noble rock, this block which was intended for the lid of the sarcophagus being still in its place. She dropped her young upon it in the sight of the whole army. Then they cut her throat upon it and brought fire. It [the block] came down in safety."† Divine direction to a special spot by means of an animal is not uncommon in Greek legend; this, however, is not related as a legend but is recorded as a fact by an eye-witness.

As so often happened in Egypt, there were years of famine; some of these occurred during this reign, the only record being in the bio-

---

* Golenischeff, *Hammamat*, xv-xvii.   † Golenischeff, op. cit., x-xv.

graphical inscription of Yty, the prince of Gebelên: "I maintained Gebelên through the years of scarcity. I made ten herds of goats with people in charge of each herd; I made two herds of cattle and a herd of asses. I raised all kinds of small cattle. I made 30 ships, then another 30 ships, and I brought grain for Yny and Hefat after Gebelên was provisioned. The Theban province had to go upstream [for provisions], but Gebelên never had to send either downstream or upstream to another district."*

During the dark period after the passing of the Old Kingdom, there are glimpses of a new form of government coming into existence. No longer was the Pharaoh the sole ruler with a little band of nobles and officials at his Court. A new class of nobles had arisen; these were the provincial governors who were virtually kings of their districts, owning only a nominal allegiance to the Pharaoh, and ruling their domains without reference to the central authority. This was the condition of the country when the xii-th dynasty came to power. The nobles were so powerful that had they combined together no monarch could have withstood them. But the first king of the xii-th dynasty was not daunted by difficulties. There was constant friction and jealousy among the nobles; and as polygamy was the rule there were often questions of disputed succession when the Pharaoh was appealed to. By wise handling of such situations Amonemhat I recovered to a large extent the ancient royal power, and by the end of his reign was ruling the country with much of the splendid autocracy of the Pharaohs of the Old Kingdom. He was a vigorous and capable ruler, and like all founders of a new dynasty his first care was to secure the frontiers of his kingdom. As a king he was in every way successful; yet at the end of his reign he wrote a cynical treatise for the instruction of his son whom he associated with himself as co-regent.† The Pharaoh gives an account of a conspiracy against him by the members of his own household, and he points out that a king can trust no one: "The evening meal had ended and darkest night had come, I lay upon my bed and closed my eyes. Sleep fell upon my eyelids, but ere my dreams began I was ware of stealthy footsteps creeping near. I awoke and seized my weapons; in the darkness, in the darkness all alone. For the men who came against me with their daggers sharp and keen, were the men whom I had trusted and enriched; they had risen by my favour, and had sworn great oaths by God that their loyalty would last while life endured. A serpent of the desert they had called me in their plots; as

* Daressy, *Recueil des Travaux*, xiv. 21.

† Known to modern Egyptologists as *The Instructions of Amenemhat*. It is a metrical composition, the division between the lines being indicated by red dots.

a serpent of the desert I was ready for the fray. Weapons gleamed and flashed around me, but I struck the traitors down."*

On the death of Amonemhat I his son and co-regent, Senusert I, came to the throne. He was one of the great military geniuses who raised Egypt from a small and insignificant country to be one of the leading powers of the ancient world. In one campaign he convinced the tribes in the south that it was better to be his friend than his enemy. Unlike many of the other Pharaohs he was not content to make one successful campaign, and then rest on his laurels. He believed in being prepared, and he kept his army ready as Yku-didi of Abydos notes in his biography: "I came from Thebes as a King's councillor, in command of young recruits, to visit the cities in the land of the Oasis dwellers."†

Senusert I (pl. liii) built his pyramid at Lisht, and erected temples at all the great centres of his kingdom. Only a few fragments of these have survived to show the splendour of his works and the ability of his architects. At Abydos he built a remarkable temple to Osiris, of which it is said that it contained a well so deep that it reached the river. This suggests that he was the original builder of the Osireion in Abydos. One of his temples appears to have survived until the xx-th dynasty, for there is a short official report upon its condition: "The House of Amon dated from Senusert I needs to be repaired."

Senusert was succeeded by his son Amonemhat II, in whose reign the copper mines of Sinai were extensively worked, and foreign trade increased. The reign of the next king, Senusert II, is of peculiar interest for the foreign connections of Egypt at that period. The town built for the workmen who erected Senusert's pyramid at Illahun yielded examples of the polychrome Kamares pottery of Crete, showing the close relations between the two countries. Egyptian objects of this reign have been found in Crete. Egyptian funerary stelæ of the xii-th dynasty have been excavated in Malta in positions which prove that they must have been brought to the island at some remote antiquity.‡ The very beads show the incoming of a fair people; dark stone, such as hæmatite, garnet, and green jasper were worn, while pale amethyst, which is only tolerable in colour when worn on a fair skin, was much in vogue. Trade must have been brisk indeed for so many foreign objects and in so great variety to have poured into Egypt.

This period of peace came to an end on the death of Senusert II, and his successor, Senusert II, was faced with trouble on the southern

---

* Griffith, Z.A.S., xxxiv. 38.
† Ausführliches Verzeichniss der Berliner Museums, p. 89.
‡ Murray, Ancient Egypt (1928), p. 45.

frontier. The chief difficulty in dealing with the enemy on the southern border was the Cataract. The Nubian tribes had always relied on the delay caused to the Egyptians by the transhipment of troops and supplies, which gave them time to take to the hills until the punitive expedition had passed. Senusert determined to remove this difficulty before he started, and he had the channel cleared of the rocks and a fairway made up which his boats could sail. The first attempt was not to his liking, and he had the work done again, as his inscription shows: "Year 8, under the Majesty of the King of Upper and Lower Egypt, Kho-kau-Rê, living for ever. His Majesty commanded to make this canal anew. The name of this canal is 'Excellent are the roads of Kho-kau-Rê'. His Majesty went upstream to overthrow the miserable Kush. The length of this canal is 150 cubits, width 20, depth 15."* The result of the speed with which he could move his troops into the enemy's country gave him victory, and he was able to say with truth, "I made my boundary south of my fathers'. I did more than was committed to me by them: I the King both say it and did it."† He built two fortresses, one at Semneh, the other at Kummeh, in which he set frontier guards, and no negro was allowed to pass the fortresses to Egypt except for trade, and even then the negro had to tranship his goods into Egyptian craft. There is only one record of a campaign in Syria during this reign, and this seems to have been successful. The Pharaoh led his troops in person, as is recorded by one of his officers, Sebekkhu: "His Majesty proceeded northward to overthrow the miserable Asiatics. His Majesty arrived at a district, its name was Sekmim. His Majesty led the van in returning to the capital, after Sekmim and the miserable Rutenu had succumbed, while I acted as rear-guard."‡ One campaign against the redoubtable Senusert was sufficient for the northern tribes to leave Egypt in peace, and the southern tribes had also had their lesson.

Of the private life of Senusert III nothing is known, but the portraits of him in later life are so tragic in expression that it would seem that some terrible misfortune and unhappiness had overtaken him. His public career was a series of brilliant successes, therefore the tragedy which must have befallen him could have been only in his private capacity as a man.

Amonemhat III, the son of Senusert, succeeded his father while still a youth (pl. liv. 2). He proved himself a capable ruler, but his genius lay in organisation, not in military campaigns. He sent regular expeditions to Sinai for copper, so regular that the miners built huts for themselves near the mines and buried their tools in the huts against the

---

* Wilbour, *Recueil*, xiii. 202. † Lepsius, *Denkmaler*, ii. 130 *h*.
‡ Garstang, *El Arabah*, pls. iv, v, pp. 32, 33.

next year's expedition. Every leader of such an expedition set up a memorial of the fact, usually giving the name of every member of the party from the highest to the lowest. One leader boasts of his success: "I opened a mine successfully. I excavated a mine for my lord, and my young men returned in full number, none among them having fallen by the way. Therefore give praise to the King, exalt his fame, laud the King and guard that which is his. The mountains bring forth what is in them [for him], and the hills bear their riches [for him]."*

Amonemhat III sent expeditions to the Wady Hammamat as well as to Sinai, but as they went there to bring back large blocks of stone, the "army" for the Hammamat expedition was much larger than those who went to Sinai. In the nineteenth year of his reign Amonemhat dispatched a large party to fetch stone for statues: "His Majesty sent to bring monuments from the valley of Hammamat of fine *bekhen*-stone for [the building called] 'Life of Amonemhat' and for the House of Sebek of Shedet, and 10 enthroned statues of 5 cubits, quarried in this year. Guards of the necropolis, 20; quarrymen, 30; sailors, 30; a numerous army, 2000."† It is generally supposed that these enthroned statues refer to the statues seen by Herodotus when he visited the lake that he calls Moeris, but which is now called the Fayum: "About the middle of the lake stand two pyramids, each rising fifty orgyæ above the surface of the water, and the part under water extends to an equal depth: on each of these is placed a stone statue, seated on a throne."‡

All these were, however, but minor works of this remarkable king. He was the builder of the Labyrinth, which excited the admiration and wonder of the Greek authors who saw it. Herodotus goes so far as to say, "The pyramids are beyond description, yet the Labyrinth surpasses even the pyramids"§ (see p. 159).

But Amonemhat's greatest achievement was the engineering work that was done in the Fayum province. The ancient name of this province was Ta-she, the Land of the Lake; it was so called from the lake which filled a deep natural hollow. It is actually an oasis, being separated from the Nile Valley by a ridge of desert. Though the lake was deep the edges were marshy, and Amonemhat set to work to reclaim some of the marsh. As the lake is due to infiltration from the Nile, it was essential for the success of the scheme to have accurate knowledge of the annual rise of the river. The careful recording of the height of the Nile as far up the river as Semneh suggests that this was done for the purpose of learning exactly what the conditions might be. The news of the first rise could have been carried by runners

---

* Weill, *Sinai*, p. 166.   † Lepsius, op. cit., ii. 138*a*.
‡ Herodotus, ii. 149.   § Ibid, ii. 148.

to some recording station, and a regular series of runners bringing news of the pace of the rise could well have been maintained, and thus a body of real information could have been accumulated. This would have been quite in keeping with the tradition of Amonemhat's ancestors, who were careful to have their preparations complete before embarking on any important enterprise, and this was the largest piece of engineering that had been undertaken since Menes of the i-st dynasty had altered the course of the Nile. It was a great undertaking brilliantly accomplished. Amonemhat built a great dam twenty miles long, and so reclaimed about forty square miles of good and fertile land. The lake was then made into a reservoir to hold the annual flood water until the dry season, when it could be released for purposes of irrigation. Amonemhat's system of canals and sluices was still in use at the time of Herodotus, who says, "the water in this lake does not spring from the soil, for these parts are excessively dry, but it is conveyed through a channel from the Nile, and for six months it flows into the lake, and for six months out again into the Nile."*

Amonemhat III was the last of the great kings of Egypt for some centuries to come. The dynasty ended with several obscure kings and queens and merged into the xiii-th dynasty of which comparatively little is known.

SECOND INTERMEDIATE PERIOD

Except for a confused list of more than a hundred kings, there is little definite information about the xiii-th and xiv-th dynasties. The reigns were short, and with each successive reign Egypt appears to have sunk lower into weakness and ignorance. There are no large works of this period, no temples, no art, and few inscriptions. At the end of this inglorious time foreigners invaded the country and took possession.

The Jewish historian Josephus has preserved an extract from the history of Manetho which gives the account of this invasion and of the invaders. "We had formerly a King whose name was Timaus. In his time it came to pass, I know not how, that God was displeased with us, and there came up from the East in a strange manner men of an ignoble race, who had the confidence to invade our country, and easily subdued it by their power without a battle. And when they had our rulers in their hands they burnt our cities, and demolished the temples of the gods, and inflicted every kind of barbarity upon the

* Lepsius, op. cit., ii. 149.

inhabitants, slaying some, and reducing the wives and children of others to a state of slavery. At length they made one of themselves King, whose name was Salatis; he lived at Memphis and rendered both the upper and lower regions of Egypt tributary, and stationed garrisons in places which were best adapted for the purpose. But he directed his attention principally to the Eastern frontier, for he regarded with suspicion the increasing power of the Assyrians, who he foresaw would one day undertake an invasion of his kingdom. And observing in the Saite nome, upon the east of the Bubastite channel, a city which from some theological reference was called Avaris; and finding it admirably adapted to his purpose, he rebuilt it, and strongly fortified it with walls, and garrisoned it with a force of two hundred and fifty thousand men completely armed. To this city Salatis repaired in summer time, to collect his tribute, and pay his troops, and exercise his soldiers in order to strike terror into foreigners." Then follows a list of some of the kings. "Some say they were Arabians. This people who were thus denominated Shepherd Kings, and their descendants, retained possession of Egypt during the period of five hundred and eleven years."*

Petrie's summary of this period is perhaps the best: "The country was disorganised, and incapable of resisting any active foe, when from the East there poured in a barbaric people, who settled, and seized on the government of the country, harrying and plundering, while the native rulers were at their mercy. After a century of this confusion they became more civilised, probably by the culture imbibed from the Egyptian mothers of the second and third generation. Then they established a monarchy of their own in the Egyptian fashion, adopting the usages of the country, and keeping native administrators in their power to claim the allegiance of the people."†

The fortress of Avaris is known in the inscription of Aahmes, the son of Abana, where it is called Het-Uart, "House of the Leg". As Manetho says it derived its name from "a theological notion", this may have been a shrine in which a relic of Osiris was worshipped. It was situated at the place now known as Tell el Yahudiyeh, "The Mound of the Jew", which was the key position to repel an invading force entering Egypt from the east, and here was built a fortified camp. This was surrounded by a great earthwork or, more exactly, a sand-bank, 41 feet high and varying in width from 80 to 140 feet at the top. The long slope down to the plain was covered with stucco so as to make a smooth surface, up which it would be impossible for an enemy to rush. The only entrance was by a sloping roadway, 35 feet wide, flanked by high walls, which made it a kind of sunk causeway. This

---

* Josephus, *Against Apion*.   † Petrie, *History of Egypt*, i. 235 (ed. 1894).

type of fortress is entirely un-Egyptian. An Egyptian was accustomed to hand-to-hand fighting, and his fortresses, like a medieval castle, had perpendicular walls. The builders of Avaris were clearly accustomed to projectiles, probably slings and bows and arrows; and this would be the meaning of Manetho's statement that the Egyptians were conquered without a battle; for to the Egyptians a battle meant close fighting with swords and daggers, not with missiles. If they could not get to close quarters with the enemy they were helpless. After the Hyksos had been long enough in the country to become Egyptianised the defences of Avaris were altered, and a great wall, standing 45 to 50 feet high, was built round the glacis. The wall was at least six feet thick, and was built of large blocks of fine white limestone, and formed a defence in the true Egyptian manner. The size of the permanent garrison, as given by Manetho, is certainly exaggerated, but there might well have been that number during the military manœuvres which Salatis conducted every summer.

It is possibly due to the Hyksos occupation that so few temples of the earlier periods have survived. According to Manetho the conquerors destroyed the temples, but whether from religious zeal against alien gods, or from sheer love of destruction, cannot be known, for no indication of their religious beliefs or ritual has been recorded and no ritual object of their time has been preserved.

Josephus quotes again from Manetho as to the end of the Hyksos: "After these things he relates that the Kings of Thebes and of the other provinces of Egypt, made an insurrection against the Shepherds, and that a long and mighty war was carried on between them, till the Shepherds were overcome by a king whose name was Alisphragmuthosis, and they were by him driven out of the other parts of Egypt, and hemmed up in a place containing about ten thousand acres, which was called Avaris. All this tract (says Manetho) the Shepherds surrounded with a vast and strong wall. And Thummosis, the son of Alisphragmuthosis, endeavoured to force them by siege, and beleaguered the place; but at the moment when he despaired of reducing them by siege, they agreed on a capitulation, that they would leave Egypt, and should be permitted to go out without molestation wheresoever they pleased. And, according to this stipulation, they departed from Egypt with all their families and effects, and bent their way through the desert to Syria."* Josephus also quotes Manetho's summary of the expulsion of the Hyksos: "(Manetho again says): After this Amenophis returned from Ethiopia with a great force, and Rampses also, his son, with other forces, and encountering the Shep-

* Josephus, *Against Apion*.

herds and the unclean people, they defeated them and slew multitudes of them, and pursued them to the bounds of Syria."*

The Hyksos were an illiterate people and have left no records, with the exception of scarabs. Even these have often only muddled hieroglyphs, showing that the wearers were not able to read them. Scarabs of earlier periods are found in great numbers in southern Palestine with other Egyptian objects, which prove that long before the invasion the Hyksos were in constant touch with Egypt.

A folk-tale of a later date professes to give the reason which caused the princes of Thebes to rebel. Unfortunately the papyrus breaks off at the most exciting point of the story, and no other copy has ever been discovered to satisfy our legitimate curiosity. The story tells that the Hyksos king, Apophis, wishing to pick a quarrel with the prince of Thebes, sends him a message to say that he cannot sleep at nights on account of the noise made by the hippopotami in the pool. The prince of Thebes is greatly perturbed on receiving the message, for he knows that he cannot control a hippopotamus and that it is only an excuse on the part of Apophis to attack; he calls his council together and explains the position, and there the papyrus comes to an end.

NEW KINGDOM

The xviii-th dynasty is not only the most important period in the history of Egypt but is the best-recorded. After centuries of the rule of foreigners there was a nationalist rising headed by the then prince of Thebes, Seqenen-Rê III. He pushed the Hyksos northwards and apparently cleared the Thebaid before he was killed in battle. He was followed by his son Kames, whose career did not last long, then another son, Aahmes, succeeded to the throne. More fortunate than his father and brother, Aahmes drove the enemy to the confines of Egypt, and finally chased them out of the country. The story of the campaigns, of the insurrection in the south engineered by Tety the Handsome, of the naval engagement, and of the siege and final capture of the Hyksos stronghold of Avaris, is told with engaging simplicity by the king's namesake, Aahmes the son of Abana. He begins proudly: "I will tell you, O all ye people, I will inform you of all the honours which came to me. I was presented with gold seven times in the presence of the whole land, male and females slaves likewise. I was endowed with many fields. The fame of a man valiant in his deeds shall not perish

* Josephus, *Against Apion.*

in this land for ever." As the presentation of gold to a warrior was only for some outstanding deed of courage, Aahmes the son of Abana had reason to be proud of receiving it seven times. He appears to have joined the navy when quite a lad, and served sometimes on boats and sometimes on land, and he remained a warrior to the end of his long life. He was in all King Aahmes's campaigns. The insurrection in the south was brief but disastrous for the rebels: "There came an enemy of the South; his fate, his destruction approached; the gods of the South seized him and his Majesty found him in Tynt-to-amu [*i.e.* the First Cataract]. Then came that miserable one, Tety the Handsome; he had gathered rebels about him. His Majesty slew him and his crew, annihilating them." Aahmes the son of Abana had his most exciting adventure in a later reign, for he served under Aahmes I, Amonhotep I, and Thothmes I. This adventure was during a naval engagement on the Nile, when one of the chiefs of the enemy flung himself into the river and was making his escape. Aahmes the son of Abana leapt after him, fought him in the water, knocked him on the head, and brought him back triumphantly as a living prisoner, a "struck-alive".*

As the mummy of King Aahmes has been preserved, his personal appearance is known. He was a strongly built man, broad-shouldered, and with curly brown hair; he was not good-looking for he had pro-jecting front teeth, and his portrait suggests an admixture of negro blood. Though he seems to have been greatly beloved and admired by his army, and though he achieved many brilliant successes in the field, his fame was overshadowed in later times by the great victories of his descendants, Thothmes I and Thothmes III.†

Aahmes was succeeded by his son Amonhotep I. The Hyksos were still a danger to Egypt for they were strong enough to attempt to regain their lost conquest, and they were near the northern frontier of Egypt. Amonhotep was forced to fight in more than one campaign against them, and the irrepressible Aahmes the son of Abana accom-panied him: "Behold, I was at the head of our soldiers, and I fought unbelievably, and his Majesty was witness of my valour." Amon-hotep's main work was the important but unspectacular task of organising his country after the horrors of war, and this he did with the energy for which his family was famous. When he died his death was expressed in the usual way: "His Majesty, having passed life in happiness and years in contentment, went forth to heaven and joined the Sun." Had he lived in another dynasty he would have been remembered as one of the great Pharaohs; but coming, as he did,

* Lepsius, op. cit., iii. 12 *a*, *d*.

† I have deliberately transliterated the name as Thoth, which is the exact trans-literation of the Greek Θωθ.

between that great soldier Aahmes I and that still greater soldier Thothmes I, his exploits and his reign tend to be forgotten.

His rock-cut tomb was mentioned in the great trial of tomb-robbers in the xxi-st dynasty. It was reported that "robbers have robbed it". Inspectors were sent to examine it, and they gave evidence at the trial: "The eternal resting place of the King Zeser-ka-Rê, son of the Sun, Amonhotep, which has 130 cubits of depth in its great hall, as well as the long passage on the north of the temple of Amonhotep-of-the-Garden, was examined this day, and was found intact by the masons."*

Thothmes I, son of Amonhotep, now came to the throne; his mother was a lady of the royal family though not the heiress. His right to the kingship was obtained, as was usual at this period, by marriage with the heiress. He was one of the great warrior-kings of Egypt, and the records of his reign show an uninterrupted series of victories. Aahmes the son of Abana, though now an old man, was still to the fore; he took part in the river battle in Nubia and so distinguished himself that "I was raised to the dignity of Captain-General of the Sailors". The Nubian campaign in which the naval battle was fought was important because its success brought the whole of the territory as far south as the Third Cataract under the sway of Egypt. The only record of it comes from the dramatic pen of Aahmes the son of Abana: "His Majesty raged like a panther of the south; his Majesty cast his javelin, and it remained in the body of that enemy chieftain, whose army was powerless before his flaming uræus, made so in an instant of time. His Majesty sailed downstream with all countries in his grasp, and that miserable Nubian chief hanged head downward at the prow of the barge of his Majesty." Old Aahmes accompanied Thothmes on that king's great raid through Palestine and Syria, when the army of Egypt reached the Euphrates. There he was again conspicuous in the hand-to-hand fighting: "I was at the head of our soldiers, and his Majesty saw my valour when I seized upon a chariot, its horses and those who were in it, as living captives." This was his last campaign, for being about the age of ninety he decided to retire from active service. "I have grown up," he says, "I have reached old age, and I shall rest in the tomb which I myself have made."

Thothmes summed up his own career in an inscription at Abydos; in it he recounts not only his conquests but his benefactions to temples: "I did more than any other king who was before me. The gods rejoiced in my time and their temples were in festival. I made the boundaries of Ta-mery† as far as the circuit of the sun, and I caused

---

* Abbott Papyrus in *Select Papyri*, pt. ii, pls. 1 to 8.   † A name of Egypt.

Egypt to be the head of every land."* When the end came, "the King rested from life, going forth to heaven and mingling with the gods."

In person he was a stocky little man, hardly more than five feet in height. Like his grandfather Aahmes I he had projecting front teeth, but he had a well-shaped nose, and when young might have been good-looking. He was about sixty at his death, and was then quite bald. He must have been endowed with an abounding energy and with an iron constitution to have endured the physical strain of long journeys and strenuous fighting, for like all the Pharaohs he led his army to battle and fought beside his men. He was certainly skilled in the use of weapons, witness the deadly stroke of the flung javelin recorded by Aahmes the son of Abana; and judging by the general appearance of his mummy he must have been quick and energetic in his movements.

By his conquests in the south and the north he so crushed all his enemies that Egypt had peace, and on the good foundations which Amonhotep I had laid she was able to rebuild her economic state. With the advent of peace and security, literature and the arts began to flourish again. Thothmes I inaugurated that wonderful era of temple-building which lasted until the xx-th dynasty and produced some of the finest buildings the world has ever seen. As prince of Thebes he naturally honoured his local god, Amon, by increasing the size of the temple of Karnak, then the only Amon-temple of any importance in Thebes, and erected at the entrance two stately obelisks, one of which still stands.

At the end of his reign Thothmes I associated his daughter Hatshepsut (pl. vii. 3) with himself as co-regent. In her records she claims to have reigned as king, but the official lists ignore her altogether, and place Thothmes II as the immediate successor of Thothmes I. Her career covers part of the reign of Thothmes I, the whole of that of Thothmes II, and a great part of Thothmes III. It is considered by modern historians more convenient to place the events recorded by Hatshepsut after the reign of Thothmes II though they were in many cases contemporary.

The accession of Thothmes II is described picturesquely: "The Falcon in the Nest has appeared as King of Upper and Lower Egypt."† He was a great contrast to his predecessor, for he seems to have been a weakling, somewhat effeminate with his artificially curled brown hair. When there was a rebellion in the south, he went towards the scene of fighting but not in too dangerous proximity to a battle. When the

---

* Mariette, *Abydos*, ii. 31.   † Piehl, *Inscriptions*, i. pl. cxxix. Q.

news was brought that "the miserable Kush have begun to rebel, his
Majesty raged like a panther of the South. Said his Majesty, 'I swear
as Rê loves me, as Amon favours me, I will not leave one of their males
alive'. Then the army of his Majesty arrived at the miserable Kush
and overthrew the barbarians; and according to the command of his
Majesty they did not leave alive one male except one of the children
of the Chief of the miserable Kush, who was taken away alive to his
Majesty with their people. They were placed under the feet of the
good God, for his Majesty had appeared upon his throne when the
living prisoners were brought in."* This was no great warrior leading
his men to battle and being found always in the thickest of the fight,
but a rather timorous young man who could make a brave show when
he could sit on his throne in all the panoply of royalty, and put his foot
on the necks of bound and helpless prisoners.

Tholmes II reigned only thirteen years; then, as Thothmes III
(pl. lix. 1) was still only a lad too young to reign, Hatshepsut became
the virtual ruler. She was a woman of great force of character; and
if her portraits speak true, she was endowed with beauty and charm as
well. Her reign is characterised by the great expansion of trade, and
by her passionate devotion to her religion, which showed itself in the
erection of one of the finest temples that even Egypt can boast of, and
by the decoration of other temples as well.

Her magnificent temple at Deir el Bahri is renowned not merely
for its beauty but for the interest of many of the inscriptions on its
walls. These inscriptions are illustrated by sculptures, and recount
among other things the story of her divine birth. Still more important
is the history of the trading expedition which she sent to Punt. The
started from the Nile and are shown floating down the river with
characteristic Nile fishes in the water. The scene then changes, and the
fishes are those peculiar to the Red Sea. As no land journey is indicated,
it is clear that there must have been a waterway from the Nile to the
Red Sea along which sea-going ships could pass. The scenes in the land
of Punt show houses built on piles, apparently in a swamp. Portraits
of the people of Punt are given, and except for the inordinately fat
Queen of Punt they were not unlike the Egyptians. One scene repre-
sents the Egyptian envoy standing beside a table on which are displayed the beads and other trade articles which he had brought to
exchange for native products. He returned to his royal mistress
bringing gold, ivory, incense, apes, birds, and trees.

Hatshepsut stimulated trade in her own country by her encouragement of architecture and other forms of art. Her account of the

---

* Sethe, *Untersuchungen*, i. 81.

setting up of two obelisks in the temple of Karnak is interesting. "I was sitting in the palace and thinking of my Creator, when my heart urged me to make for him in the Hall of Columns two obelisks whose points should reach the sky. . . . Verily, these two great obelisks that my Majesty has wrought with electrum, they are of a single stone of hard granite without any join or division. My Majesty commanded this work in the 15th years on the first day of the month Mechir till the 16th year and the last day of the month Mesori, making seven months since the ordering of it in the quarry."[*] To quarry two obelisks of a hundred feet in length by the arduous method of pounding, to transport them to the river and load them on a fleet of boats, to erect them in their places, engrave and polish them, and all in the space of seven months, was a triumph of organisation.

Hatshepsut was not buried among the Queens of Egypt, but true to her claim to the regal power her tomb is in the Valley of the Tombs of the Kings.[†]

Thothmes III's accession to the throne was partly by marriage, by which he became co-regent with Hatshepsut, and partly by divine appointment. This last was effected by the image of Amon, which when carried by the priests, stopped before him and refused to proceed farther. During Hatshepsut's reign there were no wars, and Egypt had increased so greatly in wealth that the neighbouring countries began to cast covetous eyes on her riches. When Hatshepsut died and Thothmes reigned alone he found himself faced with a coalition of the powerful princes of Megiddo and Kadesh, who were preparing for an invasion of Egypt should opportunity arise. Thothmes took action at once, collected an army and marched to attack the enemy before they were fully prepared. The record of his first campaign is very full, for his private secretary kept a diary of the events, which was written on leather rolls, and afterwards engraved on the walls of the temple of Karnak. Thothmes proved himself in this campaign to be the great military genius of his period; he relied chiefly on rapidity of movement and sudden attack, though he could besiege a key point for weeks if necessary. Megiddo was the key point in this campaign; it had to be taken at all costs. When he reached Aaruna at the foot of the hills in which Megiddo stands he called a council of all his generals, who

---

[*] Lepsius, *Denkmäler*, iii. 22–4, *a–d*.

[†] A good deal of mystery has been woven round the death of Hatshepsut by the theory, apparently evolved by modern writers, that she was murdered by Thothmes III who wished to reign alone. There is, however, no real evidence for this theory, which seems to be based on a misreading of the cartouches which were erased and re-cut in the temple of Deir el Bahri. But at all periods of Egyptian history it was not an uncommon practice to erase the name of a predecessor and usurp his work.

strongly advised that the army should take the level route round the hills and the easy ascent from the north. They were perhaps influenced by the knowledge that the Egyptian soldiers had probably never climbed a hill before. They were also aware that there was a narrow defile to be passed if the ascent was made from the south, where "horse must follow behind horse, and man behind man also, and our vanguard will be engaged while our rearguard is at Aaruna without fighting." Thothmes' reaction to the advice was characteristic of the man; he spoke his mind plainly: "As I live, as I am the beloved of Rê and praised by my father Amon, I will go on this narrow road. Let those who will, go on the roads you have mentioned; and let anyone who will, follow my Majesty." When the soldiers heard the speech, they shouted with one accord, "We follow thy Majesty whithersoever thy Majesty goes." Thothmes led the van himself, marching on foot at the head of his army. They passed through the defile, "horse behind horse, and man behind man, his Majesty showing the way by his own footsteps". They reached Megiddo where the enemy was not expecting them, and the next day fought a pitched battle in which the princes of Megiddo and Kadesh were defeated and "fled headlong to Megiddo as if terrified by spirits; they left their horses and their chariots of silver and gold. They were drawn up by hauling them by cloths into the city, for the inhabitants had shut the gates of the city upon them, and let down cloths to haul them up to the city." The Egyptian army, being young and not yet disciplined, fell upon the plunder of the battlefield and so lost the opportunity of taking Megiddo then and there. Thothmes reproached them bitterly: "If only the troops of his Majesty had not given their hearts to spoiling the things of the enemy, they would have taken Megiddo at that moment when the vile enemy of Kadesh and the vile enemy of Megiddo were hauled up in haste to get them into their city. For the capture of Megiddo is as the capture of a thousand cities." Megiddo was then besieged and did not surrender for three weeks. The terms of surrender were not harsh; a certain amount of tribute had to be paid, and an Egyptian governor was put in charge, but there was no massacre of prisoners or inhabitants and the two enemy princes appear to have escaped.

This is the only campaign which is recorded in full detail, but there were sixteen campaigns in all, in Palestine, Syria, and Nubia. Thothmes was not only a great general but a statesman as well with high ideals. His treatment of conquered countries was always humane; even the chiefs who fought against him were not executed, they were merely deposed: "The sons of the princes and their brothers were brought to be placed as hostages in Egypt. If any one of the

chiefs died, his Majesty would make his son go to stand in his stead."
He established the *Pax Ægyptiaca* over the whole of his empire; no
longer were there plundering expeditions by one little kinglet against
another little kinglet; Syria and Palestine were forced to keep the peace,
and under his benign rule they reached a degree of prosperity which
they have seldom, if ever, enjoyed since.

The Egyptian poets referred to their great king as "a circling comet
which shoots out flames and gives forth its substance in fire", and as
"a young bull, ready with its horns, irresistible". But his character is
better expressed in the words which his officers said of him at his
death: "Behold, the King ended his time of existence of many good
years of victory, from the first year to the fifty-fourth. On the 30th
of the month Phamenoth, the Majesty of the King, Thothmes, true
of voice, ascended to heaven and joined the Sun's disc; the follower of
God met his Maker."* Another records that "the King completed a
lifetime of many years, splendid in valour, in might, and in triumph.
He mounted to heaven, he joined the Sun, the divine limbs mingled
with him who begat him."† His Vizier said of him: "There was
nothing that he did not know, he was Thoth in everything. There
was no affair which he did not complete." And an officer who had
been "the Follower of the King in his campaigns to the lands of the
South and the North" so loved his old commander that in his tomb he
put a scene of the worship of Thothmes with this little prayer engraved
over the altar of offerings: "For thy *ka*, O Amon-Rê, King of the
Gods, for Rê-Harakhti, and for Hathor Regent of Thebes, that they
may give victorious courage to the royal spirit of Men-kheper-
Rê."‡

As soon as the Syrian princes learned that the great conqueror was
dead, they made an effort to return to their old and evil ways, but the
new Pharaoh, Amonhotep II (pl. xlix. 4), had inherited much of his
father's military genius, and in one campaign the princes discovered
that Egypt would not suffer the breaking of the King's peace. This was
the only attempt on the part of the foreign possessions of Egypt to
assert their right to plunder their neighbours during the whole of
Amonhotep's otherwise uneventful reign. He was succeeded by his
son, Thothmes IV (pl. l. 3), who conducted an expedition as far north
as Naharina, and had a campaign in Nubia. He was chiefly distinguished for his love of sport: "He hunted wild game on the deserts
both north and south of Memphis, he coursed the lions and the deer,
he shot arrows at a target, he drove in his chariot, and his horses were

---

* Mariette, *Karnak*, pp. 28–31.   † Piehl, *Inscriptions*, i. 87–92.
‡ Davies, *Journal of Egyptian Archæology* (hereinafter referred to as *J.E.A.*), xxvi
(1941), p. 131.

fleeter than the wind. Alone did he hunt or with two companions only."

When Amonhotep III, son of Thothmes IV, came to the throne, Egypt was at the highest point of her glory. He made one small military expedition of no importance, but it was lauded to the skies: "His Majesty returned, having triumphed on this victorious campaign in the land of the miserable Kush; having made his boundary as far as he desired, as far as the four pillars which bear up the sky. He set up a tablet of victory as far as the Pool of Horus. There was no King of Egypt who did the like except his Majesty, the Mighty."[*] The surprising event of his life was his marriage with a non-royal lady named Tyi, for by Egyptian custom the throne went to the husband of the heiress-queen. Tyi's position as "the Great Wife of the King" was so emphasised in all the inscriptions of this reign as to suggest that the position was not altogether secure. The so-called "marriage scarabs" on which Amonhotep announced his marriage show a certain defiance: "Live the King of Upper and Lower Egypt, Neb-Maot-Rê, Son of the Sun, Amonhotep, gifted with life, and the King's Great Wife, Tyi, who is living. The name of her father is Yuya, the name of her mother is Thuya. She is the wife of the mighty King whose southern boundary is as far as Karoy, the northern as far as Naharina."[†]

It is to this reign that the earliest of the letters known as the Tell el Amarna Tablets can be dated. These are the official and private letters to the Pharaoh from the independent kings, vassal princes, and Egyptian governors in Syria and Palestine. The private letters make lively reading; there are lists of presents sent and asked for, kind inquiries made after the families of the correspondents, and small items of news reported.

Amonhotep may well be called "the Magnificent". He had everything that the world could give him, and he spent lavishly on his own pleasures and on those things which enhanced his own position. His finest temple, the temple of Luxor, was built in honour of his own divine birth; his colossi still dominate the Plain of Thebes; innumerable statues of deities which he set up are never anonymous but always bear the name of the royal donor; statues of himself exceed in number those of any other Pharaoh. He encouraged art in every form, from the splendour of architecture to the more humble art of making glass beads. He reigned when Egypt was at the height of her power, the world was at his feet, and there was nothing left for him to wish for. There exists one portrait of him which, if truthful, shows him listless and disillusioned, as if life had lost all interest for him.

[*] Lepsius, op. cit., iii. 82, *a*.   [†] Mariette, *Album de Boulaq*, pl. 36.

He was succeeded by his son Amonhotep IV, later called Akhenaten*
(pls. lxi; lxx. 1, 2; lxxi. 2). His reign—known as the Tell el Amarna
period—has had more nonsense written about it than any other period
in Egyptian history, and Akhenaten is a strong rival to Cleopatra for
the historical novelist. The appeal of Cleopatra is the romantic combination of love and death; Akhenaten appeals by a combination of
religion and sentiment. In the case of Akhenaten the facts do not
bear the construction often put on them.

It was not until the fourth year of his reign that Akhenaten adopted
the religion of the Aten, to which he devoted the rest of his life to the
exclusion of all other considerations. The Aten is the actual disc of the
sun, the physical sun which emits heat and sends out visible rays;
whereas Rê is the divine element in the sun and is a more abstract,
perhaps a more spiritual, conception. Akhenaten was therefore no
heretic, for the sun in all its aspects was the royal god, and this was
recognised by him for he worshipped Rê, Horus, and the Mnevis bull.

The hatred which Akhenaten showed to Amon of Thebes suggests
some strong personal feeling, perhaps against the priesthood of that
god. It is not impossible that the religious schism and the persecution
of Amon may have been due to the priests of the Sun-god. The
removal of the capital from Thebes to Akhetaten (Tell el Amarna)
was a shrewd blow to the wealth of the priesthood of Amon by
blocking the import trade from the northern possessions of Egypt.
The riches of Syria, Palestine, and other lands of the eastern Mediterranean, which had hitherto poured into Thebes, and of course in to
the coffers of the temple, were now stopped at the new capital. The
King's imprisonment in his new city, whether self-inflicted or enforced,
cut off supplies from the royal bounty; and wealthy officials followed
the King and spent their wealth on the new temples.

The removal of the capital had another and more disastrous effect.
Akhenaten made a vow that he would never leave Akhetaten, and
this vow he kept; he therefore never travelled to inspect the administration, he knew nothing of the government of the country; he spent
his time in adoring his new god and building temples to his honour.
Even when the loyal chiefs in Palestine were imploring help, he had
no time to attend to such mundane matters, but composed hymns and
prayers to the Aten.

* Akhenaten was the son of Amonhotep III and Tyi, and this is perhaps the reason
why his name and those of his immediate successors are omitted from the official lists,
for according to Egyptian law the royal descent was in the female line, and Tyi was
not royal. The Tell el Amarna royalties were apparently regarded as usurpers, and
when the legitimate line was restored, Akhenaten is referred to as "the criminal of
Akhetaten"; hardly a misnomer if his betrayal of his faithful friend Ribaddi of Gebal
is remembered.

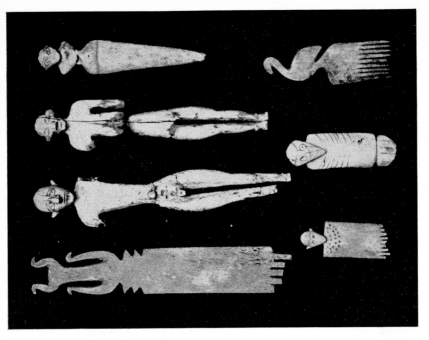

Petrie Coll.

2. Amratean ivory figures

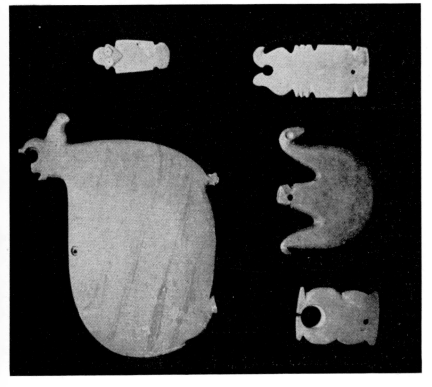

Petrie Coll.

1. Amratean slate palettes

PLATE I

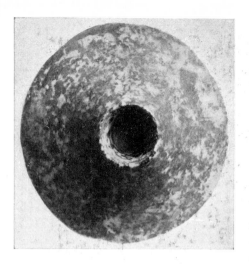

1. Amratean mace head   2. Gerzean mace head

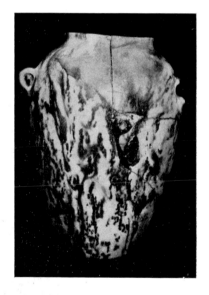

3, 4. Amratean stone vases

PLATE II

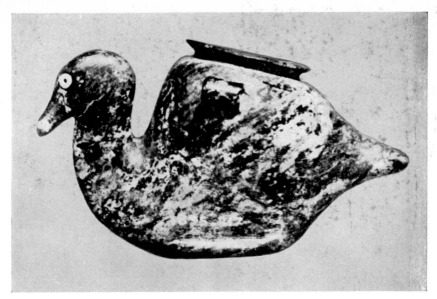

Photograph by M. A. Murray   *Petrie Coll.*

⚶ 1. Gerzean vase, diorite

Photograph by Dr. S. Pritchard   *Fitzwilliam Museum*

2. Perfume box, dynasty xviii

PLATE III

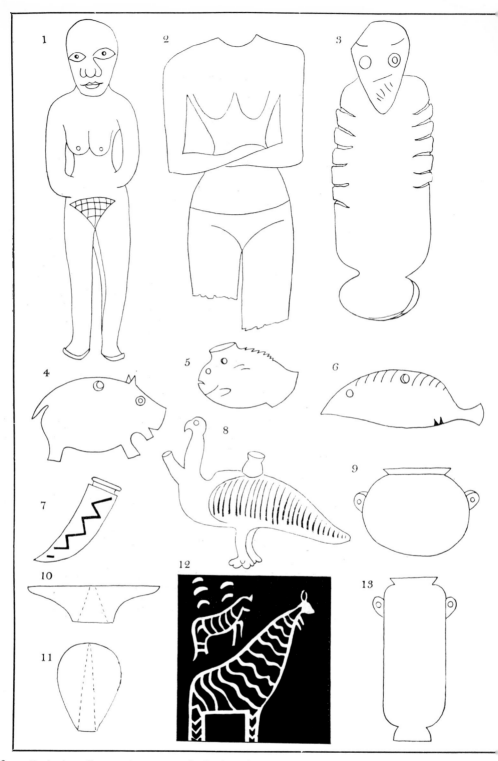

1. Badarian figure, ivory; 2. Badarian figure, pottery; 3. Amratean figure, ivory; 4. Slate palette; 5. Pottery vase; 6. Slate palette; 7. Ivory tusk; 8. Pottery vase; 9. Stone vase, Gerzean; 10. Mace head, Amratean; 11. Mace head, Gerzean; 12. Decoration on pottery, Amratean; 13. Stone vase, Amratean

PLATE IV

Petrie Coll.

Narmer (Menes), dynasty i

PLATE V

Ny-Glyptothek Copenhagen

⚱ Khafra, dynasty iv

PLATE VI

I

1. Field divided into squares, showing water runnel. *Shaduf* with bucket pulled down

2. *Shadufs* in action on canal bank

3. Alabaster sphinx of Queen Hatshepsut

4. Inundation. *Shaduf*-pole with bucket removed

Photograph by M. A. Murray

2

4

Photograph by M. A. Murray

PLATE VII

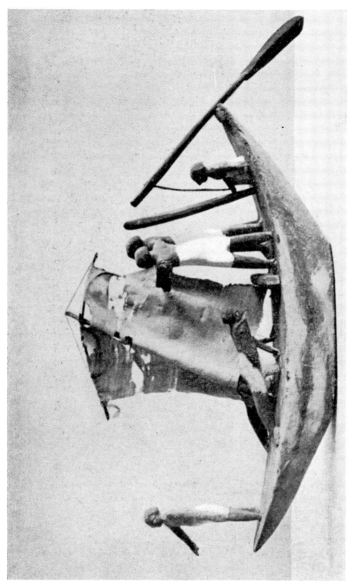

Fitzwilliam Museum

Sailing boat, dynasty xi

Photograph by Dr. S. Pritchard

PLATE VIII

Soul-house

Plate IX

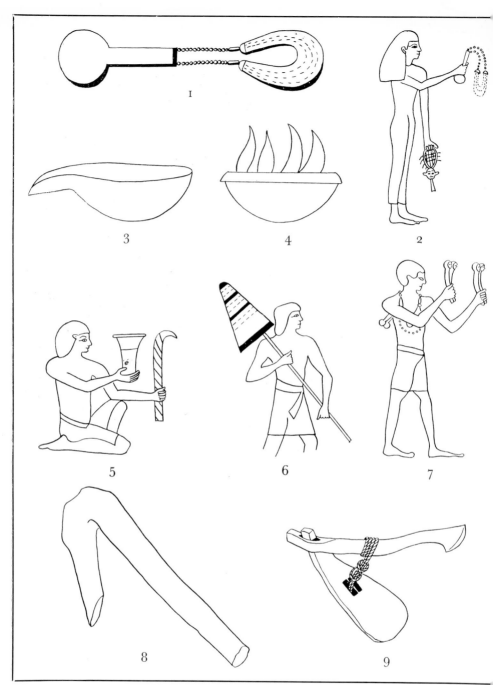

1. Menyt. 2. Priestess holding menyt and sistrum. 3. Saucer-lamp. 4. Bowl-lamp alight. 5. Priest with twisted candle. 6. Man carrying flat candle. 7. Priest holding castanets and wearing menyt. 8. Primitive hoe. 9. Egyptian hoe

PLATE X

Ritual ploughing.   Rameses III in the temple at Medinet Habu

PLATE XI

1. Framework of bed,
   dynasty i

2. Plaited string mat-
   tress, dynasty i

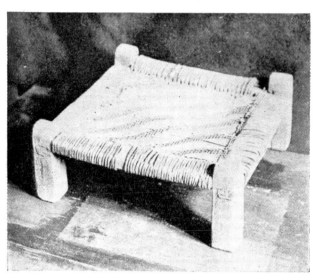

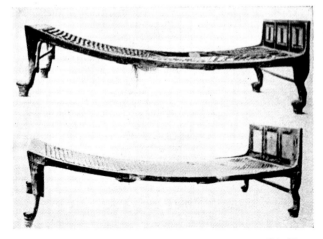

3. Stool with plaited
   leather seat

4. Beds from the
   tomb of Yuya,
   dynasty xviii

Plate XII

1. Princess's chair. Back

2. Princess's chair. Front

3. Casket of Yuya

PLATE XIII

Fitzwilliam Museum

Kitchen scene, dynasty xi

Photograph by Dr. S. Pritchard

PLATE XIV

Spinning and weaving, dynasty xi

Plate XV

1. Bronze mirror with obsidian handle

2, 3, 4. Perfume spoons, wood

5. Perfume spoon, ivory

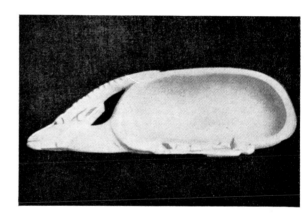

Photograph by Dr. S. Pritchard   *Fitzwilliam Museum*

6. Knitted sock. Roman

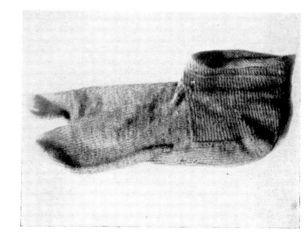

PLATE XVI   *Petrie Coll.*

It is uncertain whether Nefert-yti, Akhenaten's queen (pl. lxxii), acquiesced in the new religion. She was separated from her husband after she had borne him six daughters, and lived (or perhaps was imprisoned) in another part of his city. Her retirement seems to have been due to the fact that Akhenaten associated a young lad with him ostensibly as co-regent, and the queen found that her place in the King's life had been usurped.

After Akhenaten's death his town was deserted precipitately, and there was a general destruction of all outward signs of the new religion. The temples and palaces were deliberately gutted and smashed to pieces, hardly one stone was left standing on another. It would seem that the destroyers were bent on effacing every vestige of a hated enemy.

Details of the reign of Akhenaten are furnished by the Tell el Amarna Letters, which set forth with painful clearness the downfall of Egyptian power in the northern provinces. The letters become increasingly urgent in entreaty or demand for help against the invading Hittites and the local traitors. Each letter gives warning that unless help is sent, even if only a few soldiers, "the land of my lord the King will be lost". Many times the writers add a postscript addressed to the King's private secretary: "Tell the King frankly that his land is being lost." The most pathetic of all letters are from Ribaddi of Gebal, who wrote more and more urgently as he saw the enemy approaching nearer and closing round his doomed city. "Like a bird that is caught in a snare, so am I in this city of Gebal." He asks for only a few soldiers, a token army, a mere gesture to show that the Pharaoh was still powerful. But the Pharaoh was worshipping the Aten and worldly affairs did not interest him. Ribaddi's last letter is terrible in its despair: "If no help comes, then am I a dead man." After this there is a grim silence.

Two boy-kings followed Akhenaten. The first was Smenkh-ka-Rê, who lived and died at Tell el Amarna. The second was Tut-ankh-Amon (Frontispiece),* who by his very name shows that the worship of Amon had been reinstated. In spite of the loss of the Syrian provinces Egypt was still a power to be reckoned with and to be conciliated. In the tomb of Huy, Tut-ankh-Amon's vizier, there are representations of the arrival of ambassadors from both north and south (pl. xc. 1), bearing gifts for the young Pharaoh, who sits aloof and haughty. The tomb of Tut-ankh-Amon was found to contain many of the objects depicted in Huy's tomb.

---

* Tut-ankh-Amon's relationship with his predecessors is uncertain. His portraits show some likeness to Akhenaten, but his mummy has unusually large front teeth, reminiscent of the projecting teeth of the Pharaohs of the early xviii-th dynasty. His tomb was discovered by Mr. Howard Carter in 1922.

c

Tut-ankh-Amon died at the age of eighteen, and his young widow at once wrote to the King of the Hittites asking for his son in marriage and saying that she would make him King of Egypt. But among the entourage of Akhenaten there had been a priest of Amon called Ay; he had been ostensibly one of the strongest supporters of Aten worship and was high in the royal favour at Tell el Amarna, where he had held important offices. When Akhenaten died and the Aten religion was abolished, Ay declared publicly his attachment to Amon. Under Akhenaten he had risen as high as any subject could rise; now with the death of Tut-ankh-Amon, he saw the prize of the kingship within his grasp, with nothing but one little girl as an obstacle to his ambition. There was only one way to obtain what he desired. The young Hittite prince was met on his journey to Egypt by a party of Ay's men and murdered, and the little girl-queen disappears from history without leaving a trace.

Some modern historians end the xviii-th dynasty with Ay, and begin the xix-th with Haremheb, because Haremheb came as a great reformer, restoring order after the chaotic conditions caused by the neglect of his immediate predecessors. As, however, he was closely connected with the Tell el Amarna episode, appears to have married into that family, and left no descendants, it seems better to place him in the xviii-th dynasty.

He dated his reign from the death of Amonhotep III, thus ignoring Akhenaten, Smenkh-ka-Rê, Tut-ankh-Amon, and Ay. Under Akhenaten he had been a military commander, and being an unusually capable man he had gradually drawn into his own hands the whole government of the country, and was Viceroy for some years before he became King. His appointment as Pharaoh was made by the god Amon, and part of the coronation ceremony was his marriage with the heiress, for it was by this marriage that he legitimised his position as King.

His chief work was his legal enactments; he not only made laws but insisted on their being enforced. Though his reign was not a long one, he accomplished much in the time. He re-established law and order in the whole country, and extricated Egypt from the chaos into which Akhenaten and his co-religionists had plunged her. He rooted out Atenism, and was probably responsible for the utter destruction of the city of Akhetaten. On the other hand he was a great builder, and enriched and enlarged many of the temples dedicated to various gods. He and his wife had no children, therefore with them the direct line of the xviii-th dynasty became extinct.

In the xix-th dynasty there are only three kings who are of any importance historically, Setekhy I, Rameses II, and Mer-en-Ptah. It is these three kings whose physical characters show so marked a difference from the Pharaohs of the xviii-th dynasty that it has been suggested that they were of a different race. They were not only bigger men, but of a different build; their faces were more square than oval; the large mouths, big aquiline noses and the shape of the orbits of the eyes are quite unlike the features of the Thothmessides. They were, however, entirely Egyptian in upbringing and in outlook on life; they were warlike and devout, boastful and kindly, realising that as God they had a right to the worship of their subjects, and yet that as God mercy was their prerogative.

On his accession Setekhy I (pl. lxxiv) made a gallant attempt to recover the lost provinces, and had more than one campaign in Syria. He followed the method of that great general, Thothmes III, by taking possession first of southern Palestine; then moving northwards and seizing the whole coast at the same time; finally making an on-slaught on the country to the north. But here he found an enemy stronger than the Egyptians. The Hittites had been an insignificant people in the time of Thothmes III, but now they were the most powerful race in the whole of Syria, and Setekhy after much fighting could retain only the Palestinian provinces south of Galilee.

The record of his battles fills the greater part of the inscriptions, but there is one achievement which throws a favourable light on his character. This was the establishment of a water-station on the way from the Nile Valley to the gold mines in the eastern desert. "His Majesty inspected the hill country as far as the region of the moun-tains, and he said, 'How evil is the way without water. A traveller's mouth is parched. How shall his throat be cooled? how shall his thirst be quenched, for the Low Land is far away and the High Land is vast. The thirsty man in this fatal country cries aloud. Make haste then, and take counsel for their needs. I will make a supply for pre-serving their lives so that in after years they will thank God in my name.'" A well was dug according to the King's command, "and the water flooded it in very great plenty like the two caves of Elephantine. Then said his Majesty, 'Lo, God has performed my petition, he has brought water for me upon the mountain.'"*

Setekhy was a great restorer of ruined sanctuaries; and where he made such restorations he records the deed by only one line of inscrip-tion, merely stating the fact with his name and titles. His finest work was the lovely temple of the Seven Chapels at Abydos, dedicated to the memory and for the worship of the Osiris-kings of Egypt who were buried or had cenotaphs in that ancient royal cemetery. His own

* Lepsius, op. cit., iii. 139–41, d; Golenischeff, Recueil, xiii. pls. i, ii.

great tomb, however, was at Thebes in the Valley of the Tombs of
the Kings, and is one of the marvels of ancient Egypt. It is cut three
hundred feet into the rock; the walls and most of the ceilings of the
halls and passages are decorated with sculpture and painting, depicting the Journey of the Sun through the Realms of Night.

In the temple of Qurna his son Rameses II records Setekhy's death
in the words, "Lo, he went to his retreat, he reached heaven, he
joined Rê in heaven".*

Rameses II (pls. lxii; lxiii; lxiv. 2) is perhaps the best-known of all
the Pharaohs, partly because during his long reign he had time to
build more than his predecessors and partly because he so often usurped
the architecture and sculpture of earlier kings.

In the restlessness of the world in those early times, Egypt had
always to be on her guard against foreign aggression, which was at its
most dangerous on the accession of a new Pharaoh. Almost every
Egyptian king, when he came to the throne, had to make a display of
force on his frontiers to ensure a peaceful reign; the farther afield he
could carry his arms the less likely he was to be troubled afterwards.
Rameses was no exception to the rule, for the Hittites were pushing
rapidly southward, and threatening the whole of Syria and Palestine.
To guard his own kingdom, Rameses had to give battle, but the
Hittites were a strong enemy and Egypt was involved in war for
twenty years.

It was in the second campaign that there occurred the episode which
was the great event in the life of Rameses and which he recorded on
the walls of every temple he built. He was intending to attack Kadesh
on the Orontes, and was marching through the country with his army
divided into four sections, each called after the name of a god, Amon,
Rê, Ptah, and Setekh. Rameses with his bodyguard and the army of
Amon formed the van, the army of Rê being about a mile and a half
behind. The Egyptians were quite unaware that the Hittite army was
hidden behind "the deceitful city of Kadesh", and proceeded to pitch
their camp to the north-west of the town. Meanwhile the Hittites
moved to the south-east, and fell upon the army of Rê as it was crossing
a ford. The rout of Rê was complete, they fled in disorder, and burst
upon the unsuspecting Amon-division pursued by the Hittite chariotry.
The panic spread to the Amon-division who also fled leaving Rameses
with only his bodyguard to face the exultant enemy. The Hittite
chiefs flung the whole of their chariotry—two thousand five hundred
chariots—in an encircling movement at the little band. The situation
was desperate, and with the courage of despair Rameses put himself at
the head of his little force and charged the enemy as they came up from

* Champollion, *Notices,* i. 694.

the south. This surprise attack halted the enemy and gained the King sufficient time to look round and see that the weakest part of the line of his opponents was to the east. He charged again in that direction, driving the enemy into the river. By doing this he had to desert the newly formed camp, and this gave him some respite, for the Hittites were unable to pass such rich plunder and stopped to sack the camp. Then the unexpected happened. A large Egyptian division arrived on the scene, marching from the coast; neither Rameses nor the Hittites appear to have known that they were in the neighbourhood. They came in the nick of time, and with their help Rameses was able to attack six times and beat off the enemy's assaults. At the end of nearly four hours of stubborn fighting the vizier arrived with the Ptah-division and attacked the Hittites in the rear. Both sides were exhausted, and Rameses appears to have withdrawn his troops without molestation from the Hittites, but without any further attempt on his part to capture the deceitful city of Kadesh.

For twenty years the Egyptians were engaged in fighting the Hittites or their allies, until at last it was evident that such a state of affairs was impossible, and both sides agreed to a treaty.* The terms of the treaty were, (1) mutual resignation of all projects for further conquests in Syria, though no boundaries are mentioned; (2) mutual defensive alliance against foreign enemies; (3) mutual help in suppressing risings in Syria; (4) mutual extradition of political fugitives. With this item there was a proviso that the persons so extraditied were to be humanely treated. The witnesses to this remarkable document were "a thousand deities of the male gods and female gods of the land of the Hittites, and a thousand deities of the male gods and the female gods of the land of Egypt".

As the treaty with the Hittites secured peace for Egypt, Rameses was able to devote his time to building on a large scale. The constant wars in Syria and Palestine had shown that Thebes was too far away from the scene of action to remain the capital; even Memphis was too remote. Rameses therefore founded a new capital at Tanis in the Delta. With the encouragement of the Pharaoh new towns of some importance sprang up in all parts of the Delta, all adorned by Rameses with temples. His greatest achievements of this kind were, however, at Thebes and at Abu Simbel in Nubia. As all these sanctuaries had to be endowed, much of the wealth of the country fell into the hands of the priesthoods.

Rameses reigned sixty-four years; during the latter part of his life there were no events of any importance recorded. The Hittite treaty and his marriage with a Hittite princess are the last of any historical

* Lepsius, op. cit., iii. 146.

value. As often happened in Egypt when there was too much peace and prosperity, the country degenerated, the Pharaoh became slothful, the officials neglectful, and the peasants unhappy. Foreigners began to flock in and settle in Egypt, pushing out the rightful inhabitants, and when Rameses died his son and successor, Mer-en-Ptah, was faced with a perilous situation.

Mer-en-Ptah ("The Beloved of Ptah") (pl. lix. 2) began his reign with five years of peace, but it was the false calm which precedes the storm. The weakness of the government in the last years of Rameses II had allowed the whole of the west side of the Delta to fall into the hands of foreigners, and on the east side the Egyptians were being rapidly ousted by foreign settlers. Egypt was in danger of losing the whole Delta, first by peaceful penetration, then by armed invasion. Mer-en-Ptah appears to have spent the first five years of his reign in making quiet preparations for the struggle which he foresaw would come. It came when the Libyan chief, Meru-yu, was so convinced of an easy victory that he brought his wife and children and all his possessions with him when he decided to attack the Pharaoh and seize the Delta. The night before the decisive battle Mer-en-Ptah had a prophetic dream, a vision which was communicated to the army to encourage them. "His Majesty saw in a dream as if a statue of the god Ptah stood before his Majesty. He said, while holding out a sword to him, 'Take it and banish fear from thee'." The Libyans expected hand-to-hand fighting, but Mer-en-Ptah had prepared more modern methods. He had stationed cohorts of archers in strategic positions, and they poured their arrows on the invaders. "The bowmen of his Majesty spent six hours of destruction among them, then they were delivered to the sword."* As soon as the enemy's ranks showed signs of breaking, Mer-en-Ptah "let loose his chariotry", and "the families of Libya were scattered as mice on the dykes. They left behind them their advanced columns, their feet made no stand but ran. Their archers threw down their bows, and the hearts of their fleet ones were weary with marching. They loosed their water-skins and cast them on the ground, their food-sacks were thrown away. The prince of Libya fled by favour of the darkness. His women were taken before his face, the grain of his supplies was plundered and he had no water in his water-skin to keep him alive. His camp was burned, all his possessions were food for the troops." Mer-en-Ptah had promised his people that he would bring the enemy "like netted fish on their bellies", and he fulfilled his promise. His Triumph-Song (p. 209) shows that Egypt regarded the defeat of the Libyans as a great deliverance.

* Dümichen, *Historische Inschriften*, i. 2–6.

No further fighting took place during this reign and no other historical event is recorded. The country was exhausted with fighting, and the extravagant building programme which Rameses had carried out had impoverished the people. It was only the defeat of the Libyans which saved Egypt from utter ruin. As it was, Egypt was falling from her high estate, art had degenerated, there was no building, and except for the Triumph-Song there was little literature.

The rest of the xix-th dynasty is occupied by the struggles of the descendants of Rameses II for the throne. They were all weaklings, and the more they disputed and fought the more the country suffered. The last king of the dynasty, Setekh-nekht, made a gallant attempt to establish some semblance of good government, though the conditions were terrible: "The land of Egypt was overthrown. Every man was his own guide, they had no superiors. The land was in chiefships and princedoms, each killed the other among noble and mean." When Setekh-nekht "rested in his eternal house", his son, Rameses III, ascended the throne and was the founder of the xx-th dynasty.

History repeated itself, for during the internal troubles in the last part of the xix-th dynasty foreigners had begun their usual tactics; the time of peaceful penetration had passed, and an armed invasion was in preparation. Rameses III was the last of the fighting Pharaohs. He deliberately delayed any attack until he was ready. Then he made his assault with complete success: "The foreign lands and countries are stripped and brought to Egypt as slaves; gifts are gathered to satisfy the gods; provisions and supplies are like a flood in Egypt. As for those who invade his boundary, his Majesty goes forth against them like a flame in dry herbage. They flutter like birds in the net, their legs struggling in the basket. The land of Egypt lives with untroubled heart; a woman can go about at her will, with her veil upon her head, she can go as far as she pleases."*

Danger from another quarter soon threatened Egypt. A confederacy of the tribes of the eastern Mediterranean lands had been formed, and were pursuing a career of conquest and plunder. They were like a cloud of locusts destroying all as they passed, and before their hungry eyes lay the rich land of Egypt. In the eighth year of Rameses' reign they prepared to attack. Under the spirited generalship of the Pharaoh Egypt was ready. All the harbours at the mouths of the Nile were defended by ships manned by fighting crews, and along the coast were the infantry and chariotry, who were led, as was the custom, by the Pharaoh in person. The enemy suffered a complete defeat by land and sea: "The countries which came from the Islands in the midst of the Sea advanced on Egypt, relying on their strength.

* Dümichen, op. cit., ii. 46.

The net was made ready for them to ensnare them. Entering stealthily into the harbour-mouth, they fell into it. Caught in their places they were slain and their bodies stripped."*

Rameses followed up the naval victory by a rapid march through Palestine and Syria as far as the Hittite frontier on the Orontes. He took five "strong cities", including Amor, which had been the focus of the invading forces. Among the prisoners whom he brought back to Egypt were the chief of Amor, the chief of the Hittites, the chief of Thekel, the chief of Shardana of the Sea, the chief of the Shasu (Bedawin), the chief of Teresh of the Sea, and the chief of the Philistines.

Three years later another invasion was attempted by a coalition of the Meshwesh (Maxyes) and the Libyans.† But "his Majesty fell upon their heads like a mountain of granite", and the invasion came to nothing.

The booty from all these wars was immense. The document known as the *Great Harris Papyrus* gives the distribution which Rameses made of the plunder. The building and endowment of his temple at Medinet Habu swallowed up a large part, and other temples were also richly endowed. All the wealth, however, was not devoted to religious purposes only. Rameses sent out many trading expeditions, some of them "sailing away on the great Sea of the inverted water", *i.e.* the Indian Ocean, and reached Punt. Other traders travelled both by land and sea and brought back the products of many lands. He also spent freely in Egypt: "I caused to be planted the whole land with leafy trees, and I let the people sit in their shade." The country was so well policed that "a woman of Egypt could walk out to the place she wished, no vile persons molested her on the way".‡

Rameses appears to have died as the victim of a conspiracy in his own harem. One of the minor queens, named Tyi, joined with some other women and officers of the royal household in an intrigue to kill the Pharaoh and set Tyi's son on the throne. One of the conspirators obtained a book of magic from the royal library in order to learn "how he could strike people blind and reach the innermost parts of the harem. He made wax images." The wax images were in all probability intended as a means for killing the King, for when the case came to trial the image-maker was condemned to death. The wax images not proving successful, the conspirators tried stronger measures, and an actual attack was made upon the person of the King. He was not killed; he lived long enough to arrange for a special court to try the conspirators, but he appears to have died before the

* Dümichen, op. cit., ii. 47.
† Ibid., i. 13–15.

‡ Breasted, op. cit., iv. 204.

sentences were pronounced. A curious point is that the chief culprits were tried under false names, such as "He whom Rê hates", "The Wicked One of Thebes". Twelve of the conspirators were condemned to death and committed suicide as soon as sentence was pronounced; the rest had their ears and noses cut off and were imprisoned. The record of the death sentence and its fulfilment is terse in the extreme: "He was placed before the nobles of the Court of Examination; they found him guilty; they left him in his place; he took his own life." This was in accordance with the injunction of Rameses to the judges: "Those who should die, they shall be caused to die by their own hand." The record of the trial of the women is equally terse: "Wives of the people of the harem-gate, who joined with the men when things were discussed; they were placed before the nobles of the Court of Examination; they found them guilty; they brought their punishment upon them. Six women." Of the queen's fate nothing is known.

The rest of the dynasty consists of increasingly weak and insignificant kings, who were, one and all, the sons or grandsons of Rameses III. Each of them took the name of Rameses, and it is often difficult to distinguish between them. Historical records are almost non-existent in their short reigns; their chief claims to remembrance are their magnificent painted tombs at Thebes. As the royal power decreased the power of the priesthood of Amon increased. Towards the middle of the dynasty the heiress-princess married the High-priest of Amon, and thus transferred the right to the throne from the royal family to the priesthood. Another factor which increased the priestly power was the arrangement by which the Pharaoh relinguished his control over the finances of the temple of Amon, the riches of the priests being probably greater than those of the king. When therefore the last of the Ramessides died, the High-priest of Amon became in name what he had for years been in fact, the Pharaoh of Egypt.

LATE PERIOD

The xxi-st dynasty consists of two lines of kings, (a) the priest-kings of Thebes, and (b) the royal kings at Tanis in the Delta. As the royal descent was always reckoned through the women, the marriages of the princesses were of great importance, and the names of these royal ladies have been preserved.

There are no historical facts recorded during this dynasty;* the principal events are connected with some form of religion, such as a

* The recent discoveries of royal tombs at Tanis have added to our archæological knowledge, but no new historical facts have emerged.

careful inspection of the tombs and mummies of the dead Pharaohs, and a certain amount of repairs to the temples. The northern frontier, always a potential danger-zone, was quiet, for the old Palestinian enemies of Egypt were engaged in fighting the invading Israelites and could not attempt any invasion on their own account. The priest-kings were not warlike, being indolent, and the country under their rule sank into a slothful and miserable state. Ignorance and superstition are the marks of this period; never before had Egypt sunk so low, and never had her prestige in the eyes of the world suffered so great a fall. The story of the travels of Wen-Amon in Syria (p. 216), whither he was sent to fetch timber for the temple of Amon, shows the estimation in which the Egyptians were held at that time; the obstacles which were thrown in his way and the contempt with which he was treated tell their own tale. The chief of Byblos went so far as to say to Wen-Amon, "I am not the servant of him who sent you". How different from the tone of the Tell el Amarna Letters, when the princes of Syria are to Pharaoh "your servant and the dust upon which you tread".

The xxii-nd dynasty began with Sheshank I (the Biblical Shishak), a ruler of character. He descended from a Tanite princess, and was himself the prince of Bubastis in the Delta. As there is no account of his rise to the kingship of all Egypt, it is supposed that he obtained the kingdom by right of marriage with the heiress. He is best known by his spectacular exploit against Jerusalem in the fifth year of Rehoboam. The Biblical historian, with the usual exaggeration of the Oriental where numbers are concerned, says that Shishak "came up against Jerusalem with twelve hundred chariots, and threescore thousand horsemen, and the people were without number that came with him. . . . And he took away the treasures of the house of the Lord, and the treasures of the King's house, he took away all."* It is only necessary to read the Biblical account of the riches lavished by Solomon on the Temple and the Palace to realise the amount of booty that fell into Egyptian hands.

Besides Jerusalem, Shishak took also a number of "fenced cities", and in his record of the campaign these cities are represented as battle-mented ovals surmounted by a human head and torso; within the oval is the name of the city. The arms of the human personification of the town are tied at the back to indicate capture, and round the neck of each figure is a rope, the other end of which is held in the hand of a gigantic figure of Amon, who presents the captives to the King.

In spite of the enormous sums that must have been spent on the burials of the Pharaohs and on the endowments of the temples, the

* 2 Chron. xii. 2-4, 9.

fabulous wealth of Egypt was not exhausted. The plunder of Jerusalem had brought a further mass of treasure into the country, and it was perhaps because of this increase that Shishak's successor, Osorkon I was able to make his donations to the temples on almost the same lavish scale as the Pharaohs of the xviii-th dynasty.

The remainder of the kings of this dynasty are of no importance historically. The country was splitting up into small principalities, as Egypt was prone to do under weaker rulers, though the Pharaohs still maintained a semblance of authority over the local dynasts. Finally Egypt became a congeries of little states, not unlike Greece in classical times. This was the opportunity for a foreign power to attack and take possession. Ethiopia was in a flourishing state, and the Ethiopian kings had a certain claim to the throne of Egypt. Piankhy of Napata* therefore set out to enforce that claim, and has left a detailed account of his invasion. He appears to have taken the Thebaid without difficulty, and claimed, though he did not exercise, control over the north. But Tafnekht, prince of Saïs, was also desirous of being Pharaoh and began a career of conquest. He soon held the whole Delta, and many of the southern princes submitted to him. Piankhy then sent an army northward; his address to the soldiers has been preserved: "Delay not, day or night, as if at a game of chess, fight at sight. Force battle from a distance. Yoke the war-horses! Draw up the line of battle! Amon is the god who has sent us! He makes the weak strong, so that a multitude flees before the feeble, and one man takes a thousand captive.† Say to Him, 'Give us the way that we may fight under the shadow of Thy sword. When the young men whom Thou hast sent out make their attack, let multitudes flee before them." Piankhy's troops had besieged Hermopolis for four or five months before Piankhy arrived in person to direct operations, and the city was already "foul to the nose". The king at once encircled the city with an embankment on which was set a high wooden structure manned by archers and slingers. These active measures soon reduced Nimrud, prince of Hermopolis, to submission. The terms were unconditional surrender by Nimrud in person, and Piankhy entered the city in triumph and went into Nimrud's palace as a conqueror. Nimrud's "wives and daughters were brought before him but he turned his face from them. His Majesty proceeded to the stables of the horses and the stalls of the foals. When he saw that they had suffered hunger, he said, 'I swear as Rê loves me, as my notrils are rejuvenated with life, it is, more grievous to my heart that my horses have suffered hunger than

---

* The stela which records the conquest was set up in the temple of Napata (Barkal). Mariette, *Monuments divers*, pls. 1–6.

† Cf. Isiah xxx. 17. "One thousand shall flee at the rebuke of one."

any evil deed which thou hast done." Before arriving at Memphis, Piankhy sent a message to that great fortress: "Shut not up! Fight not! Those who wish to come, let them come in; those who wish to go out, let them go out. The people of Memphis shall be safe and sound, not even a child shall weep! Look at the provinces of the South, not a single person has been killed, except those who were slain as rebels." Memphis, however, was prepared to hold out, being strongly fortified with great walls on three sides, and the river on the east. Piankhy swore a great oath, "As Rê loves men, as Amon favours me, this shall happen. I shall take Memphis by a flood of water!" He organised a flotilla, which he sent stealthily across the water to capture the boats, which were moored by their bow-ropes to the houses inside the town. This operation was successful, all the enemy boats were captured without any casualties, and Piankhy's troops embarked. The king harangued them before they started to the assault: "Forward against it! Mount the walls! Penetrate into the houses across the river!' Thus Memphis was taken by a flood of water. Multitudes were slain therein or brought as living captives to his Majesty." The final triumph was the submission of Tafnekht, who sent an abjectly humble message to Piankhy offering to become his vassal. Piankhy who was a kindly man, accepted the offer and sent two of his officers to receive the oath of allegiance. The words of the oath have been preserved: Tafnekht "went to the temple, he worshipped God, he purified himself by a divine oath, saying, 'I will not transgress the command of the King, I will not violate the King's orders, I will do no hostile act against another prince without thy knowledge, I will do as the King orders, I will not disobey the King's commands.' "

Though Piankhy returned to his own country, the Ethiopian domination continued till the end of the xxv-th dynasty, with a break of six years, which constituted the xxiv-th dynasty. There is a certain amount of mystery surrounding Bocchoris, the only kind of the xxiv-th dynasty. He was the son of Tafnekht, the old enemy of Piankhy, and Diodorus calls him "Bocchoris the Wise". Manetho mentions a remarkable happening in this king's reign: "Bocchoris the Saïte, reigned six years, in whose reign a sheep spoke." It is possible that this may have been regarded as an omen foretelling the dreadful death of Bocchoris, for Manetho goes on with an account of the next king, "Sabacon, having taken Bocchoris captive, burnt him alive".*

The earlier kings of the xxv-th dynasty are of little importance, for the shadow of that grim kingdom, Assyria, was beginning to fall across the countries of the Near East, and on every place that it fell it brought

* See Wainwright, *Sky Religion in Egypt*, for suggestion that the fate of Bocchoris was a religious sacrifice.

ruin and devastation. In the reign of Taharka (the Biblical Tirhakah) the shadow fell on Egypt. Taharka joined with Hezekiah of Judah against the advance of Sennacherib, and both were saved un-expectedly.* But under Esarhaddon the devastating course of Assyria continued. His conquest of Palestine was a triumphal march, and he took Memphis and the whole of the Delta in the space of three weeks. Taharka retired to the south, and when the Assyrians had departed he returned and tried to recover his kingdom. The Assyrians sent another army with the result recorded in the significant inscription of Ashurbanipal: "Tirhaka fled to Ethiopia, the might of the soldier of Ashur my lord overwhelmed him, and he went to his place of night."

Tanutamon (Tandomanu in the Assyrian inscriptions), the successor of Taharka, recovered part of the lost dominion of Egypt, and held it till Ashurbanipal returned in force and drove him out: "Tandomanu heard of the progress of my expedition, and that I had crossed the border of Egypt. He abandoned Memphis, and to save his life he fled to Thebes. I took the road after Tandomanu; I went to Thebes, the strong city; and he abandoned Thebes and fled to Kipkip. My army took the whole of Thebes; silver, gold, precious stones, the furniture of the palace, costly and beautiful garments, great horses, men and women; two lofty obelisks covered with beautiful carving, which were set up before the gate of a temple, I wrenched and brought to Assyria." This was the terrible Sack of Thebes which sent a shudder of horror through all the countries within reach of Assyria. When the prophet Nahum inveighed against Nineveh—"Woe to the bloody city! It is full of lies and robbery"—he instanced Thebes as an example of what might befall. "Art thou better than populous No,† that was situate among the rivers, that had waters round about it, whose ram-part was the waters, and her wall was from the waters? Ethiopia and Egypt were her strength, and it was infinite; Put and Lubim were thy helpers. Yet was she carried away, she went into captivity; her young children were dashed to pieces at the top of the streets; and they cast lots for her honourable men, and all her great men were bound in chains."‡

It is clear from the records of Taharka, Tanutamon, and Ashur-banipal that Egypt was again split up into small principalities.

* Herodotus, ii. 141; Isaiah xxxvii. 36.
† This was the colloquial appellation of Thebes; the Assyrian inscriptions give Ni as the name. The Egyptian word (perhaps pronounced Nu) merely means town, and was used for Thebes as we use the same term for London.
‡ Nahum iii. 8-10. Isaiah's description of desolation might well apply to Thebes during the centuries that followed: "Thorns shall come up in her palaces, and brambles in the fortresses thereof; and it shall be an habitation for dragons and a court for owls" (xxxiv. 13).

Herodotus, in relating a folk tale concerning the first king of the xxvi-th dynasty, says, "The Egyptians established twelve kings, having divided Egypt into twelve parts". Psamtek, one of the twelve, drove out the others by the help of Aegean mercenaries, and became Pharaoh. As he had to reward these soldiers of fortune without offending his legitimate subjects, who always had a strong jealousy of foreigners, he established them as frontier guards: "To the Ionians and those who had assisted him, Psammetichus gave lands opposite each other, with the Nile flowing between them. Besides these lands he gave them all that he had promised. . . . Even in my time garrisons of the Persians are stationed in the same places as they were in the time of Psammetichus, for they maintain guards at Elephantine and Daphnai."*

Psamtek was succeeded by his son Necho II, whose first act was an attempt to re-establish the Egyptian dominion over Palestine. He made a raid over that country, and King Josiah as a dutiful vassal of Assyria opposed him. "Necho king of Egypt came up to fight against Carchemish by Euphrates; and Josian went out against him. But he sent ambassadors to him, saying, What have I to do with thee, thou King of Judah? I came not against thee this day, but against the house with which I have war; for God commanded me to make haste. Forbear thee from meddling with God, who is with me, that he destroy thee not. Nevertheless Josiah would not turn his face from him, but disguised himself that he might fight with him, and hearkened not to the words of Necho from the mouth of God, and came to fight in the valley of Megiddo."† Josiah was killed in the ensuing battle, and Jehoahaz became King of Judah, "and Pharaoh-Nechoh put him in bands at Riblah, that he might not reign in Jerusalem; and put the land to a tribute of an hundred talents of silver and a talent of gold. And Pharaoh-Nechoh made Eliakim King and turned his name to Jehoiakim, and took Jehoahaz away, and he came to Egypt and died there."‡ Necho's dominion over Palestine did not last long for the Assyrians were still sufficiently strong to drive the Egyptians out of the country. Necho then turned his attention to improving the trade of Egypt. To this end he began a great water-way from the Nile to the Red Sea; it was intended to be wide enough for two triremes to be rowed abreast, and the journey would take four days. This stupendous undertaking was stopped on account of an adverse oracle. Nothing daunted, Necho then set about building ships on both sides of the Isthmus, some in the Mediterranean for the European trade, others in the Gulf of Suez for trade with the East. The docks for these ships were still to be seen in the time of Herodotus.

* Herodotus, ii. 151, 152, 153.   † 2 Chron. xxxv. 20-3.   ‡ 2 Kings xxiii. 33, 34.

The reign of Apries (the Biblical Hophra) has a certain dramatic quality which distinguishes it from the other reigns of this dynasty. The prophecy of Jeremiah* concerning this king strikes a tragic note: "Thus saith the Lord, I will give Pharaoh-Hophra king of Egypt into the hand of his enemies, and into the hand of those who seek his life." Apries sent a military expedition into Cyrene, where the Egyptians suffered a severe defeat. The exasperated army mutinied against Apries, and set up one of their officers, named Amasis, as king.† Civil war resulted, Amasis leading the Egyptians, Apries an army of thirty thousand Ionians and Carians. One battle decided the war, Apries was defeated and taken prisoner. He remained a captive for three years, then escaped and raised another army of mercenaries. Finally, in a naval battle, Apries was surprised on one of the ships and killed.

Amasis, having secured the throne, proved himself a capable ruler. His enactments conduced to peaceable and quiet lives among his subjects. One of his laws was so much admired by Solon that that wise man introduced it into Athens. This was that "every Egyptian should annually declare to the governor of his district by what means he maintained himself; and if he failed to do this, or did not show that he lived by honest means, he should be punished with death".‡ Amasis owed his throne to the Egyptians' hatred of foreigners; at the same time he was keenly aware of the importance of foreign trade and the necessity of keeping on good terms with his nearest neighbours, the Greeks. He solved this difficult problem by giving the city of Naukratis to the Greeks as their own possession, with special trading facilities, so that Naukratis had a monopoly of all goods coming by sea from Mediterranean lands. This gratified the Greeks; at the same time he destroyed the other Greek settlements in Egypt and so gratified his own people by confining the foreigners to the one port. This is one of the few examples in history when two diametrically opposing parties have been completely satisfied with the same arrangement; Amasis must therefore be ranked as one of the greatest diplomatists in the history of the world.

PERSIAN PERIOD

Persia was now rising into power, and embarking on a career of conquest. The fertile Nile Valley was an obvious objective, but the main difficulty in attacking Egypt from Persia was the waterless desert, to march over which took three days. Cambyses, the Persian king, made a treaty with the King of Arabia, who arranged to send

---

*Jer. xliv. 30.   † Herodotus, iv. 159.   ‡ Herodotus, ii. 177.

out sufficient water in water-skins on the backs of camels all along the route, and so enabled the Persian army to pass through the desert. Amasis was now dead, and his son Psamtek IV was on the throne. The Persians entered Egypt, and after one battle and the storming of Memphis they took possession, and Cambyses became king of Egypt. Psamtek became a guest of Cambyses in his palace, but as he intrigued against the conqueror he was condemned to death. Like the conspirators in the reign of Rameses III, he committed suicide; he "was compelled to drink the blood of a bull, and died immediately"*

Cambyses left no heir, and the Persian throne was seized by an impostor who passed himself off as a brother of Cambyses. But an able man arose in Persia and cleared his way to the throne by the murder of the impostor. This was Darius the Great, who proved to be one of the best of all the foreign rulers of Egypt. He came in person to visit this outlying province of his empire; and when he saw that trade was the high-road for its prosperity, he at once set about preparing the way. He finished the canal that Necho had begun, thereby making a waterway from the Nile to the Red Sea and eliminating the troublesome land journey. He rebuilt the temples and promoted the worship of the gods; he established schools, he reopened quarries, and in every way he encouraged trade and raised the standard of living. The successors of Darius did not find Egypt an easy province to handle, as insurrections headed by members of the old royal line gave much trouble. The leaders of these insurrections form Manetho's xxviii-th dynasty. Neither the xxviii-th nor the xxix-th dynasty has left many remains, for the country was torn with civil war. The Persians had other wars on their hands, and it was not until the beginning of the xxx-th dynasty that they made a determined attempt to recover complete control of Egypt. The native Pharaoh then on the throne was Nectanebo I (Nekht-Horheb), a resolute man, and a good commander. The Persians found much of the Delta strongly fortified; and when they succeeded in landing, it was at the beginning of the inundation. The Persians being ignorant of the ways of the river were easily out-manœuvred in the marshes by the Egyptians, and were driven out, leaving Egypt at peace for some years. The next two reigns are a record of continuous fighting until finally the Persians entered the country victoriously and the last native king, Nekhtanebo II (Nekht-neb-ef), fled to Ethiopia, abandoning Egypt to the plundering and ravages of as brutal and rapacious overlords as ever ruined a country. So much were the Persians hated that, when Alexander the Great defeated them and took possession of the Persian Empire, Egypt hailed him as her saviour and gave him divine honours.

* Herodotus, iii. 15.

PTOLEMAIC PERIOD

Alexander's great monument in Egypt was the magnificent city which still bears his name. His stay in Egypt was short and there was little time for much to be done, but that time was well spent, for he seems to have conciliated his new subjects by conforming to their religion and bringing back to them a certain amount of peace and good government. His early death was a disaster for his kingdom, for his heir was a little child of four years old; or, in default of the child, Alexander's half-brother Philip Arrhidaeus was the next heir. Philip is said to have been half-witted, and it was not long before he and the little child were both murdered. Alexander's empire had been divided among his generals as guardians for the child, and it was easy for each general to make himself king of his vice-royalty. Ptolemy was the general in charge of Egypt and became the founder of the Ptolemaic dynasty. He showed his astuteness even while viceroy, in his action on Alexander's death. As Alexander had been invincible in life, his body was regarded as a talisman to ensure victory, and it was believed that any country which possessed it would be secure from invasion. But the great conqueror was to be buried in the Oasis of Amon, a no-man's-land, a neutral territory. He had died at a long distance from Egypt, and his body was being brought southward through Syria and Palestine in order to pass through Egypt on its way to the Oasis. Ptolemy collected his army and marched out to meet the funeral cortège under the pretence of acting as escort and doing honour to his dead master. When the funeral procession reached Egypt, Ptolemy threw off the mask, took possession of the body, and buried it with pomp in Alexander's own city. The size of Ptolemy's army stifled any protests that might be made.

The early Ptolemies devoted themselves very successfully to making Alexandria the centre of intellectual life for the whole of the eastern Mediterranean area. Ptolemy II Philadelphus founded the great museum and library which made Alexandria famous and attracted most the learned men of the time to study there. The city itself was one of the most beautiful of its time, and filled all visitors with admiration. Scientific and literary work was carried on with energy at the museum, and the library was the largest in the world, containing nearly half a million volumes. The temples of Upper Egypt were repaired or rebuilt, and vast sums must have been spent in order to conciliate the priesthoods.

But the kings of this dynasty gradually degenerated, becoming sunk in luxury and increasingly vicious until the name Ptolemy became a

byword for wickedness and incapacity. Towards the end of the period
the shadow of Rome falls across Egypt when that mighty power began
to arise. As regards Egypt that power culminated in the reign of the
last of the Ptolemies, the great Cleopatra (pl. lxxvii. 2).* Julius Cæsar
took possession of the country in name only, leaving the actual government in the hands of Cleopatra; and it is doubtful if Antony took any
real part in the government though he had the status of king. But
when Octavius defeated Antony and entered Egypt as a conqueror
and demanded Cleopatra as his wife, that spirited woman preferred
death to such a fate. Octavius then took the country as the private
property of the Roman Emperors, putting in a bailiff (who was called a
prefect) to manage the estate, and using the taxes as the private Imperial
income. From that time Egypt ceased to exist as an independent kingdom, and her history is only that of a private estate, hardly rising to the
position of a province of a larger empire.

* For Cleopatra's marriages see pp. 70-1.

III

SOCIAL CONDITIONS

ORGANISATION

In early times the organisation of the country was fairly simple: the Pharaoh was the head of the administration, both nominally and actually. He was the Chief Judge in peace, the Commander-in-Chief in war; he was the head of the Treasury, the High-priest of every temple, and the Controller of all temple property. As civilisation advanced and life became more complicated he appointed officials under him to whom he delegated the work that he could not do himself. The royal princes were probably the first deputies of the king, and it is perhaps significant that the title of the Egyptian Viceroy of Nubia was "Son of the King".

By the time of the Old Kingdom the organisation of the country was fixed. The Pharaoh was, as always, the supreme head, but under him were numerous officials appointed by himself. Many of these officials were scribes or clerks in the government offices, for there was a vast amount of writing to be done in regard to taxation owing to the peculiarities of the country. Taxes were paid in kind, chiefly corn, flax, or farm animals. As agriculture depended entirely on the inundation, the assessment for taxation varied from year to year, and these calculations had to be made locally. A census of farm animals was made every second year, and this again was made locally. To do all this required local organisations, and the country was then divided into twenty nomes or provinces, each with its own governor (known as "the First under the King"), its own assessors, tax-collectors and all other officials necessary for government. On the legal side there were local courts for trying local offences; from these there was always the appeal to the High Court, and finally to the Pharaoh himself. Though inspectors were appointed to see that the government was properly carried on, the Pharaoh journeyed up and down the river constantly, inspecting everything himself, and redressing wrong where he found it. It was probable that these tours of inspection showed Khufu and Khafra how hardly the temple dues pressed on the people, hence their ban on sacrifices and the closing of the temples. So much depended on the king personally that when Egypt was afflicted with *rois fainéants* the country lapsed at once into chaos, and foreigners took advantage of

the condition to invade. Of that welter of disorganisation in the First
Intermediate Period little is known; few inscriptions remain to show
the miserable condition of the country.

With the rise of the Middle Kingdom the Pharaoh had to contend
with the fact that the governors of nomes had now become petty
princes, and it was the business of the energetic rulers of the xii-th
dynasty to reduce these arrogant princes to the subordinate position
which their predecessors had occupied in the Old Kingdom. To do
this Memphis could no longer be the capital as it was too far north to
control the princes of the south. The centre of government was
then moved to Middle Egypt, to the city known as Ithet-Tawy. By
rousing the military ardour of the country the Pharaohs of the xii-th
dynasty brought Egypt into line again; the local princes became military commanders under the Pharaoh as Commander-in-Chief; the
Pharaoh had his own army, "the Followers of his Majesty", who were
professional soldiers; and the provincial militia became part of a regular
army under the orders of their local chiefs but also under the supreme
command of the Pharaoh. The law-courts, "the Six Great Houses",
were in the capital, and all cases, with the exception of petty local
offences, were tried there and the Pharaoh had the report of every case
sent to him and decided on the punishment of all offenders who were
found guilty. Reports were sent to him regularly from all the high
officials in all parts of Egypt; and he himself travelled throughout his
kingdom and was acquainted with all the details of administration
everywhere.

The Middle Kingdom fell for the same cause that brought about
the fall of the Old Kingdom. Short reigns, combined with the weak
or idle characters of the kings, brought the country low, and the
Hyksos invaded and held Egypt for two or more centuries. After
they were driven out, the old organisation was continued with certain
developments made necessary by changed conditions. The Pharaoh
was obliged to delegate some of his functions to a deputy, a Vizier,
for it was physically impossible for one man to fulfil all the manifold
duties of his high position. All cases concerned with land were heard
in the Vizier's Court, the Chief Treasurer reported daily to the Vizier,
all local authorities reported three times a year to the Vizier, and he
made tours of inspection and supervised the local authorities. The
Vizier was the minister of war, of agriculture, of irrigation, no timber
could be felled except with his permission (for timber was of great
value in Egypt), and he administered the estates of the temples. In the
Vizier's office were filed all wills, records of trials concerning land, con-
tracts concerning land, lists of criminals awaiting trial, observations on
the Rising of Sirius (for this had a bearing on the inundation). Prac-

tically all the details of administration were in his hands.* When the Pharaoh was in the capital the Vizier reported to him every day, taking the Chief Treasurer with him to the palace. Yet though he took so much of the work off the king's hands, the monarch was fully employed; for as the final authority on all matters concerned with the government and with law, he had to understand all the details of any affair that he was called upon to decide. The Pharaoh was also perpetually on the move, whether in campaigns outside his own borders or on tours of inspection in times of peace.

The Vizierate seems to have come to an end when the kingdom of Egypt was split in two in the xxi-st dynasty, with Smendes ruling in the north and the High-priest, Herihor, as king of the south. But the regal power was not curtailed and survived even the disaster of the Assyrian invasion. Every Egyptian king was, until the very end, as truly a Pharaoh as any of his predecessors. It was this position of the Pharaoh, both King and God and therefore supreme, that enabled the Ptolemies to exploit the country as they desired.

The glittering façade of Alexandria as the centre of all the intellectual activity of the period has blinded the eyes of later generations to the conditions that lay behind that proud frontage.

Under their native Pharaohs, the Egyptians were subject to a divine ruler to whom they and all they possessed belonged. This was, however, a personal relation; it was possible for anyone, even the poorest of the poor, to approach the god and make known his complaints. The rather happy-go-lucky method of administration suited the country, and though it depended in great measure on the personal character of the administrator in each district it was possible for individuals of every class to attain an ordinary degree of comfort and prosperity and to live averagely happy lives.

But when the Egyptian ideas were translated into the Greek concept of government, the result was disastrous. By changing the intimate relation of the Pharaoh to his people into the rule of the State which owned everybody and everything, the Greeks transformed the personal element of the Pharaonic rule into the soulless domination of State control. It was a deliberate and well-thought-out policy, carried out with efficiency and ruthlessness. Centralisation and exploitation were the two principles on which the Ptolemies acted. Thus the wealth of the country came into the hands of the few, and enabled those few to build great temples inspiring wonder among visitors, and to make Alexandria the leading city for the whole of the Near East.

* The Vizier of Rameses II was with the king in the Kadesh campaign; there is no record as to which official acted as the king's deputy in the absence of the Vizier.

This was done by an adroit and crafty interpretation of the theory of the absolute authority of the Pharaoh. Theoretically the Pharaoh had been the sole owner of Egypt and all that was in it, practically he had been like most other rulers, merely the head of a country where private property and private rights were respected. But the theory was there and the Ptolemies acted on it.

The Crown had of course large estates, but the greater part of the land was in private hands. This was now registered with great exactness and was placed under the control of the State, whether it was arable land, orchards, vineyards, or even gardens. In practice the result was that all land-holders merely leased their land from the State, with this anomaly, that the lessee was bound to the land but the State could dismiss the tenant at will. The farmer was forced to remain at the place where he was registered; and for permission to work his farm he had to cultivate the land, sow, reap, and transport his crop at his own expense. The State made a pretence of regarding the house and the agricultural implements as the private property of the farmer, but it could at any time sell them up as payment to itself for arrears of taxes.

From the beginning of the dynastic period there had always been a biennial census of cattle, though possibly not of other animals. Under the Ptolemies all farm animals were subject to a yearly census, and could at any time be commandeered by the State.

Besides his own legitimate work, the State required the farmer to keep all the canals in repair, and to be ready to transport State property; all without pay.

It would seem that State interference could hardly go further if the government wished to induce men to take up the profession of farming; the work being hard and the profit inconsiderable. But as the State was both theoretically and practically the owner of the land and the farmer merely the serf under the State, he received every year orders as to what he should grown on his land, and how much of each crop should be sown. The produce was then heavily taxed; his rent and taxes were usually paid in corn which he had to transport at his own expense to the State granary. After this the State had the right to buy from him at a fixed (not the market) price as much of his produce—corn, oil, fruit, flax, wool—as it wished. Even the green fodder which—as has always been done in Egypt—was grown on the fields after the harvest belonged so entirely to the State that the farmer could only obtain the amount sufficient for his cattle by paying a heavy tax.

The keeping of the canals in repair was also a heavy drain on the farmer's resources. If a new canal had to be made or an old one cleared, he had to find the labour for the work. The banks had to be supported by timber; the farmer had to provide the trees, look after them, in due course fell them, and prepare the timber for use.

The State was as absolute in the industrial as in the agricultural life of the country; and it had the same power over all forms of trade, internal or external. Every detail of industry and trade was accurately registered. Certain branches of manufacture and trade were State monopolies. All private industries were heavily taxed, and all raw materials belonged to the State from which they had to be bought by private concerns. Even sales were under control. The State was also a trader, and by its agents free-trading was finally crushed out.

In order to maintain this rigorous system of taxation, inspection, and registration, immense hordes of officials were required. The Civil Service of the Ptolemies was gigantic in size.

The result on the people at large of this systematic nationalisation of the country is peculiarly interesting. "The spirit of the nation was one of indifference—the dull obedience of serfs who possessed no initiative, no animation, no patriotism, whose thoughts were wholly concentrated on the problems of daily bread and economic interests. . . . The Greek officials became submerged in a mire of bureaucracy and bribery. . . . Serfdom lay heavy upon the people, but protests were seldom heard. Dissatisfaction assumed a form typical among serfs. When they found that conditions were no longer tolerable, groups of men, agriculturists, workmen, sailors, or officials, said 'We can bear no more', and fled to the temples to claim the protection of the gods, or disappeared in the swamps of the Delta. From the commencement of the third century B.C., these strikes were of common occurrence. They were a constant terror to the officials, since force was useless in dealing with a psychology born of dull despair. The government was rich in money, but the country was poor in spirit, and hardly knew happiness. True, the country occasionally revolted, under the banners of the old gods and temples or under the influence of national feeling. But these insurrections invariably ended in massacres, and only when the energetic elements in them had been destroyed was an amnesty granted to the survivors."*

The Romans carried on the policy of the Ptolemies by making the country the private estate of the Emperor. This precluded any criticism or interference by the Senate. All the hardships of the Ptolemaic system were intensified by the disadvantages of an absentee landlord,

---

* Rostovtzeff, "Foundations of Social and Economic Life in Egypt", *J.E.A.*, vi (1920), p. 170.

for the country was governed by a Prefect in the Emperor's name, and the taxes went to fill the private coffers of a Caligula or a Nero.

LAW

From the xviii-th dynasty onwards, there is a considerable amount of information as to the legal procedure. Before that date the records are more scanty, and only great trials are mentioned, though with few details. The harem trial at which Uni was the judge (p. 17) fails to satisfy the curiosity which the mention of it arouses. In Egypt as in all other countries, the punishment of treason was death; and torture was certainly used to make the accused confess.* Perjury was also a capital crime, for the great oath in the law-courts was by the life of Pharaoh,† and to swear falsely meant an injury to the king. How important the life of the king was is seen in the curse: "There is no tomb for one who is hostile to his Majesty; but his body shall be thrown into the water." To be without a tomb where prayers and offerings could be made meant total extinction after death.

For serious crimes which were not punishable by death, there were various punishments. One was the cutting off of the nose and ears; another was hard labour at the mines, and this was a punishment worse than death on account of the terrible conditions under which the prisoners lived.

For lesser offences, such as stealing, the culprit when convicted was sentenced to restore the stolen goods and was fined double or treble the value, but if the owner of the stolen goods was merciful he might remit the fine. Beating, however, was the usual punishment for almost all minor offences, and was much in favour for evasion of taxes (see pl. lxxix. 2 for a skit on the subject).

Civil cases were chiefly in reference to land and inheritance, and these were tried before the Vizier. As they were almost entirely among people of some consequence, it was essential that the Vizier should be an impartial judge. Thothmes III made a great point of this when he appointed Rekh-mi-Rê to that office: "It is an abomination towards God to show partiality", and he warned the new Vizier to treat friend and stranger, rich and poor, alike, "for the true dread of a prince is to do justice".

---

* In the trial of the tomb-robbers in the xx-th dynasty, "the thief Nesumontu was brought in, the examination was held by beating with a rod; the bastinado was applied on feet and hands; the oath of the King was administered that he might be executed if he told a lie".

† Cf. Joseph's oath, "By the life of Pharaoh surely ye are spies." Gen. xlii. 16.

AGRICULTURE

The plough, and the hoe from which the plough was evolved (pls. x. 8, 9; xi), have always been the agricultural implements of Egypt. Fields were divided up into small squares by means of mud walls a few inches high (pl. vii. 1); in hieroglyphs the sign of a province is written or determined with the picture of a field so divided. The system is continued at the present day. Between every two squares is a runnel to convey the water from the *shaduf* (pl. vii. 2). Each square can be watered separately by blocking the runnel with a mud wall at the desired place, then breaking an opening in the mud enclosure of the square to be watered. When that square has been sufficiently watered, the opening is closed, the block in the runnel removed, and the same procedure is followed for another square. In this way one field can be made to grow at the same time various crops which require different amounts of moisture.

In ancient Egypt all agriculture was at a standstill during the inundation, that is for at least three months of the year. When the river subsided in November or early December, ploughing began, and sowing followed at once. The seed was trodden into the soft mud by animals, sheep or pigs. The harvest was about March or April. Then, unless the field was near the river or a canal, it lay fallow till after the next inundation, for everything is dried up under the burning sun in the "evil days of summer". The ground becomes as hard as a stone, and every sign of vegetation disappears on the fields, while dust devils sweep across the dreary flats. There is then practically little difference between the desert and the cultivation.

The farm animals of the ancient Egyptians were cattle, sheep, goats, antelopes (especially oryxes), and pigs; in the Old Kingdom hyenas. Birds bred for the table were geese, ducks of various kinds, cranes, and pigeons. The birds were fattened by having food put down their throats, so also were some of the animals. Farm scenes are common on the walls of the tomb-chapels of the Old and Middle Kingdoms; the whole process of agriculture is seen there, ploughing, sowing, treading in the seed, reaping, treading out the grain, winnowing, loading on donkeys, and depositing in granaries with scribes checking the amount brought in. In the farmyard scenes the whole method of looking after the cattle is shown, including the fight of two bulls of rival herds, each bull urged on by its own herdsman.

The careful selection of animals in the temple herds must have had effect in improving the breeds of cattle and sheep in all parts of Egypt. The Apis not necessarily the calf of the old Apis, and was not always even from the herd belonging to a temple, but he had to be a fine ani-mal without blemish. What became of the calves that Apis sired does not seem to be recorded. The calves of the Mnevis-bull were not allowed to be sold, but the legal records show that the priests of the Mnevis were not averse to turning a sacrilegious penny by selling the calves; for which they probably got a good price.

TRADE

Trade being the chief means of transmitting civilisation from one country to another, it becomes one of the most important subjects to study in the life of an ancient people. The actual interchange of goods, whether as raw materials or as manufactures, brings countries into con-tact. But the material imports and exports, however valuable they may be, cannot be regarded as the only exchange when trade is once established. The immaterial, the invisible, the imponderable, often have more effect than the interchange of goods. Such imports, as the countries grow closer with the increase of trade, insensibly affect the mental and spiritual outlook of each country.*

Egypt had trade with foreign countries from the earliest times of which there are any remains in the Nile Valley. This was due to her geographical position, lying as she does where Asia and Africa meet, and within easy reach of the countries of Europe; on one side touch-ing the Mediterranean with its various cultures, on the other side in contact with the East.

Two essentials are required if trade is to be carried on with success; the routes must be safe and transport comparatively cheap. Water transport being always the cheapest, boats came into use very early. As the river was the highway in Egypt, trade was carried on there almost exclusively by boat. Boats were in fact a necessity of life during the annual inundation, when in Upper Egypt whole villages were islanded (pl. vii. 4), while in the Delta the network of water-ways through the marshes made foot-travel impossible in many parts.

The earliest boats were undoubtedly little skiffs or rafts of papyrus reeds lashed together, and made waterproof with pitch; they were propelled by oars or paddles. Boats of this kind remained in use throughout the historic period, chiefly for the use of fishermen, for travelling in the marshes, or for ferries across canals. They were even used for sea-going traffic as late as the time of the prophet Isaiah:

---

* Cf. e.g. the introduction of Christianity and Islam into the countries where they took root.

"Woe to the land shadowing with wings, which is beyond the rivers of Ethiopia: that sendeth ambassadors by the sea, even vessels of bulrushes upon the waters."*

The earliest representations of boats are on the white-lined pottery of the Early Amratean period; these were small rowing boats, intended for river traffic only. But already in the Gerzean period the paintings on the vases show that large vessels of wood were plying between Egypt and other countries (fig. 1). These were certainly seagoing craft and carried cargoes; they were propelled by at least two banks of oars, and had mat-work sails, which, however, seem to have been only for use on rare occasions as they are never represented as hoisted. It is not likely that these big boats were built in Egypt, for the real difficulty in such construction was the scarcity of timber at that time. The Egyptians themselves were alive to this difficulty, and began to import large timber in, probably, the Semainian period, for in the i-st dynasty there is evidence of great wooden beams being used in building. As soon as suitable timber arrived in Egypt the Egyptian carpenters showed themselves experts in ship-building, for it is obvious that wooden boats must have been used from the i-st dynasty onwards to bring stone down or across the river for all the buildings of the Pharaohs.

By the end of the iii-rd dynasty imports of timber were on a comparatively large scale. Snefru built a fleet of sixty ships of one type, and as he had no wars these could not have been war-galleys; the only alternative is that they were for trade. Later on he imported forty ship-loads of timber. This implies a considerable volume of trade with those countries of the eastern Mediterranean where large timber could be obtained, the Lebanon being the nearest and the easiest of access. By this time the type of boat for trading both in the Mediterranean and the Red Sea was practically fixed, and there was little alteration for many centuries. The river boats and barges had been stereotyped before the dynastic invasion (pl. viii), and though foreign forms may have been introduced from time to time they were speedily abandoned in favour of the type that suited the conditions.

The river was so essentially the highway, and boats so invariably the recognised means of travel, that pictures of them were used as hieroglyphic signs with certain well-defined meanings (pl. xcvi. 11). The importance of boats to the living is reflected in their importance to the dead, for the Voyage to Abydos was an integral part of the funerary ritual, and many Pharaohs had large wooden boats buried near their own burial places. In religious beliefs and the ritual of the gods, boats played a large part. The sun crossed the sky in a boat,

* Isaiah xviii. 1, 2.

and passed through the countries of the Night in a boat (pl. xxvi. 1, 2, 3); Amon had a boat-shaped shrine (pl. xxx. 1) and went in a boat on his great festival. Boat-shaped shrines were a common form of shrine for many of the gods; and the sacred lakes which were made within the precincts of the temples seem to have been intended for the deity of the temple to take his pleasure in a boat. Even at the present day the boat of Abu Haggag is kept at the mosque in the temple of Amon at Luxor (pl. xxx. 2) and is carried in procession at midsummer.

Though boats were often for pleasure, the main use of them was for trade, and there seems little doubt that Egyptian ships passed down the Red Sea, calling at the trading ports on either side of that great waterway, and may perhaps have even reached India. Trade was the objective of all these early voyages and travels; and, as has been pointed out before, foreign trade can be traced in Egypt from the earliest human habitation of the Nile Valley. The foreign pottery among the Badarians; the copper, turquoise, and lapis lazuli of the Amrateans; the gold, silver, and perfumes of the Gerzeans; not to speak of the foreign plants such as wheat and the vine; all these show the extent and variety of trade in prehistoric Egypt. The foreign pottery was from the Mediterranean area; copper and turquoise came from Sinai; lapis lazuli is Asiatic; gold may have been brought from Nubia or Asia Minor or India; silver from Asia Minor; perfumes may have been Asiatic or African; wheat and the vine possibly came from the Caucasus.

When written and pictorial records begin in the i-st dynasty it is clear that there was already a well-established and regular trade with Sinai for copper, malachite, and turquoise. The journey to Sinai could be made by land or water; the route chosen would depend on the season of the year. The evidence of trade with Crete is conclusive; the brown polished ware found at Abydos is the same as the Neolithic ware of Crete, and in the islands off the coast of Crete are found locally made clumsy copies of the Egyptian stone vases of this period. The trade route through Koptos and the Wady Hammamat to the Red Sea was of the greatest importance at this time, for the waterway, which was so marked a feature of Hatshepsut's trading expediton to Punt, was not in existence. Egypt was already importing raw materials and exporting manufactures in addition to consumer goods.

One of the great periods of foreign trade was in the xii-th dynasty, when the connections were with the Mediterranean and the Black Sea. Vases from Crete are found in Egypt, and Egyptian scarabs occur in Crete; stelæ of the xii-th dynasty have been found in Malta, and the spiral decoration so common in the early temples of Malta is equally common on scarabs of the xii-th dynasty in Egypt. At

Tripolye on the Dnieper were found offering-trays approximating so closely to the Egyptian soul-houses, which occur only in the xii-th dynasty, that they are proof of close connection between the two countries.* The foreign god Bes (p. 115) makes his first appearance at this period, and the evidence points to his being of Mediterranean origin.

In the xviii-th and xix-th dynasties trade was more fully developed. All countries within Egypt's sphere of influence desired to have commercial relations with her, and foreign rulers sent gifts† to the Pharaoh to obtain entrance for their traders and their goods. There is also a certain amount of evidence of connection with the Middle East and India. Letters and goods travelled freely from and to Mesopotamia by way of Syria and Palestine, for in the early xviii-th dynasty Egypt was the overlord of both countries, and (omitting the disastrous episode of Tell el Amarna) retained that position in Palestine till the xx-th dynasty. The great conquests of the xviii-th dynasty kings brought into Egypt new handicrafts, conspicuous among which was glass-making. The ripple-cloth of the Ægean and tablet-weaving were introduced, and the latter craft remained in use for more than fifteen hundred years. The descriptions of the temples at this the most luxurious period of Egyptian history show that gold was imported in large quantities, chiefly from the south. Egypt had so great a reputation for the possession of gold that the Mesopotamian kings believed that "gold in your country is as common as dust".

Rameses III of the xx-th dynasty recorded many trading expeditions; some of the most successful were to Sinai for copper. "The mines were found abounding in copper, it was loaded by tens of thousands into the galleys. It was sent to Egypt, and arrived safely. It was carried and made into a heap under the palace windows, hundreds of thousands of bars of copper, the colour of gold. I allowed all the people to see them."

The account which Wen-Amon gives of his disastrous expedition to Syria in the xxi-st dynasty, though probably fictitious as to his adventures, at least gives a clear picture of the continuity of trade with that country. The father and grandfather of the prince of Byblos had had dealings for cedar-wood with the priesthood of Amon, and had kept day-books or ledgers in which all the transactions were entered. The prince also declared that there were twenty ships then in his harbour which were in business association with Smendes, the prince of Tanis, and fifty ships at Sidon which did business with Birket-el, who appears to have been an Egyptian trader.

* Murray, *Antiquity*, xv (1944), p. 384. See also Appendix 1.
† This word is often translated "tribute"; the literal meaning is "bringing".

The disturbed state of the country during the Ethiopian occupation and the Assyrian invasion accounts for the loss of trade and of documents connected with trade in those periods, but in the xxvi-th dynasty Egypt came in contact with the Greeks and other coastwise sailors of the north. Naukratis and Daphnai were the two centres of the Mediterranean trade, the eastern trade in the Red Sea was carried on from Kosseir and probably from Suez. The enterprise of the Egyptians at this time is shown by their desire for new markets for their wares, and Necho sent out ships to circumnavigate Africa, and he also began a waterway from the Red Sea either to the Nile or to the Mediterranean direct. But for the disastrous civil war at the end of the dynasty, Egypt might have re-established her great trading reputation. But civil war weakens a country, and Egypt fell a victim to the Persians, and the revival of her trade was only as part of a flourishing empire. The terribly efficient state-control of the Ptolemies crushed all initiative, and though there was a façade of prosperity at Alexandria and at the royal court, the whole of the country was rapidly relapsing into barbarism and poverty, so that when the time came Egypt fell an easy prey to Rome.

POSITION OF WOMEN

In any sociological study of ancient Egypt the status of the women must be clearly understood. Though they had the usual importance which mothers of families have in any country, they enjoyed a peculiar position from the fact that all landed property descended in the female line from mother to daughter. The entail in the female line seems to have been fairly strict, and nowhere so strict as in the royal family. The practical result was that the husband enjoyed the property as long as his wife was alive, but on her death her daughter and the daughter's husband came into possession. It is inconceivable that any man, certainly not a Pharaoh, would give up his position to another man merely on a question of marriage. The marriage laws of ancient Egypt were never formulated, and knowledge of them can be obtained only by working out the marriages and genealogies. It then becomes evident that a Pharaoh safeguarded himself from abdication by marrying every heiress without any regard to consanguinity; so that if the chief heiress died, he was already married to the next in succession and thus retained the sovereignty. The age of the heiress was of no account, she might be a grandmother or a new-born infant. As long as she was the heiress or likely to be the heiress later on, she was married off to the king; and when the king died his successor married all the heiresses also. Even among small officials in the xii-th dynasty this close intermarriage was practised, as their genealogies show. It is, however, more difficult to trace the working of this law of inheritance among the lesser folk than in the royal family where the records are more abundant. But even among these lesser folk the genealogy is almost invariably traced back to an ancestress, not to an ancestor, who was possessed of property, which property descended in the female line, and extraordinary intermarriages resulted.

A concrete example will show how the system worked (fig. 3). This example records the family of a small official in charge of a government storehouse at Abydos in the xii-th dynasty: the stele is to the memory of Wah-ka, who is the only male mentioned, therefore

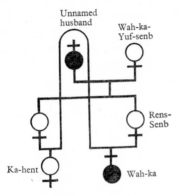

Fig. 3

the relationships are with him. His mother was Rens-senb, and the mother of his mother was Wah-ka-Yuf-senb. So far it is plain sailing, but his sister Bebu was also born of Yuf-senb, and his sister Kahent was born of Bebu. These two sisters show that the unnamed husband of Yuf-senb must have been the father of all the ladies, for in these genealogies the Egyptians were meticulously careful to give the exact relationships. Rens-senb and Bebu must have been sisters as they were both born of Yuf-senb, but Bebu could not have been Wah-ka's sister unless both had the same father; and Bebu's daughter could not have been Wah-ka's sister unless she also had the same father as Wah-ka. It would then mean that the unnamed husband of Yuf-senb married all the heiresses of Yuf-senb and so kept the property of the elder lady in his own hands. As his name is not mentioned he was probably a person of inferior status, not worth considering.*

* See Appendix 2 for comments on these marriages of small officials.

The royal marriages give the same conditions, for the throne went strictly in the female line. The Great Wife of the king was the heiress; by right of marriage with her the king came to the throne. The king's birth was not important, he might be of any rank, but if he married the queen he at once became king. To put the matter in a few words: the queen was queen by right of birth, the king was king by right of marriage.

The marriages of Rameses II are very clear. He married Ystnefert, by whom he had a daughter, Bint-Anath, whom he married; she died childless. The mother of Rameses was Tuya, and on her statue her titles are: "The King's Mother, she who bore the Mighty Bull, User-Maat-Rê, Wife of the God, Mother of the King, Great Wife of the King, whom he loves." In another inscription she is called "The living Wife of the King". And on yet another statue of her, she has beside her the small representation of a queen, who is said to be "born of the Queen Tuya, daughter of the King of his body, whom he loves, Great Wife of the King". Such closely consanguineous marriages can be explained only by the custom of matrilineal descent, the crown going in the female line. Tuya must have carried the succession, therefore she and all her daughters had to marry the Pharaoh, no matter what their relationship to him.* Another set of marriages of this much-married Pharaoh are also known. He married Nefertari Mery-Mut,† by whom he had two daughters, Meryt-Amon and Nefertari, both of whom he married. It had been the custom from early times that one of the king's sons should succeed his father and marry the heiresses, but until the time of Rameses II there is nothing to show whether the choice of his successor rested with the reigning king or whether birth or primogeniture had any influence. In the case of the family of Rameses II the position is clear; the sons of the chief heiress were the successors and had a right to marriage with the heiress. Rameses was succeeded by his thirteenth son, though some of the elder sons were still alive; but Mer-en-Ptah was also the son of Ystnefert who carried the succession, and the mothers of the other sons were inferior heiresses.

The custom of matrilineal descent also explains the many marriages of Cleopatra; she was married first to her eldest brother, who reigned by right of that marriage; on his death she was married to the younger brother, a peculiarly vicious youth, who also reigned by right of that marriage. By those two marriages she had no children. When Julius

---

* See Appendix 2 for marriages in the House of David, and also for cases of matrilineal descent in royal houses of other countries.

† Nefertari was so common a name that the royal ladies are often distinguished by an epithet of some kind; Mery-Mut means Beloved of the goddess Mut.

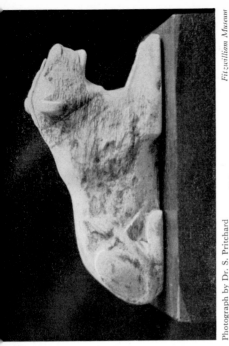

Photograph by Dr. S. Pritchard

Fitzwilliam Museum

1. Lion

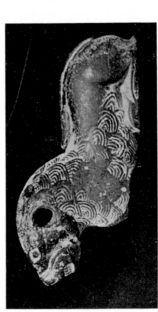

Petrie Coll.

Photograph by Dr. S. Pritchard

Fitzwilliam Museum

2. Lioness

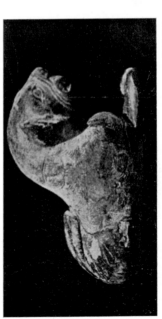

Petrie Coll.

3, 4. Lion. Two views of the same piece, showing that the carving on the shoulders is worn away by use.
Pieces for a game. Ivory

PLATE XVII

1. Dance by men

2. Dance by women

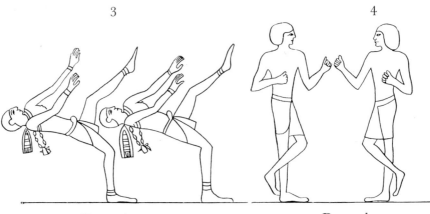

3. Dance by women

4. Dance by men

PLATE XVIII

Sport in the Marshes

PLATE XIX

Social party

PLATE XX

Petrie Coll.

1. Osiris garden

Photograph by Dr. S. Pritchard *Fitzwilliam Museum*

2. Bronze cat with gold eyes

Hildesheim Museum

3. Mask of Anubis. Painted pottery

PLATE XXI

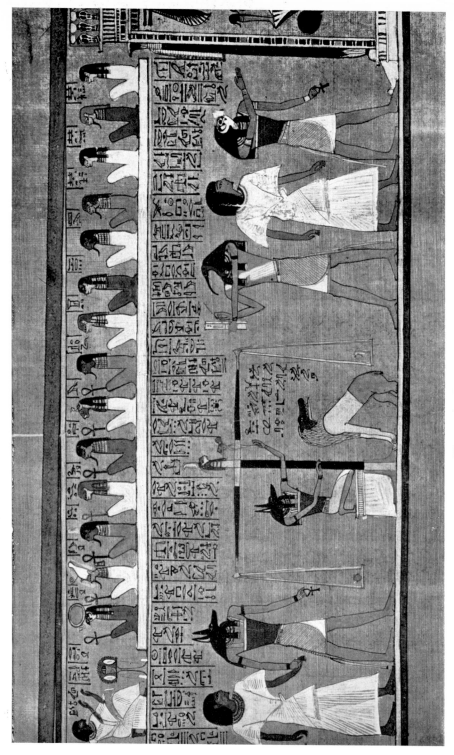

The weighing of the heart

PLATE XXII

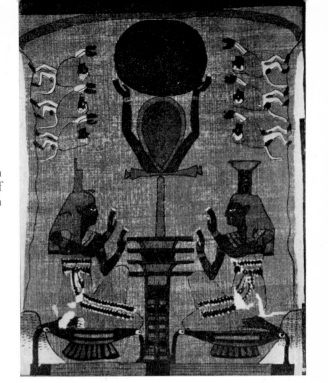

1. Emblem of Osiris, from which springs the sign of Life, upholding the Sun which gives Life to the world

2. Osiris enthroned as Judge of the Dead

PLATE XXIII

△ Isis and the infant Horus

PLATE XXIV

1. Birth dance by men disguised as the god Bes

2. Men disguised as the god Bes dancing round Ta-urt, goddess of birth

PLATE XXV

1. Boat of the Sun, guarded by deities. Tomb of Setekhy I

2. The dead Sun in shrine, guarded by a serpent Tomb of Setekhy I

3. The sunset Sarcophagus of Setekhy I

PLATE XXVI

Soane Museum

Portrait coffins. Dynasties xviii and xix

Plate XXVII

⚓ 1. Queen Meryt-Amon

2. The Lady Thent-Amon

Cairo Museum

3. Queen Mut-em-het

Cairo Museum

4. Queen Isi-em-kheb

PLATE XXVIII

1. Doll with earrings and
movable arms

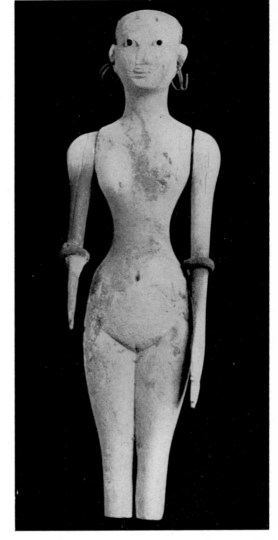

Photograph by Dr. S. Pritchard   *Fitzwilliam Museum*

2. Wooden figure with face carved
separately and pegged on

Photograph by M. A. Murray   *Petrie Coll.*

PLATE XXIX

1. Boat of Amon. Temple of Abydos

Photograph by M. A. Murray

2. Boat of Abu Haggag. On the roof of the mosque in the temple of Luxor

PLATE XXX

Temple of Deir el Bahri, dynasty xviii

PLATE XXXI

Outer court, temple of Hatshepsut, Deir el Bahri

PLATE XXXII

SOCIAL CONDITIONS 71

Cæsar took Egypt, the only way by which he could be acknowledged
as the ruler was by marriage with the queen; and by that marriage
there was one son, Cæsarion. When Antony was aiming at the purple
his first step was to secure Egypt, the granary of Rome; he took the
only course possible in the circumstances, and married the queen.
The fact that he already had a wife in Rome would mean nothing to
the Egyptians; the queen would be the Great Wife and her husband
would be the king. There were two children of the marriage, a boy
and a girl. When Antony was killed and Ocatavius entered to take
possession of Egypt, he was quite prepared to marry Cleopatra, but
she very wisely preferred death. The classical historians, imbued as
they were with the customs of patrilineal descent and of monogamy,
besides looking on women as the chattels of their men-folk, completely misunderstood the situation and have misinterpreted it to the
world. The action of Octavius after the death of Cleopatra shows the
kind of man he was. By Roman law, the boy Cæsarion, son of
Julius Cæsar and Cleopatra, was the rightful heir; by Egyptian law, the
girl was the heiress and should have been married to one of her brothers
who would thus have become king. What Octavius did was to bribe
the guardian of Cæsarion to deliver the boy to him, and the child was
promptly killed. Having got rid of the heir by Roman law, Octavius
turned his attention to the children of Antony. Young Alexander's
guardian was as venal as Cæsarion's, and little Alexander shared his
half-brother's fate. As Roman law did not recognise the rights of the
girl, Octavius had now made himself safe in the eyes of his own people,
but in order to safeguard himself in Egypt he sent the girl out of her
own country, and married her off to a kinglet at a long distance away.
Octavius was an extremely astute person.

Women's position was high, due perhaps to their economic inde-
pendence. They went about freely, except of course in time of war;
but more than one Pharaoh boasts in his Triumph-Song that he has
not only driven out the invaders but the country is so peaceful that a
woman can go where she will without molestation. In ordinary
times of peace, the scenes of daily life show the wife accompanying
her husband in all his inspections of his estates, she watches the craftsmen at their work, is present at the counting of the cattle, and oversees
the harvesters in the fields. In the xviii-th dynasty mixed parties of
men and women were not uncommon (pl. xx); the guests sat on
chairs and were served by young girls, who handed the refreshments
and put garlands of scented blossoms round the necks of the guests or
anointed them with perfumed ointment. When the party was of
ladies only it was less formal; the ladies sat on the ground and talked
familiarly with the handmaidens. The husband's outdoor sports

D

were often shared by the wife and children, as in the famous fresco in the British Museum, where the man is killing wild fowl in the marshes, accompanied by his wife and little daughter and his favourite cat (pl. xix). It is worth noting that in scenes where both parents are present, the child is usually a girl.

With Isis, the divine wife and mother, as their model, women were held in great respect. Even in late times, when foreign ideas were beginning to influence Egypt, there is a charming record of a beloved lady. She was "profitable of speech, agreeable in her conversation, of good counsel in her writings, all that passed her lips is like the work of the Goddess of Truth, a perfect woman, greatly praised in her city, giving the hand to all, saying that which is good, repeating what one loves, giving pleasure to all, nothing evil ever passed her lips, most beloved by all".

Four professions seem to have been open to women: the priesthood, midwifery, mourning, and dancing. There is a little known of the training for these careers. The royal priestesses entered the profession when quite young and learned to dance the sacred dances and sing the sacred songs (pl. x. 2). Midwives must have been held in some esteem, for according to the legend the great goddesses had once acted in that capacity. In all probability the human midwives were entirely untrained, which may account for the high rate of maternal and infant mortality. Professional mourners began as young girls; they are shown in company with the grown women with their arms upraised and apparently shrieking as loudly as they could. Dancers were trained from very early childhood, so young that they are still represented nude (pl. xviii. 2, 3), in contrast to the apprentice-mourners, who are always shown fully clothed. There is no evidence as to how the men dancers were trained (pls. xviii. 1, 4; x. 7), yet theirs was an important profession as some of the dances at a funeral had to be performed by men. Allied to the dancers were the acrobats, girls who turned somersaults, either singly or in groups.

In all great houses there were women servants, whose duties were the same as in great houses everywhere. In houses where the occupants could afford only one servant this was always the woman to grind the corn, the most laborious of all the household tasks, and the woman was often a slave. The grinding was done on a saddle-quern, for the rotary mill was not introduced till considerably later. Women did all the spinning and weaving, and the women of the farm went to market with their wares.

EDUCATION

The education of the children, especially of the boys, was considered to be of great importance. They appear to have been sent to boarding-school at the age of four, but food does not seem to have been supplied by the school, for the mothers went every day carrying bread and beer for their little sons. The subjects taught at school were chiefly reading, writing, and arithmetic. Great pains were taken that the boys should be well trained as they were all being educated to be clerks in government offices, or priests, or artists; reading and writing were essential for these three professions, and for the government service arithmetic was of great practical value on account of the complicated system of taxation. Each department of the government service had its own school, to which the members of that department had the right to send their sons. In the upper forms a boy was given some of the work of that department, so that he was partially trained by the time he was old enough to enter the service. There was, however, no compulsion on a boy to enter the department in which his father served; he could strike out a new line for himself if he wished, but usually he followed his father in the department where the paternal influence would be of use to him.

Good handwriting was considered essential, and copies were set for this purpose. Composition was also important, as a good scribe often had to write letters in which style was of more consequence than matter. A scribe might have to write petitions for illiterate persons, and if these were couched in beautiful language and flowing periods, the great man to whom the petition was addressed would be more influenced by them than by the urgency of the grievance. The document known as *The Eloquent Peasant* gives models of different forms of petitions, from the fulsomely flattering to the subtly threatening. This document belongs to the xii-th dynasty, and shows that the petition-scribe was making a handsome living at that early time.

Writing had to be practised on cheap materials until the budding scribe could be trusted with papyrus. Like the artist the scribe began on pieces of limestone picked up on the desert, or on broken pot-sherds from the village dust-heap. And again like the artist he used a brush made of a slip of reed with the fibres of one end a little teased out. Arithmetic was taught on severely practical lines. Much of the work in the government offices dealt with taxation which was in kind, chiefly corn; and this was complicated by the estimate that must be made on the corn-fields before they were sown. Each year this

D2

estimate had to be made, and it was based on the height of the previous inundation which often removed the previous landmarks. Thus every scribe had to be able to calculate the cultivable area of a field and the cubic contents of a heap of corn. The method would have been simple but that the Egyptian never seems to have mastered the multiplication table; he did everything by addition. On the few arithmetical problems which survive the scribe has written out at the top his version of the multiplication table to help him to the solution. The method was by counting first the left-hand column, and then counting the opposite numbers. The example given below is the twice-times table.

$$1\ldots\ldots\ldots 2$$
$$2\ldots\ldots\ldots 4$$
$$4\ldots\ldots\ldots 8$$
$$8\ldots\ldots\ldots 16$$
$$16\ldots\ldots\ldots 32$$

Thus to find the multiple of five, count on the left hand column 4 and 1, then count the opposite numbers, 8 and 2, which gives the answer. Of the method of training in the higher forms of mathematics there is no trace, though a few mathematical papyri are known.

Lessons in the schools began early in the morning before the heat of the day, and were over at noon, when the "children rush out, shouting for joy". Punishments were much the same as in all schools, impositions and caning. Some of the impositions have survived and show that they were the same as the "lines" of the present day, *i.e.* a certain number of lines from some classic written over and over again. These are perhaps the most tantalising of all the documents which have been preserved, for they are invariably of some exciting story of which only the beginning has been transcribed, and of which this wretched child's imposition is the only copy. Beating was, of course, the chief punishment for idleness, and was freely used. Some of the grim old teachers seem to have taken a delight in applying it, and say, "The ears of a boy are on his back, he hears when he is beaten".

Royal children, of whom there must have been a considerable number in the Pharaoh's harem, were taught by private tutors, but as the children of great nobles were admitted to share the lessons, there was formed a sort of royal school. There are several records of boys who had their education in the palace. As early as the iv-th dynasty Ptah-shepses records that he "was born in the time of Men-kau-Rê, and was educated among the royal children in the King's palace, in the private apartments and the royal harem; he was more honoured by the King than any child". This last remark shows that there were other children of non-royal rank, sharing the education with the little princes. When they grew older, the young princes were put to some profession and were not allowed to be idle.

There were many moral books written "for the young", full of copybook maxims. They are painfully like some of those which afflict youth in all countries and in all periods. Some of the maxims are very sound, as when a boy is told always to love his mother because of what she has done for him. "Always to mother be loving and tender; God will be angry if love you don't render." Good manners were always insisted upon, and it is interesting to find that even in the time of Herodotus the manners of the young Egyptian men impressed him very favourably: "The young men when the meet their elders give way and turn aside; and when they approach, rise up from their seats."* This carries out the injunction of the moral writer: "Manners, remember, will make people love you. Rise for your elders and those set above you."

One of the most important lessons that a budding scribe had to learn was the composition of letters, and for this purpose he was given either a real or a model letter to copy. There are several of such letters extant, mostly of the New Kingdom (1600–1150 B.C.).

A private letter, probably one actually written for the purpose and not as a model, relates to personal affairs:

The scribe Ammomes enquires after his father, the commandant of the Auxiliaries, Bekenptah. In life, prosperity, health, and in favour of Amon-Rê, King of the gods. I say to Rê-Harakhte and to Atum and his Ennead: Mayest thou be in health every day. Furthermore: Pray write to me as to the state of thy health by the hand of any persons who are coming here from thee, for I desire to know daily how thou farest. Thou writest to me neither good nor ill, and no person of those whom thou sendest passes by me, that he may tell me how thou farest. Pray write to me as to how thou farest, and how thy servants fare in regard to all their concerns, for I have an exceeding longing for them. Furthermore: I had brought to thee only fifty good kyllestis-loaves, for the carrier threw away 30 of them, saying "I am too heavily laden". And he would not wait for me to have vegetables brought from the storehouse, though he had not informed me what evening he would be coming to me. I send to thee two plates of fat for unguent.†

When a superior or a fellow-officer obtained promotion it was most important to know how to word a letter of congratulation; the following is probably a model:

* Herodotus, ii. 80.
† Papyrus Anastasi, v. 20, 6 ff. Erman, *Egyptian Literature*, transl. Blackman, p. 201.

The Commandant of Auxiliaries and Overseer of the Foreign Country, Pen-Amon, to the Commander of Auxiliaries, Pehripide.

In life, prosperity, health, and in favour of Amon-Rê, King of the gods, and of the Ka of King Setekhy II. I say to Rê-Harakhti, Keep Pharaoh, our good Lord, in health. May he celebrate millions of Sed-festivals whilst thou art daily in his favour.

Furthermore: I have heard what thou hast written, saying, "Pharaoh, my good Lord, has carried out for me his good designs. Pharaoh has appointed me chief captain of the Auxiliaries of the Well." So hast thou written to me. It is the kindly disposition of Rê that thou art now in the place of thy father. Bravo again and again! When thy letter reached me I rejoiced exceedingly. May Rê-Harakhti grant thee a long life filling thy father's place! May Pharaoh regard thee yet again! Mayest thou grow stronger and write to me again how thou farest, and how thy father fares, by the hand of the letter-carriers who come hither from thee. Furthermore: All goes well with me, and all goes well in the domain of Pharaoh. Have no anxiety about me. Farewell.*

A business letter conveying unpleasant news is of some interest as showing something of the state of the country:

The scribe Pe-uhem informs his Lord Anhur-rekh.

Life, prosperity, health! This is written to let my Lord know.

A further matter to inform my Lord. I have heard the order that my Lord sent me, that I am to give fodder to the horses of the great stable of Rameses Mery-Amon [Rameses II], likewise to the horses of the great stable of Ba-en-Rê Mery-Amon [Mer-en-Ptah]. A further matter to inform my Lord: the peasants of the domain of Pharaoh, which is under my Lord's charge, three men of these ran away from the superintendent of the stable, Neferhotep, when he beat them. Now the fields of the domain of Pharaoh which are under my Lord's charge, are neglected for there is no one to till them. This is written to let my Lord know.†

An inscription of the vi-th dynasty shows how a man gradually rose from one office to another. This was a man called Nekhebu who in the end held the highest office of his profession. "His Majesty found me a common builder, and his Majesty appointed me to the offices of Inspector of Builders, then Overseer of Builders and Superintendent of a Guild. And his Majesty placed me as King's Architect and Builder, then Royal Architect and Builder under the King's Supervision. And his Majesty appointed me Sole Companion, King's Architect and Builder in the Two Houses." Nekhebu's brother had held all these appointments previously, and Nekhebu had his early training under his brother: "When I was in the service of my brother, the Overseer of

Works, I used to do the writing, I used to carry his palette. When he was appointed Inspector of Buildings I used to carry his measuring rod. When he was appointed Overseer of Builders, I used to be his companion. When he was appointed King's Architect and Builder, I used to rule the city for him, and did everything excellently. When he was appointed Sole Companion, King's Architect and Builder in the Two Houses, I used to take charge of all his possessions for him. When he was appointed Overseer of Works, I used to report to him concerning everything about which he had spoken."*

As the priestly training was the highest form of education, the career of Bak-en-Khonsu is of interest. He says, "I passed four years as a little child; I passed twelve years as a youth as chief of the training stables of Men-Maot-Rê" (Setekhy I of the xix-th dynasty). He went direct from the training stables to the temple, where he became a libation priest, being then sixteen. He held that office for four years, and at the age of twenty he became a "divine father", and remained in that position for twelve years; he then held the post of third prophet of Amon for fifteen years, then second prophet of Amon for twelve years, and finally when nearly sixty he obtained the highest office of all, the first prophet or High-priest of Amon, and died at the age of eighty-seven. All the Pharaohs had a priestly training, and therefore were highly educated according to the standards of the time. They were great travellers also, and had a considerable knowledge of other countries besides their own. The queens were certainly able to read and write, and appear to have been often well-educated.

HOUSES AND TOWNS

The earliest representation of a house is of the Gerzean period; this is a model showing the door and two windows. Lattice shrines but no houses are represented in the i-st and ii-nd dynasties, yet there must have been brick-built houses, for the royal tombs of the i-st dynasty at Abydos show that brick buildings of large size were well within the capacity of the Egyptian builder. In the iii-rd dynasty, a great official, named Methen, had a house 200 cubits long and 200 cubits wide; he mentions that the house was "built and furnished". He had large grounds, in which "fine trees were planted, and a very large lake made; figs and vines were plentiful. Very plentiful trees and vines were planted and a great quantity of wine was made there. A vine-yard was made, 2000 stat† of land within a wall, and trees were planted.

---

* Sethe, *Urkunden*, i. 215–21; *J.E.A.*, xxiv (1938), p. 4.
† A stat is equal to about seven-tenths of an acre.

In the temples of King Zoser of the iii-rd dynasty there are representations of folding doors made of wood and working on a pivot, which show the advance of comfort in the house quite in keeping with the rise in the standard of living. On the beautiful sarcophagus of a great noble of the iv-th dynasty is carved the façade of his house. This was a two-storied building; on the ground floor was the front door in the middle with a fresh window on each side; the upper story has five windows set in a straight line; the effect is that of a modern villa. In the vi-th dynasty Harkhuf, the caravan leader, boasts that he had his own house: "I built a house, I set up the doors, I dug a lake, I planted trees."

The houses of the xii-th dynasty belonging to all classes of the population (with the exception of those of the very poorest) are well known. The "soul-houses" found at Rifeh, are models of the types of houses inhabited by small traders and lesser officials (pl. ix). Though some of these houses have only one story while others have two, all are alike in having a spacious courtyard in front. The one-storied houses have three rooms and a veranda which opens on the courtyard; the two-storied houses have six rooms, and the veranda is on the upper floor; there is also a stair leading to the flat roof. In the courtyard of the larger houses there is a stand of water-jars, and in a few instances there is also a woman-slave engaged in grinding corn on a saddle-quern. At Beni Hasan the great feudal princes lived in state like the feudal princes of medieval Europe; though no representation of their splendid mansions exists, the number of their servants shows that the establishments were commensurate with the rank and wealth of their owners.

The towns, however, give the best examples of the housing of gangs of workmen and their families.

The workmen's town of the xii-th dynasty at Kahun is the earliest known example of town-planning. It was laid out in two parts, divided from one another by a wall. The east side contained the houses of the chief people of the town, and the better class of workmen's houses. On the west side were the houses of the poorer men. The town was of considerable size and was intended for the men engaged in building the pyramid of Senusert II. They lived there with their families until the death and burial of the king, then as there was no more work there they drifted elsewhere and the houses fell into decay.

The town was walled all round, and the streets were laid out in straight lines crossing each other at tight-angles. Down the middle of each street ran a shallow stone channel, about 22 inches wide, serving the same purpose as the kennel of a medieval town. Five great houses, all built to the same plan, were on the north of the town; four were joined together, only one was detached. Each house covered an area of 138 feet by 198 feet, and contained about seventy rooms and passages, including servants' quarters and storerooms. The entrance was from the street, with the porter's room opposite the front door. Inside the door the passage to the left led to the public rooms, the master's office and business rooms; these had no connection with the rest of the house. Two other passages, running parallel with each other, led from the front door into the interior of the house. The more westerly of the two led to a large open court with a colonnade on the south side; this was probably for the same purpose as the similar court or *mandara* in a modern house, and was used for the reception of visitors and for sitting in the shade and "enjoying the sweet breezes of the north wind" in summer. The private rooms, which backed on to the business rooms, opened on the *mandara* and could be approached only from the *mandara*. The easterly passage also led to the *mandara* and had rooms opening on it along its eastern side. These were probably the women's rooms as they could be entered easily from the front door or from the *mandara*. A door at each end of the passage would ensure complete privacy if required. Some of the rooms were vaulted with barrel-roofs of brick, but mostly they were covered with thatch resting on wooden beams; large rooms had a column in the centre to support the roof. Some roofs were probably flat as there were stairways leading up, but a brick-built second story was not indicated by the remains. The doorways were arched, the thresholds were of wood and the doors also were of wood; in fact there was a great deal of wood in the construction of these large houses. From its size the wood must have been one of the conifers, and therefore imported. The doors worked on a pivot, the pivot-hole being in a block of stone set beside the threshold. By constant use the pivot-hole became so worn down that the door would not work, and many devices were used to raise the door to its proper level again; the usual method was to put a piece of hard leather—generally a piece of an old sandal—into the hole; this was a temporary alleviation which had to be renewed constantly. The interior decoration of the rooms was interesting and unexpected; there was a band of dark-brown paint about a foot high all round the rooms at the bottom of the walls where they touched the floor; above that, to the height of about four feet, was a dado of vertical stripes of red, black, and white; the wall above was colour-washed in a light shade of buff. Some of the rooms had been adorned with frescoes. The workmen's dwellings had either four or five rooms with stairs leading up to the roof. As the town had been deserted voluntarily the people had taken away all their possessions that were of any value to them, and only fragments of furniture and pottery remained to show how they had lived.*

Another workmen's town was found at Tell el Amarna. This little settlement was tucked away in a fold in the hills, out of sight of the main city of Akhetaten, and like Kahun it was within a stone's throw of the work on which the men were employed, which was the quarry-ing of tombs for the poorer class of inhabitants of the town. Though there were many centuries between Kahun and Tell el Amarna there is little difference in the two towns. Both were walled all round, both had a central wall dividing the town into two unequal parts, both were laid out with straight streets intersected at right angles by cross streets. At Tell el Amarna all the houses were exactly alike and exactly the same size, with the exception of one large house, which probably was for the overseer of the work. The houses appear to have been put up by contract and were cheaply built. The architect must have forgotten the stairs, for they are crammed either into the kitchen or into the entrance hall as an after-thought; in either case they are so large that the room was unusable. The stairs led up to the flat roof; when in the hall they half-filled it, but when in the kitchen there was no room for any-thing else, and the oven and other cooking paraphernalia had to be put behind a screen in the hall. Each house had a frontage of five metres and a depth of ten, and the ground floor was divided into four rooms, a hall opening on the street; at the back of the hall was the *mandara* or living-room, and at the back of the house were two small rooms, one a bedroom, the other the kitchen. On the flat roof was a little light erection of wood and mat-work which served as an extra room. The front door was of wood, and worked on a pivot; it had a sliding latch moved from the outside by a string, and when the door was shut it could be fastened on the inside by a heavy wooden bar which slipped into sockets in the door-jambs.

Everything in the little town shows that this was entirely a work-men's settlement; the pottery was for use and is hardly ever orna-mented; the walls of the houses are thin, the partition walls being only one brick thick. This is very different from the gentlemen's houses or the painted palaces in Akhenaten's city. But in all probability the houses and their contents were as good there as a workman might have expected anywhere else in Egypt.

* Petrie, *Kahun, Gurob, and Hawara*, p. 23. *Illahun, Kahun, and Gurob*, p. 7.

FURNITURE

Among the earliest furniture known is a bed of the 1-st dynasty. This was a low framework of wood resting on four legs. The intervening space within the frame was filled by soft linen-string closely plaited and lashed to the sides and ends of the frame, forming a mattress. Beds of this kind, more or less elaborately decorated, are found at all periods in Egypt (pl. xii. 1, 2, 4).

Chairs are also early, though in the beginning it was only royalty that was enthroned. The two enthroned figures from Hierakonpolis* are the earliest representations of any kind of seat; Narmer is also enthroned when, as Osiris, he sits under a canopy to watch the running dance. The thrones are little more than blocks of stone hollowed out for a seat, they had no backs or arms. After the time of Zoser chairs came into use among the nobles and their wives. These chairs were clearly of wood, the seats being probably of plaited leather over which a thin cushion was placed; they might be single-seated for use by one person only, or double to accommodate a husband and wife sitting side by side. In course of time chairs were made more comfortable and fitted with arms and backs. Footstools occur in use with chairs. The royal footstool was usually decorated with the figures of two bound captives, a Syrian and a negro as the traditional enemies of Egypt, in order that the Pharaoh might symbolically crush his foes beneath his feet.† Low stools for the use of workmen are also found (pl. xii. 3).

Tables do not appear to have been used; in all cases where food is shown the "table" is merely a stand with a tray on it. Wooden stands, however, for holding water- or wine-jars were common in the Old Kingdom. The water-jars were placed at the side of the entrance door ready for any thirsty soul who entered. Wine-jars were kept in the storeroom, or were sometimes set in the garden under the shade of a tree with stands of cakes beside them, for a pleasant alfresco meal.

All cloths or other objects which had to be kept tidily were laid in boxes (pl. xiii. 3).

In the Middle Kingdom the amount of furniture increased, and even in the "soul-houses" of the poorer people there are representations of beds and chairs and stands for water-jugs. In the houses of the nobles, though the amount of furniture is greater than in the Old Kingdom, there are no new forms.

* *Ancient Egypt* (1932), p. 70.
† "The Lord said unto my Lord, Sit thou on my right hand, until I make thine enemies thy footstool." Ps. cx. 1.

The New Kingdom is the chief period in which to study Egyptian furniture (pls. xii. 3; xiii. 1, 2, 3). The great number of actual pieces found in the tombs of Yuya and Tut-ankh-Amon are more instructive than any number of pictures. The princess's chair from the tomb of Yuya is an interesting piece of construction. Like many chairs of this period it has two backs; the inner back is a panel which slopes outward from the seat and is highly decorated with religious scenes. The real back of the chair is hidden by the panel; it consists of three uprights held in place by horizontal bars at top and bottom; being rigid, the sloping panel, which rests against it, is unable to slip. The legs of the chair are strengthened with bars across, and where the seat meets the legs there are wooden angle-pieces.* The seats of this and another chair found in the same tomb are of plaited leather, and there was also a leather-covered cushion filled with feathers. In the beds of the period the wooden framework slopes up in a fine curve at the head, and the foot is finished with a high foot-board. Tut-ankh-Amon's tomb supplies a greater variety of furniture than any other single excavation, for in it were found stools, chairs, beds, footstools, and boxes.

As an important part of the Pharaoh's duty consisted in travelling about the country and as he accompanied his army on their campaigns, he had a certain amount of travelling equipment. When household gear was still rather primitive his equipment would be simple, but in the xviii-th dynasty luxury was found in all homes in peacetime, therefore the Pharaoh would require a maximum of comfort in travelling. In the tomb of Tut-ankh-Amon was a folding bed; it is made of a light wood, painted white, and folds up by means of heavy bronze hinges. This could be easily carried by one man, and could be used on a boat if the travelling was by water.

Of the same period, but belonging to a private person, was a folding head-rest,† also intended for travelling. And folding stools of the modern camp-stool type are also known at this time. The anti-splash silver bowl (see p. 280) is clearly part of the royal travelling equipment, but of a later date.

GARDENS AND FLOWERS

All large houses had gardens attached to them, for the ancient Egyptians were fond of flowers and shady trees. Throughout the long

---

* There is nothing to show that at this period the Egyptians knew how to bend wood by steaming, but there is no other way to account for the bent-wood frames of the chariots, or the wooden angle-pieces.
† Petrie, *Kahun, Gurob, and Hawara*, pl. xviii. 17, p. 15.

history of Egypt there are frequent mentions of gardens, sometimes as belonging to a temple, but more often to a private house. The chief difficulty of maintaining a garden in Egypt was the watering. This was a matter of necessity if the trees and plants were to survive, yet there is seldom any reference to this essential part of the work. In the xix-th dynasty there is a scene of gardeners engaged in watering; they are using a *shaduf* to raise the water from a pond or canal in exactly the same way that a modern Egyptian labourer raises the water for the benefit of the fields (pl. vii. 1, 2, 4).

The feeling of the Egyptians for gardens is shown in their belief that the first object to meet their eyes on entering the world of the dead was a beautiful and shady tree, from which a goddess welcomes them with food and water, the food being the fruit of the tree. The Egyptians loved their gardens so much that one of the usual prayers was that after death they might return and sit in the shade and eat the fruit of the trees they had planted.

Among the flowers the blue lotus was the favourite, partly for its colour but chiefly for its scent. In the piles of offerings depicted on the walls of the tomb-chapels there are often bowls of lotuses, and the offering-bearers carry long stems of lotus twined round their arms. Ladies wore wreaths of the blue or the rose lotus round their heads, and boatmen often slung a blue lotus with a piece of string round the neck like a pendant. Dancers wore the lotus and it is possible that a crown of this flower was part of the royal insignia.

In the New Kingdom (from which so much of our knowledge is derived), palaces, private houses, and tomb-chapels often had sculptured or painted friezes of alternate buds and blossoms of the lotus, or of lotus petals strung together. At parties garlands of lotus were hung round the necks of the guests. One of the favourite devices in jewellery was the blue lotus, for the narrow petals could be successfully imitated with strips of turquoise set in cloisons of gold. In and after the New Kingdom the lotus is so closely connected with women that on women's tombstones the sign which follows the name is of a woman holding a lotus in her hand; the stem curls stiffly forwards so that she may inhale the fragrance of the flower.

Other flowers were also known and represented. The forget-me-not crown of a princess of the xii-th dynasty (pl. lxxxiv. 1) shows beauty of colour and delicacy of design; so also does the buttercup crown of Queen Ta-usert of the xix-th dynasty. At Tell el Amarna the wall decoration shows a great variety of flowers; the flowers were made in glazed ware and inlaid in the walls or were painted on the walls and floors. The blue centaurea was the favourite, but there were also daisies with white petals and yellow centres, red poppies, flowering rushes, and various kinds of foliage. At Medinet Habu a battle is represented as having been fought in a flowering meadow.

Plants, including full-grown trees, were freely imported, even in the prehistoric period, for according to the legend Osiris brought in wheat, barley, and the grape-vine. The subjugation of Libya, which occurred just within the historic period, is recorded on a slate palette, and among the spoils are olive trees. The pomegranate was also introduced early, perhaps from Palestine. Incense trees and other sweet-smelling woods are often mentioned as being brought from abroad to plant in the gardens of the temples.

Of smaller plants one of the most important was flax, which seems to have been imported in the i-st dynasty, for the cloth of the prehistoric periods was made of other fibres. Clover, now one of the main crops of Egypt, has its original habitat in Asia Minor, and was probably introduced in the i-st dynasty with so many other useful things. Henna was also an early importation, and was used by ladies for staining the nails and palms of the hands. Thothmes III brought back many strange and rare plants from his campaigns in foreign countries; these are depicted on the walls of one of his little temples at Karnak.

Many remains of flowers have been found in the tombs, as wreaths were always laid upon the mummies of important persons. The grave of Horuta at Hawara in the xxvi-th dynasty contained flowers and leaves of the following plants, which are not native to Egypt: pomegranate, flax, clover, vine, currant, peach, henna, castor oil, walnut, lychnis cœlirosa, myrtle, woody nightshade, immortelles, sweet marjoram, bay laurel, and polyanthus narcissus. There were also roses—"the roses had been picked unopened and shrivelled up, but when put in warm water they opened out".* The wreaths in the coffin of Tut-ankh-Amon show fewer foreign plants than those at Hawara. There were olive leaves, petals of blue lotus, flowers of the blue cornflower, willow leaves, wild celery, berries of the woody nightshade, mandrake fruit, and picris coronopifolia. Judging by the wreaths the burial took place either in late March or early April.

SERVANTS

In the i-st dynasty it is evident that women-servants were sacrificed at the grave of the dead master, but in later times a statue of the maid-servant was placed in the master's tomb. These statues show the woman in the act of performing the hardest of all the household tasks, that of

* Newberry in Petrie's *Hawara, Biahmu, and Arsinoe*, p. 52.

grinding corn on a saddle-quern. Slaves were common at all periods (pl. lxxiii. 1).

In large houses there were of course many servants, both indoor and outdoor, as well as all the people connected with the farms and estates. In the kitchens, which are shown crowded with men and women (pl. xiv), bread-making only was done by women; the rest of the cooking was men's work. Roasting was done over a brazier filled with glowing charcoal, the meat being turned on a horizontal spit. In a scene of the xii-th dynasty an ox is being roasted whole, the spit turned by two men; and in the same kitchen another cook is roasting a duck and keeps his hand up to shield his face from the fire; he grumbles to his assistant, "I have been over this blaze since the world began. I never saw such a duck!"* The kitchens were also used for cutting up the joints, which are sometimes seen hanging up in the larder.

There is at Tell el Amarna a little painting of the arrival of a noble at his house; he has just alighted from his chariot, and the fat old cook is hurrying out of the kitchen carrying a covered dish containing the master's dinner.†

Fuel was always a difficulty in Egypt. For cooking large joints charcoal must have been the fuel; for smaller fires it is likely that dry reeds were used. Reeds give a fierce heat for a short time but the fire needs constant replenishing and must be as constantly fanned. In all the kitchen scenes there is always at least one cook engaged in fanning his fire.

HORSES AND CHARIOTS

When horses and chariots came into use at the beginning of the xviii-th dynasty, grooms and charioteers were added to the outdoor establishments of the wealthy. Amonhotep I is the first king to be shown in a chariot; Thothmes III drove in a chariot at the battle of Megiddo, but the king who was the most addicted to driving was Akhenaten. He and his court drove furiously all round the deserts near Tell el Amarna with running footmen beside the chariots. Tut-ankh-Amon seems to have been equally fond of driving for he had six chariots in his tomb. These chariots had a framework of a light wood artificially bent into shape to make the curved front; canvas was fastened round the frame, and was covered with gesso and modelled with scenes of bound captives kneeling before the Pharaoh who was represented as a sphinx; the whole front was then covered with sheet

---

* Blackman, *Rock Tombs of Meir*, iii. pl. xxxi., pp. 30, 31.
† Petrie, *Tell el Amarna*, pl. v, p. 14.

gold with a border inlaid with coloured stones and glass. The floor of the chariot consisted of a mat of interlaced leather thongs, over which was stretched either an animal's skin or a linen rug of an unusually long pile. The two wheels were large in proportion to the body and were set far back. The harness of the horses was of leather, and all the metal used was gold, much being inlaid with stones and glass. Two horses were always driven; the driver stood up and so did the passenger when there was one, for no seats were provided. Occasionally in the king's chariot, when the Pharaoh did not drive himself, the charioteer squatted uncomfortably on the pole. As the horses were always driven with bearing reins there was little danger of their running away. There are many sketches of horses and chariots at this period, for the artists were apparently delighted to have some new thing to draw other than the stock subjects. The little outline sketches show the horses with bearing reins, and also stretching their necks after the reins have been taken off.

FOOD

Our knowledge of the food that the Egyptians ate is taken chiefly from the lists of offerings in the tomb-chapels of the Old Kingdom, which give the name of the food and the amount offered.*†

Except for a few items at the beginning of the lists, the food is divided into classes; different kinds of bread and cakes are together, then the meats, then the poultry, then fruit and drinks. Fifteen different kinds of bread and cakes are mentioned; some were large loaves, others so small that two hundred were required for an offering. Roasted bread, of which four large circular pieces were offered, was probably some kind of biscuit. The most interesting of the cakes was the *shat*-cake, as there is some indication of its manufacture. It was always made in an unmistakable shape, like an isosceles triangle, so tall for its width that it had to be laid on its side, and when stacked together they were laid heads and tails in a pile. In the tomb of Rekhmara of the xviii-th dynasty there is a kitchen scene in which *shat*-cakes are being made. Some of the cooks are sifting date-flour, and as a large jar of honey is a conspicuous object it is safe to assume that honey was an ingredient. Other cooks are dropping the mixture into pans over the fire and frying the cakes, which when finished are piled up in the usual manner.

* Murray, *Saqqara Mastabas*, i. 32–40.
† In a royal tomb of the i-st dynasty at Sakkara was a complete meal, of which the dried-up food still remains, each item in a separate dish. W. B. Emery, *A Funerary Repast*. Scholae Adriani de Buck Memoriae Dicatae I.

Baskets of onions are listed after the bread. This is the only vegetable, other than fruit, that is mentioned. Nine kinds of meat follow, including kidneys and one special dish of roast meat, which must have been prepared in a peculiar way to be mentioned separately. The poultry consisted of two kinds of goose, duck, teal, and pigeons. Two kinds of cheese (or perhaps sour milk) conclude the list of solid eatables.

The drinks were water, beer, and wine. Osiris was credited with the introduction of beer into Egypt; Diodorus says that if Osiris "found any territory unsuitable for the vine, he caused the people to make beer, a drink composed of barley and water, not much inferior in taste, savour and strength to wine". There was more than one kind of beer, but the black beer was considered the best. The making of wine was also attributed to Osiris. There were at least five different kinds of wine, but usually only the black and the white are mentioned in the lists. Wine of the Oasis was a specially fine kind, though the wine of the north was also much esteemed. Drunkenness among the Egyptians was not only common but was regarded as a pleasant sensation. So much so that in the xii-th dynasty poem where an angel is expatiating to a man on the sweetness of death he likens it to a drunk man. And in the picture of a party in the xviii-th dynasty, a maid, who is handing round cups of wine, says persuasively to a lady guest, "Drink this and get drunk". The lady replies with great animation, "I shall love to be drunk".

The fruit eaten at the end of the meal consisted of figs, sycamore-figs, and a juicy fruit called *sekhept*, probably the large green-striped melon, so often figured among the offerings.

The peasant was content with bread and onions, some cheese and fish, and his drink was water.

The lists are, however, incomplete, and the classical authors help to fill some of the gaps. Herodotus tells of salted and dried fish and of bread made from the lotus, and also mentions the papyrus as being edible.

LIGHTING

The Egyptians must have learned the art of making fire long before they peopled the Valley of the Nile, for there is no trace of any sanctity being attached either to lights or to fire. There is in Egypt no god of fire and no god of a light that had to be kindled. When the Ship-wrecked Sailor (p. 213) arrived on the island, he made himself a fire drill with which he kindled a fire; this is recorded as a natural proceeding requiring no comment. The Badarians were well acquainted with fire as they could melt copper in crucibles, and it is a very short step from a fire to artificial lighting. The earliest lamps were pottery saucers or bowls (pl. x. 3, 4), the wicks were of twisted grass, and the oil was either animal fat (probably tallow) or castor oil. In historic times these lamps were set on high stands, and are often shown in domestic scenes. In religious ritual lighted lamps were offered by the king to the God, and occasionally the food-offerings were set on fire so that the smoke might ascend as "a burnt offering of a sweet savour, a sacrifice made by fire unto the Lord". Akhenaten was peculiarly addicted to this form of sacrifice. At certain festivals of commemoration of the dead, lights were carried in procession, and in the xviii-th dynasty little saucer lamps with burning wicks were placed at the head and foot of the coffin in the burial chamber. Candles were known in the New Kingdom (pl. x. 5), and torches were carried when out of doors. There is also a peculiarly shaped "candle" which is found occasionally in the New Kingdom, which was perhaps used only in bridal processions, for it is the same shape as the candles for that purpose still used in some parts of Palestine at the present day (pl. x. 6).

DRESS

It is a curious fact that though needles are found, there are never any scenes of sewing, yet the women's dresses were certainly sewn. The invariable dress of the women was a long straight linen garment falling from the armpits to the ankles; it was held up by straps over the shoulders (pl. l. 1, 2). The length of the straps varied according to the period. If they were short the dress was cut in a V at the neck and was slightly hollowed under the arms. Such a garment must have had at least one seam at the side and a hem at the bottom, while the straps, the edges of the V, and the cuts under the arms must have been overcast or hemmed to prevent fraying. Ladies often wore a thin cloak over the frock, but there was little variation till the New Kingdom when "accordion pleating" came into fashion (pls. l. 4; lx). Then the skirt was made fuller, and the bodice had cape sleeves, and a sash was worn round the waist, falling in long ends almost to the feet (pl. xc. 2).

The men wore a short loin-cloth fastened with a belt round the waist, and reaching to about the knee (pl. xlix. 1, 2). In the Old Kingdom the front fold of the loin-cloth was often pleated. In the Middle Kingdom the loin-cloth was much longer and reached to mid-calf, like a petticoat. At the end of the New Kingdom, under Akhenaten, the long loin-cloth came into fashion again, very closely pleated with a great many folds in the front. Rameses II in the xix-th dynasty wore a pleated garment covering the body from neck to ankles; it has short bell sleeves with horizontal pleating (pl. lxii; see also pl. lx). There is no doubt that this dress must have been cut out and sewn, so also must Mer-en-Ptah's close-fitting garment have been shaped and sewn.

Embroidery was not known in Egypt, and it was not until the xxvi-th dynasty that crochet is found. It was probably a foreign introduction for it never became common. Knitting was also foreign, and is found in the Roman period, in the form of socks. These are interesting as being of the so-called hygienic type, *i.e.* with a separate compartment for the big toe (pl. xvi. 6).

Decoration of the person was practised from the earliest times. In prehistoric Egypt painting of the eyes with malachite was a common practice; in historic times antimony (kohl) was used instead. At all periods ladies had beautiful little pots or other containers to hold their eye-paint (pls. iii. 2; xvi. 2–5; lxxxvi. 3), which was applied to the eyelids with a round-ended rod of hæmatite. Under the Hyksos when the country was poor, a piece of hollow reed was all that could be afforded as a container for the paint, and when in the New Kingdom Egypt again became wealthy, the ladies had the reed copied in more costly materials, ebony, alabaster, and multi-coloured glass (pl. lxxxvi. 4, 5). Henna was used for staining the hands and nails, and there seems to have been some form of lipstick applied with a brush, as is seen in a caricature of the xviii-th dynasty (pl. lxxix. 4); the colouring matter was probably red ochre. Tattooing was another form of personal decoration much in vogue in prehistoric Egypt, but there is nothing to show that it was practised in historic times.

Except for the Pharaoh, fashions in hairdressing changed as often as fashions in dress. The royal mummies prove that the Pharaoh wore his hair short, but in representations of him his head is always covered and the hair is not seen. This suggests that there was so strong a taboo or superstition concerning the head or hair of the king that he had to wear some covering to conceal it from his subjects. After he "assumed the Double Crown" he was never again seen bare-headed. He was always clean-shaved, but on state occasions he wore a long and narrow false beard of plaited hair held at the point of the chin by a strap on each side, which passed round the jaw and in front of the ear and was attached to the crown itself. The form of the beard is precisely the same as the natural beards of the men of Punt, and it is one of the insignia of the gods. Men of high rank occasionally wore a false beard, but this was always short, little more than a tuft. In the Old Kingdom certain high officials wore moustaches, but this was rare. With these few exceptions the men were always clean-shaved. Foreigners, especially Syrians and Libyans, wore natural beards trimmed to a point.

From early in the historic period both men and women wore wigs and cut their own hair short. The shape of the wig varied according to the period; in the Old Kingdom they were small like those of Nefert (pl. li) and the wife of Ka-Aper, very different from the gigantic erections of the New Kingdom, which are so large as to make the figure top-heavy (pls. l. 4; lx). Few wigs have survived, for they were probably destroyed on the owner's death. Those that remain are of sheep's wool, black or very dark brown.

That the women of ancient Egypt were proud of their hair and cared for it is evidenced by the recipes for strengthening the hair and preventing its turning grey. As such recipes could not have a divine origin—goddesses being always young—they are often ascribed to a queen of ancient times and so bear that stamp of antiquity so dear to the heart of the Egyptian. "Recipe for making the hair grow, which was made for Sesh, the mother of the Majesty of the South and North, Tety, deceased. Paws of a dog, one part; kernels of dates, one part; hoof of a donkey, one part. Cook very thoroughly with oil in an earthen pot, and anoint therewith."

Mirrors (pls. xvi. 1; lxxix. 4) are known from the Old Kingdom. They were of copper or bronze highly polished, and usually set in a wooden handle; sometimes the handle was of ivory and often exquisitely decorated. As the polish on the mirror was important, ladies had leather cases lined with soft linen in which the mirror was kept when not in use. In many mirrors the linen lining has been found rusted on to the metal, and has thus been preserved.

PASTIMES

Outdoor sports were much favoured by men of all classes. For the wealthy there was hunting in the desert with bows and arrows and with hunting dogs; spearing big fish, or knocking down birds with a boomerang in the marshes (pl. xix). After the introduction of horses, driving in chariots was very popular. There were, however, no outdoor games in the modern sense; the sportsman enjoyed himself alone or in company with his wife and daughter, who took no part in the man's actions. The chief amusement for lads and young men among the peasants was wrestling. It was evidently so popular that many scenes of wrestling are found in the tomb-chapels of the wealthy, especially in the xii-th dynasty. Sometimes the scraps of conversation between the two opponents are recorded: " 'By your leave,' says one as he gets his arm round his adversary's leg. 'And now,' he adds, 'you will find yourself on your nose! I'll make you do that. See! you are coming a cropper.' " In another scene two men are rolling on the ground in their struggle: " 'Don't talk so big,' says the man on top. 'See! here we are! Now then, look out for yourself,' but his apparently-falling opponent thinks that, after all, he will turn the tables on his all but victor, 'Come, wretch,' he ejaculates, 'I have wriggled round. See! It is you who are yielding.' "*

For soldiers there were war-dances, which were really a form of physical drill, and as probably the local prince enlisted all the able-bodied young men in his militia, these dances were part of the regular outdoor sports of a village.

For indoor games two at least are recorded, the game on a chequer board (p. 9), which in the protodynastic period appears to have been played with pieces in the form of lions (pl. xvii), and a game of jackals and hounds of the xviii-th dynasty.

* Blackman, Rock Tombs of Meir, i. 26, 27.

IV

RELIGION

O NE of the chief difficulties in the study of the religion of ancient Egypt has been the method of its presentation to the world. The plurality of gods and the representation of the Deity, whether as an animal or as a human being with an animal's or bird's head, was shocking to the prophets of Israel, from whose denunciations many of the modern ideas of Egyptian religion have been taken. Other adverse commentators were the Greek authors, the early Christian Fathers, and may later Christian writers. Milton voices the general feeling when he speaks of "the brutish gods of Egypt", and says of Osiris "Naught but profoundest hell can be his shroud". The more modern writer is apt to be either shocked at the resemblances to Christianity or to treat the whole subject with slightly contemptuous levity, forgetting that this same religion had for thousands of years brought to its believers help in time of trouble, comfort in sorrow, and courage in the face of death. Though the outward forms may be grotesque or repulsive to our eyes, their gods were as real to the ancient Egyptians as Shiv is to the Hindu, Allah to the Moslem, and Christ to the Christian.

Though it is impossible in this chapter to give more than the barest outline, it must be borne in mind that the Egyptian religion was never static. Social conditions affect religion as much as, perhaps more than, religion affects social conditions; and as those conditions change, the spirit and therefore the outward form of religion changes also. During those many centuries through which the history of Egypt can be traced, religious changes occurred as they occurred in any other country, and these must be taken into account.

Ancient Egypt grew, as other countries have grown, from an aggregation of little states, each little state being entirely independent and having its own chief and its own deity. The early deities of Egypt—often in animal form—numbered more goddesses than gods; but whether male or female the local deity was supreme in his or her own district. This was, of course, the form of monotheism common to all primitive societies. The deity had, however, no jurisdiction outside his own principality, and in war it was the god and not the tribe that was defeated or victorious.* In course of time one district tended to

* Cf. 1 Kings xx. 23.

merge into another; the result to the deities of the districts concerned depended upon whether the union was due to peace or war. If the union had come about by peaceful means the deities, according to their reputed sex and age, became either husband and wife, or parent and child. On the other hand, a victorious invading tribe often degraded the god of the vanquished, and he became a hostile and terrifying power.

By dividing the deities of Egypt into four categories, the bewildering pantheon becomes intelligible, for the religion was not confused until foreign conquerors—Persian, Greek, and Roman—forcibly altered the condition of the country.

1. Local gods, originally animals, later represented with human bodies and animal heads.

2. Osiris and attendant deities.

3. Deities without temples, originally belonging to the Pharaoh only.

4. The Sun and other solar deities.

These are far from being watertight compartments, for in the evolution of the religion the democratisation of ritual and beliefs is very marked. Gods who in early times belonged only to the Pharaoh, in the later periods are common to all the people. This is particularly noticeable in the burial ritual and the deities connected with death. Yet even to the end of paganism and the coming of Christianity, there were still certain distinctions between the gods of the ruler and the gods of the people, and between the royal festivals and the popular festivals. In the main, however, and especially in and after the xviii-th dynasty (when the theologians had tried to unify the pantheon), the boundaries between the four categories given above are not rigid; they often so blend into each other as to be practically indistinguishable, but at least they give a framework in which the Egyptian religion can be studied without confusion.

Of the local deities I give only four of those who remained independent and were of importance to the end. Others were merged into the greater gods, or sank into insignificance and became obscure godlings, whose names occur only in magical spells.

LOCAL GODS

The greatest of the local gods was Amon of Thebes, whose career is peculiarly interesting as showing his evolution from an insignificant local deity to the high position of supreme god of the known world. When Thebes was merely a remote provincial town, hardly more than a mud village, Amon was represented as a goose or a ram. By the time the records begin the goose form had almost disappeared; little remained but the two pinion feathers worn on the head of the god when in human form, the epithet of the "Great Cackler", and rare representations of him as an actual goose. On the other hand the ram form lasted until the final extinction of the pagan religion, not only in the representations on stelæ but in the cult. Herodotus gives the legend of the ram form and also details of the special ram sacrifice to the god.*

Amon's career followed the fortunes of his city. In the xi-th dynasty Thebes was the capital of Egypt and Mentu-hotep III built there his pyramid and the imposing temple which surrounded it. During the splendid period of the xii-th dynasty the greater number of the Pharaohs bore names compounded with that of Amon, Amon-em-hat, "Amon as the Chief". Amon had now become the most important deity in Egypt. Though with the rest of the country he suffered eclipse under the Hyksos rule, he came rapidly to the front again when the warlike princes of Thebes drove out the invaders and made themselves masters of the whole of Egypt. Magnificent temples dedicated to Amon sprang up at Thebes on both sides of the river, and wealth such as had never been seen before was his.

Seeing that a battle was regarded as a combat between two gods rather than as a fight between two countries, the conquests of Thothmes III raised Amon to the position of supreme god of the known world, a position never before achieved by any deity. The idea of a supreme deity, ruling not merely his own district or even his whole country, but the whole world, now first appears; Amon was thus God of gods, Lord of lords, King of kings, and King of the gods. Though the Pharaoh was officially the son of the Sun, in popular belief he was the physical son of Amon. So strong was this belief that when Alexander the Great came to Egypt, and desired to consolidate this position in the eyes of the Egyptians, he went to the Oasis of Amon and there went through a ceremony by which, though already a grown man, he became the son of Amon, and wore the curved horns of the Theban ram in proof of his divine descent. This, however, was all that then remained of the glory of Amon, for when the Pharaohs moved the capital to the north Thebes gradually decayed, and with his city Amon also became of less and less account.

But even at his proudest and most exalted times Amon was always the Vizier of the poor, caring as much for them as for the Pharaohs; he was the gracious god who lent an ear to the voice of their humble petitions, but because they were humble they were seldom recorded. Two little addresses to Amon have survived, which show the feelings

* Herodotus, ii. 42.

of the suppliant towards this great and mighty god, who was equally ready to succour a king in battle or a poor man in trouble.

"O Amon-Rê, first of Kings, God of the Beginning, Vizier of the poor, who takes no unrighteous reward, who speaks not to him who brings false evidence, nor looks on one who only makes promises. Amon-Rê judges the earth with his finger, and speaks to the heart. He assigns the wicked to punishment, but the righteous to the West." The second is in the nature of a prayer: "O Amon, lend thine ear to one who stands alone in the court, who is poor while his adversary is rich. The people of the court oppress him; silver and gold for the scribes of the accounts; clothes for the attendants! But it is found that Amon has changed himself into the Vizier in order that a poor man shall not be crushed."

In spite of being the supreme God, there is little known of Amon. It is perhaps because he was so immensely great, so far above all other gods, that there was no necessity for the adventitious aid of legends or miracles to enhance his importance. He was the physical father of every Pharaoh, including the Ptolemies, and therefore received benefits at the hands of his grateful sons. He gave victories to Thothmes III, and he appeared in person to Rameses II in that dark hour when the king found himself deserted in the face of the enemy. "At the cry of my despair, swiftly came the God to me, took my hand and gave me strength till my might was as the might of a hundred thousand men." Except for a few occasions, when the tide of wealth was turning and flowing more towards the northern cities and Amon had to perform miracles to show that his power was not abated, he is strangely aloof. Unlike the Greek Zeus, there are no stories connected with him of amorous adventures to evoke laughter or disgust. When the theologians of the xviii-th dynasty were seized with the desire to marry their deities together and give them children, Amon was paired with Mut and their son was Khonsu, but in reality he was never connected with them in the popular mind; and to the end he remained passionless and alone.

Bast, the cat-headed goddess of Bubastis, also rose from the lowly position of a purely local deity to be one of the most popular divinities of Egypt (pl. xxi. 2). The fact that she was in origin a local goddess shows that her cult was very early; a further proof is that her city took its name from her temple. Bubastis was an important centre among the principalities of the Delta in early historic times, so important that the great Khufu was responsible for some of the building of her temple.

Bast was known and worshipped in other parts of Egypt besides her own little kingdom, but the great wave of cat-worship did not occur till the xxii-nd dynasty, when Shishak I, the then prince of Bubastis, suddenly rose to power and became the Pharaoh. Then his local deity rose with him, and her cult was popularised throughout the country, and she remained one of the most important of Egyptian deities when Greek travellers and authors began to frequent Egypt. The priests in the temples attempted to fuse her with the lioness-goddess, Sekhmet of Memphis, but among the people she retained her own individuality and her own rites.

Herodotus, without giving any reason, equates her with Artemis: "In the language of Egypt, Apollo is Horus; Demeter, Isis; and Artemis, Bubastis." He has also given a description of her temple and her festival from his own knowledge and not from hearsay of the priests.* The orgiastic ceremonies at the festival can be paralleled in many other parts of the ancient world.

Though the lioness-headed statues dedicated in a temple might be labelled Bast by the priests, the little figures made for private devotion always have the unmistakable round head and pointed ears of the cat. There are certain peculiarities of the bronze figures of Bast of the xxvi-th dynasty which have not as yet been explained. In these she wears the long straight dress of the Egyptian woman, but instead of being plain as in other female figures it is always represented as patterned all over, either a woven pattern or embroidery; this suggests some foreign influence. In her right hand the goddess carries a sistrum; over her left arm is slung a basket or bag, and in her left hand is the so-called "ægis of Bast". This is in no sense a shield; it consists of the head of a lioness surrounded with necklaces which spread in a wide semicircle round the head. The writing of Bast's name is not easy to explain; from the earliest to the latest times it is written with the picture of a jar of perfume (fig. 4), either standing alone or with the letters of her name written out.

Fig. 4

The Romans carried the worship of Bast to Italy, and traces of her cult are found in Rome, Ostia, Nemi, and Pompeii. At Nemi there was a statue of the goddess, and the inventory of its garments is still extant: "A robe of silk, purple and turquoise-green; a shirt of purple

* Herodotus, ii. 156.

linen with two girdles, one gilt; two robes; two mantles, a tunic, and a white dress."*

A local god who owed his immense celebrity to the trade of his worshippers was Thoth. His name, as written in its earliest form, was Zehuti,† *He of Zehut*, showing that in the beginning he had no special name but was a small local godling. Thoth was essentially the god of learning; he was the Master of the Words of God, *i.e.* the hieroglyphs, he was the Scribe and Messenger of the gods, he was the Measurer of time, the Mathematician and therefore the Magician. All scribes, engineers, astrologers, astronomers, and all whose work lay in applied mathematics and all dealers in magic, were devotees of Thoth. As the scribes were in all the key positions in Egypt, Thoth looms large in the official religion. He introduces Amon to Queen Aahmes, he assists Horus at the baptism of the Pharaoh, he stands by the scales at the Last Judgment‡ and records on his tablets the result of the weighing of the heart of the dead (pl. xxii), while his sacred animal sits on the upright or the tongue of the balance to ensure the accuracy of the weighing.

As the Lord of magic and of writing Thoth was credited with having written with his own hand, in forty-two volumes, all the wisdom of the world. Some of these volumes contained all the laws of Egypt, and during the xviii-th dynasty, when the Vizier sat to hear cases in the High Court of Justice, these precious rolls were always brought into court to be consulted if any disputed point of law arose. From the words of this divine Scripture there could be no appeal. A Ptolemaic story shows that Thoth also wrote a book of magic.§

As the moon is the natural measurer of time, Thoth is often regarded as the god of the moon, and then wears the horns of the crescent moon on his head. He could be invoked in illness, not because of his knowledge of medicine but on account of his being the god of magic and the supreme author of spells.

In the theology of the xx-th dynasty, Ptah is regarded as the pure Intellect which is the ultimate origin of all creation; and Thoth is the Tongue, the Word, by whom all creation came into existence.|| This is an early example of that theory of the Logos, the Word "by

* *Recueil*, xxxvii (1915).
† By the time his worship had moved from his original habitat in the north to Eshmunen in the south, the pronunciation had changed and he was called Tehuti, which the Greeks spelt with the o, presumably pronounced as an aspirated T.
‡ When the idea of the weighing of souls was introduced into Christian art the Arch-angel Michael takes the place of Thoth.
§ Griffith, *Stories of the High Priests*; Murray, *Ancient Egyptian Legends*.
|| Breasted, *Development of Religion and Thought*.

whom all things were made", which had so profound an effect on Christian theology.

As the whole learned world of Egypt were initiates and devotees of Thoth, it is not surprising that the Greeks venerated him also. They identified him with Hermes, under the name of Hermes Tris-megistos, and by that name he was honoured by medieval alchemists.

Thoth is usually figured as an ibis or an ibis-headed man. His sacred animal was the cynocephalus, the dog-headed baboon; in this form Thoth is always entirely animal, never a man with an ape's head.

The cult of Apis, the bull of Memphis, is of very early date. There were four bulls which were worshipped in the primitive periods: Apis of Memphis, Mnevis of Heliopolis, Buchis of Hermonthis, and the Golden Bull of Canopus. Apis was the most famous of the four. "This Apis is the calf of a cow incapable of conceiving another off-spring. This calf, which is called Apis, has the following marks: it is black, and has a square spot on the forehead; and on the back the figure of an eagle; and in the tail double hairs; and on the tongue a beetle."* This shows that the creature was a piebald, the marks being in certain definite shapes. Herodotus says that when a new Apis was born there was great rejoicing, "the Egyptians immediately put on their richest apparel and kept festive holiday".†

Apis, in Egyptian Hapi, was a form of the river Nile, and therfore so closely connected with Osiris as to be called the incarnate Soul of Osiris. As the Soul of God was in him, he was worshipped as God, and suffered the same fate as the human incarnation of the divine Spirit. He was not allowed to die of old age, but was ceremonially killed and a new bull installed in his place; this fact was what made the appearance of a new Apis of such importance to the people of Memphis. When the new bull was identified, the old bull seems to have been drowned, and there is some evidence to show that the flesh was eaten at a ritual feast; the skin, bones, and some parts of the body were mummified and then buried with royal honours. The drowning, the dismember-ment, and the royal burial show the close connection with Osiris.

The burial place of the Apis-bulls, the Serapeum at Saqqara, is an underground structure, which was begun in the xviii-th dynasty and continued in use till the end of the Pharaonic period. Each bull was buried in a sarcophagus in a separate burial chamber, in which a tablet was set up stating the regnal year of the Pharaoh in whose reign he was born, the regnal year in which he died, and the length of his life. These tablets are of great value in determining the sequence and length of the reigns of the kings in an obscure period of Egyptian history.

* Herodotus, iii. 28.　　　　† Ibid., iii. 27.

In Ptolemaic times Osiris and Apis were fused together into one great god, Serapis, who is not so much the dead Apis as the chthonic god to whom belongs all the wealth that lies hidden in the earth; for that reason he was identified by the Greeks with Hades, the god of riches.

The other bull-gods are of less importance than Apis. Mnevis was entirely black, and of a different breed from Apis; he was a heavily built animal with such high shoulders as to be almost humped like the zebu. He was the incarnation of the Sun-god, and as such was worshipped by Akhenaten as well as by other Pharaohs, but he never entered into the popular worship like Apis.

OSIRIS AND THE PHARAOH

In all countries local deities were the foundation of religion. Time always brings changes, and belief and ritual must change with the times if they are to keep any hold on the people. In other words, ideas of religion must keep pace with the advance of knowledge. Three great epochs in the evolution of religion can thus be traced in ancient Egypt.

The first was in one of the prehistoric periods, probably the Gerzean, when the worship of the God who rises from the dead was introduced. This was not so much the beginning of agriculture as the introduction of new types of grain and of the vine, of the making of intoxicants from these new plants, and of the suppression of cannibalism. In other words, by the impact of a foreign culture there was an increase of civilisation by the assimilation of foreign ideas, by the growth of knowledge, and a consequent raising of the standard of living. The combination of these new ideas becomes manifest in the cult of Osiris.

The second epoch was the invasion* of the dynastic kings. They had as their totem the Horus-falcon, and they fought with the people whose totems were the crocodile and the hippopotamus, revered under the name of Setekh. From this war there developed the saga of Horus and Setekh, which was originally distinct from the Osiris-legend of the Dying God, but was gradually incorporated into it.

The third epoch began in the iii-rd or iv-th dynasty when sun-worship was imported (probably from a cloudy northern country) into an almost rainless land, where the sun was regarded as inimical. By the v-th dynasty this cult was completely established as the prerogative of the Pharaoh; and though it was later accepted by some of the nobles,

* In view of the recent studies of the i-st dynasty it is preferable to use the word "rise" instead of "invasion".

it never became the religion of the people. Its fullest development was under Akhenaten.

The underlying basic religion and the three great changes in creed and ritual affected one another. New ideas of God and of the relation between God and man were evolved by the clash or combination of the varying forms of religion, and this growth from a primitive and savage cult to the highest religious ideals can be best studied in the worship and ritual of Osiris.*

The cult of Osiris is also the most important of all the Egyptian cults because it belonged to all classes from the highest to the lowest. It is perhaps the most perfect example of that belief which is found in so many countries, *viz.* that God is incarnate in man, which belief is usually accompanied by the rite of killing the Divine Man.

The chosen man is almost invariably the king. In him dwells the Spirit of God, and he thus becomes God Incarnate. The indwelling Spirit is that of the Creator, the Giver of Life, and to the Incarnate God was therefore ascribed the power to give fertility to his people and land. In the eyes of his subjects the king was actually God. The appeal of such a belief is obvious, God Himself living and moving among His people, visible to their eyes, a man amongst men but at the same time possessing the mystic and mighty power of God. With this belief there went another belief, which to the primitive mind was the logical corollary. The Spirit was not necessarily immortal, any more than the body in which it was incarnate; nor was it exempt from the failure of the bodily powers which come with age. If the Divine Man grew old and became weaker, the Spirit within him also grew weaker; if the Divine Man died a natural death or was accidentally killed, the Spirit shared the same fate. If the Creator Spirit, the Force of reproduction, were dead, what could happen to the worshippers but death and destruction: they themselves and all their belongings were doomed. To prevent so disastrous a fate, some means had to be devised for removing the Spirit from its ageing home and housing it in a younger, stronger body. The only way by which the Divine Spirit could be removed was by the death of the man in whom it was incarnate; and as he could not be allowed to die a natural death, he had to be killed. This had to be done with every kind of precaution, every kind of religious ceremony, for it was equivalent to killing a god. It follows then that while the king was young and active he was sacrosanct, not a finger might be raised against him, and his subjects, literally his worshippers, were ready to die in his defence; but when he showed any sign of age and his time had come, not a finger could be raised to save him.

* See Wainwright, *The Sky Religion in Egypt.*

In many countries the Divine King was allowed to reign for a term of years only, usually seven or nine or multiples of those numbers. The custom altered, as all customs do, with the lapse of years and the change in conditions, and the Divine King instead of being sacrificed himself was permitted to appoint a substitute who suffered in his stead. For a few days or weeks the substitute acted as king, enjoying all the pomp and privileges of that high estate, and at the end of the appointed time he was killed with the same ceremonial rites as if he had been the actual king. It is a remarkable fact that wherever there is any record of these practices, there is never any indication that the Divine Victim, whether the real one or his substitute, shirked his fate when the time came; each undertook the office knowing what the end would be.

There were three methods of killing the Divine Victim: (a) by bloodshed, when it was essential that the blood should fall on the ground; (b) by burning, when the ashes had to be collected and scattered on the fields, or more rarely strewn on running water as a rain charm; (c) by asphyxiation—strangling, drowning, hanging— when the body was dismembered and the fragments buried in different parts of the country. In this rite the insistence that the mortal remains of the dead god should come in contact with the earth indicates that this was a custom belonging to the age of agriculture; life had been taken out of the ground by the crops, so life had to be put back again, for even the corpse of the Giver of Life was still instinct with life.

Though Osiris united in himself all the deified natural phenomena which were regarded as producing fertility, it was his aspect as the ruler of both the Living and the Dead which has been most fully recorded. The god of fertility, incarnate in the king, was naturally the object of worship to every inhabitant of the country. His very name, written with the throne and the eye (fig. 5) reading Us-yri, means the Occupier of the Throne, and shows him as the Pharaoh.

Fig. 5

Round the Pharaoh, the living Osiris, clustered a group of deities who belonged to him and not to the rest of the Egyptians; round Osiris, the dead Pharaoh, was another group of deities, who originally belonged only to him, but later were adopted by people of lesser rank when all the dead were fused with Osiris.

It becomes impossible, therefore, to make a hard and fast distinction between the Osiris group of deities and the Pharaonic group in the later forms of the religion. It is only by studying the religion in its earlier aspects, preferably in and before the xii-th dynasty, that the difference can be observed.

The Osiris group consists of those five deities who were regarded as the children of the Sky-goddess Nut, Osiris, Isis, Nephthys, Horus (or Anubis), and Setekh. These were not so much the brothers and sisters of Osiris as deities connected with his death and burial. Anubis was the god of death; Setekh was the killer; Horus devised the obsequies; Isis and Nephthys together were the mourners at the funeral.

The legend and cult of Osiris show the belief in the Incarnate God and also the custom of the ritual killing of the king. Though Plutarch* is a late writer, his account of Osiris can be checked by the records of Osiris-worship, and is proved to be substantially correct.

In the legend there are found the introduction of new forms of agriculture by the god of fertility, the death by asphyxiation of that god, the dismemberment of the divine body, and the burial of the fragments in the earth. Another legend states that Isis collected the fragments of the body, raising a cenotaph in the places where they were found, and that she and Nephthys united the fragments together and by their magic power endued the body with life so that the god rose from the dead. He was thus the god of the dead and of the resurrection, typified as the grain which is buried and springs alive out of the ground. In the cult of Osiris it was this aspect of the god which was emphasised, his death, burial, and resurrection. The details of his life on earth before he was killed are not represented, except in his aspect as the Pharaoh.

As often happens, the dead and buried god becomes the ruler of the Underworld, the king of the dead (pl. xxiii. 2). The ruler of a kingdom, especially when like Osiris he governs the realms of bliss, has the right to grant or refuse admission into his kingdom. The god of the dead thus becomes the great and terrible Judge to whom the dead must answer for their deeds on earth. As our knowledge of Egyptian beliefs of the Hereafter comes from inscriptions and pictorial representations in tombs, it is this aspect of Osiris which is most familiar to the student of ancient Egypt. But in his aspect as god of fertility, Osiris was also the moon and the Nile and as such he could be worshipped as the great Creator (pl. xxiii. 1).

The cult of Osiris included human sacrifice; in the beginning it was the ruler who suffered, later a substitute was put to death (fig. 6). This ritual killing is the cause of much of the confusion which exists

* *De Iside et Osiride.*

Granite temple of Khafra, dynasty iv

2. Ruins of Christian church in the temple of Luxor

3. Statue of Rameses II, temple of Luxor

Avenue of ram-headed sphinxes, Karnak

Plate XXXIII

1. Papyrus column with lotus-bud
capital, dynasty v

2. Capital of rose lotus,
dynasty v

PLATE XXXIV

2. Foliage capital. Ptolemaic

1. Palm-leaf capital

PLATE XXXV

1, 2. Capitals from Coptic churches

PLATE XXXVI

Temple of Karnak showing flower capitals

PLATE XXXVII

Temple of Luxor, dynasty xviii

Photograph by P. Hart

PLATE XXXVIII

1. Hathor-head capitals, temple of Dendera. Ptolemaic

2. Foliage capitals, temple of Esna. Ptolemaic

PLATE **XXXIX**

1. Temple of Kalabsheh

2. Temple of Edfu

PLATE XL

Brick
rches,
nesseum

2. Pan-bedding,
   brick.
   Kahun

3. Detail of Step-
   pyramid

PLATE XLI

Photograph by Captain M. M. Barker

⚐ 1. Wavy wall, Abydos. Dynasty xii

2. Entrance pylons. Temple of Luxor

PLATE XLII

Photograph by M. A. Murray

2. Modern Coptic church

1. The Red Monastery.   Coptic

PLATE XLIII

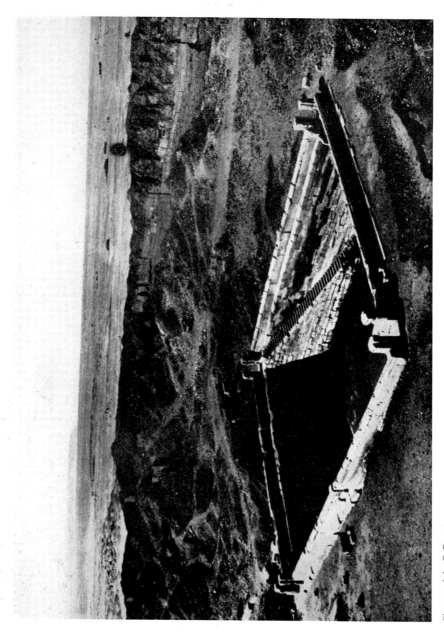

Photograph by G. Brunton

Sacred lake, Dendera

Plate XLIV

1. The Step-pyramid, dynasty iii

2. Temple of the Step-pyramid

PLATE XLV

Pyramid of Meydum, dynasty iii

Plate XLVI

After Borchard

Pyramid field of Abusir, dynasty v

PLATE XLVII

1. Statuette of Khufu.
   Ivory

2. Statue of Khafra.
   Diorite

PLATE XLVIII

in the accounts of both the god and his cult. The confusion, which extends also to the explanatory legend, arises from two deities having the same name; these were: (*a*) Horus, god of the dynastic kings, who fought against Setekh, god of the aboriginal people, and (*b*) Horus the Child, son of Isis and Osiris. To explain the rite of human sacrifice to Osiris (which was originally the sacrifice of Osiris himself), Horus the Child is supposed to have grown up and become the Avenger (or Protector) of his Father; the campaigns of the other Horus against Setekh became wars of vengeance against the murderer of Osiris; and the human victims slain in the presence of Osiris were the prisoners, the Companions of Setekh, taken in battle by Horus. But at the same time the original meaning of the rite was not forgotten, for the sacrifice

Fig. 6 (i-st dynasty)

was made on "that night of ploughing the earth in their blood".* In the xviii-th dynasty animals could be substituted for human victims: "The Coming of the Companions of Setekh, when they take their forms as antelopes. Then they are slain in the presence of the gods, they are smitten down, and their blood pours from them."† The sacrificer, who must sometimes have been the Pharaoh in person, identified himself with Horus, the Avenger of his Father, and in that character struck down the foes of Osiris. In this rite Osiris was no longer the gentle much-loved deity, mourned and lamented yearly, but was the primitive Red God of a savage people, a god who delighted in blood: "Behold this god, great of slaughter, great of fear! He washes in your blood, he bathes in your gore!"‡ As the God of Life he could give life, and Horus, the Royal Sacrificer, bought his own life by the life of others, a life for a life.

* *Book of the Dead*, ch. xviii.   † Ibid., ch. xviii.   ‡ Ibid., ch. cxxxiv.
E

The cult of Osiris became in the end a mixture of the primitive rites of a savage community and some of the highest ideals of an advanced form of religion. Even as late as the Ptolemies the killing of a god was still practised, though that god was called the enemy of Osiris. And though the figure of the god was probably made only of bread, the worshippers were still called to the cannibal feast: "Eat ye the flesh of the vanquished, drink ye his blood." Yet not so long afterwards, Plutarch could write of "the most pure and truly holy Osiris" who could not be seen by the eyes of flesh, "for the souls of men are not able to participate of the divine nature whilst they are encompassed about with bodies and passions. . . . When they are freed from these impediments and remove into those purer and unseen regions, 'tis then that this God becomes their Leader and King; upon him they wholly depend, still beholding without satiety, and still ardently longing after that beauty, which 'tis not possible for man to express or think."*

The change in the explanation of a ritual is seen also in another sacrifice connected with Osiris, the sacrifice of the pig. In early times the pig seems to have been taboo; and, as Frazer has shown, taboo becomes either holy or unclean, in either case with the meaning of un-touchable. Herodotus shows very clearly that originally the pig was the sacred animal of Osiris: "The Egyptians consider the pig to be an impure animal, and therefore if a man in passing by a pig should touch him only with his garments, he forthwith goes to the river and plunges in. . . . On the eve of the festival of Bacchus [i.e. Osiris] every one slays a pig before his door."† In this account it is interesting to note the various aspects of Osiris in connection with the pig. A passer-by, i.e. not one of the initiated, who accidentally touched a tabooed animal had to be cleansed at once by plunging into the Nile, which river was in itself another form of Osiris; the sacrifice had to take place at the full moon and it was essential to eat the sacred animal on that day that if poverty prevented the worshipper from having a real pig, he made one of bread and ate that. It seems also that it was obligatory for every householder to slaughter the animal at his own door, presumably that the blood might be on the threshold or the sides of the door.

The chief centres of Osiris-worship were Abydos in the south and Busiris in the north; the difference in ritual shows that at Abydos the emphasis was laid on the death of the god, at Busiris on the resurrection. At Abydos there seems to have been a mystery play, showing forth the passion, death, burial, and resurrection of Osiris. In Ptolemaic times this was a puppet play, but under the Pharaohs the performers were

* Plutarch, *De Iside et Osiride*, Squire's translation.   † Herodotus, ii. 47, 48.

living actors and there is little doubt that in early times the men who took the parts of Osiris and Setekh were actually sacrificed. The later ritual at Abydos was an elaborate symbol of seedtime and harvest, centring on the burial of a hollow golden figure of the god, which was filled with sand and barley. With this figure were buried four small figures, representing the four Children of Horus; these also were hollow and were filled with sand, barley, fourteen different kinds of spaces and fourteen different kinds of precious stones. The burial took place in a stone trough filled with earth and sown with barley, which was carefully watered; when the seeds germinated, the springing plants represented the resurrection of the god.

The symbolising of the resurrection by the growth of vegetation is plainly seen in some of the burials of the xii-th dynasty. "Gardens of Osiris", *i.e.* bowls of earth in which barley had been sown and had sprouted, were found at the entrance to the pyramid at Lahun (pl. xxi. 1).★ In the xviii-th dynasty "beds of Osiris" were placed in the tombs of great persons; these were beds on which the figure of Osiris had been sketched in outline, and the sketch filled with earth, sown with barley and watered until the germination of the seed.

The cults of Isis and Osiris are so inextricably mixed that it is impossible to disentangle them completely. The writing of her name (fig. 7) shows that she was the queen, "She of the Throne", and therefore naturally her partner was Osiris, the Occupier of the Throne. Her cult spread far and wide, so that there was a Thames-side temple of Isis in London and an altar to Isis at Chester. Her aspects were so many that she was known as the Myriad-named, but her chief epithets are "Mother of God, Lady of Heaven". As the devoted wife she travels over sea and land to find and bury her husband's body, she mourns and laments over his bier, she raised him from the dead, she stands beside him in the Judgment. She is also the Mother, she bears the child Horus, she protects him in infancy and childhood, she advised him when Setekh brings a legal action against him, and by her magical spells she gives him the victory in his hand-to-hand combat with his great enemy. She is the wife of the Occupier of the Throne and the mother of the king who is to come. But as Horus the heir becomes himself Osiris when he succeeds to the throne, she is both mother and wife of the reigning king. There is little doubt that this is what actually happened, that when the successful claimant came to the throne he consolidated his position by marriage with the chief heiress no matter how closely related.

She was the greatest of all the goddesses, for she was "the Great

★ Petrie, *Lahun*, ii. pl. xv. 7, p. 14.

Enchantress, the Mistress of Magic, the Speaker of Spells", she alone knew the secret name of Rê, and by that knowledge all things were subject to her. She was invoked in all illnesses, especially those of children, for she had protected Horus her son from all the dangerous illnesses of childhood. She was the great Mother to all who worshipped her (pl. xxiv).

Nephthys is a goddess whose origin and *raison d'être* are obscure. By her name, which means *Lady of the House*, she should be the goddess of the household and therefore early; but when she appears in the pantheon she is merely a co-mourner for Osiris with her sister Isis. She has no special attributes except her name worn as a headdress; no temple, not even a small shrine in a temple, was dedicated to her worship. Yet as one of the mourners for Osiris she has a definite position as a protector of the dead. As early as the Pyramid Texts she is often mentioned, but without sufficient detail to give any real indication of her special position or cult. The theologians of the xviii-th dynasty in their passion for tidying up the pantheon married

Fig. 7   Fig. 8

her to her brother Setekh, the killer of Osiris, but in order to bring her back into the immediate circle of Osiris they gave her to him as a concubine and made her the mother of Anubis. She was evidently in origin one of the many virgin goddesses who were worshipped without consorts; and in essence she remains alone in spite of the efforts of the theologians. As a mourner for Osiris she stands at the head of the corpse; as protector of the less august dead her place is at the head end of the coffin, her companion in that position being Neith. Of the four goddesses who protect the dead in the grave, she is the second in importance; the others are Isis, Neith, and Selket.

The god Setekh is one of the most important of all the gods of Egypt, and yet less is known of him than of any other of the great gods. In papyri of the xii-th dynasty he is always alluded to as "the Majesty of Setekh", an epithet not applied to any other god except Rê until a late epoch. He is represented as an animal, though of no known species, for he has a long curving snout, square-tipped upstanding ears, and his tail sticks up stiffly at an angle with the body and ends in a kind of tuft. The earliest example of this animal occurs on the mace-head of the Scorpion-King, where it is the totem of one of the tribes who

were allied with the incoming dynastic people. His worship seems to
have been very primitive, and included human sacrifice, possibly the
sacrifice of the king. His sacred animal was the ass, which was sacrificed to him—as were horses to Helios in Greece—by being thrown
down a cliff.

The earliest form of the name is spelt Setesh or possibly Setech
(fig. 8), which became hardened into Setekh.* He had no consort and
no offspring, and even to the end he seems to have been independent
and aloof. In the early religion he is one of the helpers of Osiris, of
whom he was a brother, and he amicably divided the kingdom of
Egypt with the Horus-falcon† of the invaders; he retaining the south
while Horus took the more fertile north. As the chief seat of his
worship was the city of Nubt ("the Golden") he was known also as
Nubti, written in the usual way with the sign meaning Gold. Among
the early titles of the Pharaoh was one which showed that the king
was under the direct protection of the goddesses of the south and north,
but when the gods began to dispossess the goddesses in the official
religion, the king took a new title compounded of Horus and Setekh,
thereby placing himself under the protection of the gods of the north
and south. This title was *Nebui*, "He of the two Lords", in which
Setekh appears as Nubti, "He of the city of Nubt", while Horus is
represented in his usual form of a falcon.

Setekh is closely connected with the sacrifice of the king. That
strange priest, Kha-bau-Seker, who appears to have been the chief
officiant in the shrine of Anubis, also held high office in the shrine of
Setekh; on both accounts I take him to be the executioner of the king
or of the royal substitute. He belongs to the iii-rd dynasty. Then in
the vi-th dynasty, the evidence of the Pyramid Texts shows that
Setekh was connected with the "escape from death" of the king and
that this escape was due to ploughing the earth.

The original enemy of Setekh was not Osiris but Horus, and this
was due to the division of the country. There were probably tribal
battles between the Followers of Horus and the Companions of
Setekh, in which the Setekh people were defeated. And there was also
a very ancient legend that Setekh brought a legal action against Horus,
but by the wily advice of Isis Horus gained the day. In the account of
this law-suit Setekh is always called "the Majesty of Setekh", and

* As the name begins with S, one is inclined to suspect a causative as in the name of
the crocodile god, Se-bek, "He who causes to be pregnant". Se-tekh would then
mean "To intoxicate, to cause to be drunken", and would imply a cult of the same
type as that of Bacchus, where drunkenness was regarded as possession by the god.
See above, p. 87, for Egyptian views on drunkenness.

† See footnote, p. 99.

appears as a gross bully, while Horus is represented as a young and rather helpless stripling.

In the xix-th dynasty there seems to have been a recrudescence of Setekh-worship, for three of the kings of that dynasty incorporated his name in their own; two were called Setekhy, "He of Setekh", and one was Setekh-nekht, "Setekh is victorious". At some period later than this, probably in the xxii-nd dynasty, Setekh became the Principle of Evil, and in an excess of religious zeal his name and figure were erased from all monuments as far as possible, and images of him were destroyed. His worship seems to have been confined to a few places only, and his figure was often replaced by that of the crocodile god or by Thoth, whose long beak has almost the same curve as the snout of the Setekh-animal. Owing to the iconoclastic outbreak against him, few figures or representations of this god have survived.*

As the chief sky-god Setekh was appealed to by Rameses II to grant fine weather when the Hittite envoys were coming to Egypt in the depth of winter. Rameses offered a sacrifice to every god, "and his father Setekh heard every word".

The Greeks called him Typhôn or Bebôn; the latter is an interesting name, for the root meaning of *Beb* is "eddy", either of water or air, and connects the god with the whirling pillars of sand which race across the burnt-up fields of Egypt in summer. Though the name is rare in the official religion it was common in compounds for personal names at certain periods. In the vi-th dynasty there is a variant pronunciation and there were two kings called Pepy, a name of the same type as Amony; the late Hyksos kings were also called Pepy, Helenised as Apophis, which was also the name given to the great serpent of the Nether World who was the enemy of Rê.

Much of the confusion which arose in the legend of Osiris is due to an attempt to reconcile the saga of Horus and Setekh with the Osiris legend. As is not uncommon the ritual affected the legend, and the legend which explained the ritual altered insensibly, till a mass of confusion resulted. But if the facts are carefully examined an explanation can be found.

The dynastic kings had for their totem a falcon, and from the i-st dynasty onwards every Pharaoh had his falcon-totem with which he was identified in life and in death. He came from the egg, he was the Falcon in the Nest, he sat upon the Horus-throne of the Living, he was Horus in all battles whether real or figurative, and at death he flew as a falcon to be united with his Maker.

After the invasion† of the Horus-people, the *Shemsu-Hor*, the whole

---

* Cf. the persecution of the god Amon under Akhenaten.
† See footnote on p. 99.

of Egypt, which had formerly been under the protection of the two goddesses Nekhebt and Wazt, was now put under the protection of two gods, Setekh and Horus. Setekh, the greatest of the aboriginal gods, retained his hold on the south; Horus, whose worshippers made their capital at Memphis at the head of the Delta, became the god of the north. One proof that Horus did not belong to the Osiris cycle originally is that, unlike his rival Setekh, he is not invariably included among the deities of the five intercalary days which were inserted into the calendar in Gerzean or Semainian times.

Every Pharaoh was one with his totem, therefore every Pharaoh was Horus; at the same time, every Pharaoh was Osiris, the Occupier of the Throne. A further complication set in when it became customary for the Pharaoh to appoint one of his sons to succeed him, this son being the child of the chief heiress, *i.e.* of Isis, She of the Throne. He was thus Horus the Child, whose duty it was to arrange the obsequies for Osiris when the Occupier of the Throne died.

When it was once established that Horus the Falcon was the same as Horus the Child, the son of Isis and Osiris, the battles of Horus and Setekh were explained by making Setekh the murderer of Osiris, possibly because the priest of Setekh was the appointed executioner of the divine king. The attitude of Horus towards Setekh then became that of a son avenging his father's death.

If it is realised that the Pharaoh represented three of the chief actors in the Osirian drama, some of the confusion disappears. He began his career as Horus the Child, who grew up to be Horus the Protector of his father, and he ended as Osiris the Occupier of the Throne who is finally killed by Setekh and rises from the dead.

Horus the Child (Har-pa-khred, or Harpocarates as the Greeks called him) (pl. xxiv) is of little account in the Osiris legend or in the religion. In fact he is little more than a kind of lay figure to emphasise the motherhood of Isis and to give point to the magical spells and remedies with which she, the Great Enchantress, successfully cured all his childish ailments or more serious accidents.* It was not until the Late periods, especially in Ptolemaic times, that he was regarded as of any importance, when he became identified with the newly born, or rising, sun.

Horus the Elder (Har-wer, the Aroeris of the Greeks) was one of the great gods, being closely connected with the king. His battles with Setekh were recited in almost all temples, and were performed as mystery plays on the days devoted to the memory of the death of

---

* The so-called "Cippi of Horus" are magical protections against all creatures "biting with their mouths or stinging with their tails". They are sometimes inscribed with the charms used by Isis to cure the child Horus.

Osiris, his funerary arrangements for Osiris were reproduced in the burials of the Pharaohs, and he took a leading part in all ceremonies connected with the official ceremonies of the Pharaoh. At Edfu, which was one of the great temples dedicated specially to his worship, the inscriptions on the walls of the girdle passage give as a drama the account of the fight between the two gods.

THE PHARAOH

In any study of the Egyptian religion the position of the Pharaoh is of the utmost importance, for the monarch was himself God. He was all-powerful because he was God; he was king because he was God; to swear falsely by his name was blasphemy as well as perjury, and was punishable with death; "to fear God and honour the King" was one and the same act. All the land and all the people belonged to him because he was the Giver of fertility, the Preserver of all.

This feeling is continually expressed in the inscriptions; Amonemhat III was called "the Generator who creates mankind". Another inscription of the xii-th dynasty says, "Adore the King! Enthrone him in your hearts! He makes Egypt green more than a great Nile. He is Life! He is the One who creates all which is, the Begetter who causes mankind to exist." Queen Hatshepsut, who ruled as king, puts her position in plain language, "I am God, the Beginning of Existence".*

The Pharaoh, then, was a dual personality, both God and man. Without any feeling of incongruity he could, as a man, give worship to himself as God. As God he was the Giver of all to his subjects; as a man he was like other men, the creation of his own God. He was on an entirely different level from the ordinary human being, and his God differed from the gods of the people. To his subjects he was the incarnation, the living embodiment, of the god of any district he happened to be visiting; he was their actual God in living form, whom they could see, speak to, and adore. But the king himself worshipped the Sun, to whom he alone owed allegiance, of whom he alone was the physical son, by whom he alone was loved, and whose name he incorporated in the title he took when he became Osiris, the Occupier of the Throne.

The divine birth of the Pharaoh was a dogma insisted upon at almost every period. As a man he acquired the throne by right of marriage with the heiress, but as Pharaoh he was God, and divinity could only be attained by physical descent from God. This, of course,

* Naville, *Temple of Deir el Bahri*, pl. lxxxvi, line 7.

was theoretically the case from the v-th dynasty onwards, when the Pharaoh was first called the Son of Rê, but to the Egyptian in general Rê was the royal god and not one to be worshipped by the people. It was essential that the god should visit the queen in visible form, that he should be seen in all the majesty of godhead entering her chamber. How this was effected is made clear in the inscriptions of Hatshepsut and Amonhotep III. The account begins by the god Amon consulting with twelve other deities as to the human mother he shall choose to bear his child. Thoth then suggests that the wife of the Pharaoh is the appropriate woman; he takes Amon by the hand and leads him to the palace. Amon "made his form like the majesty of this husband, King Thothmes, he found her as she slept in the beauty of her palace. She waked at the fragrance of the God, all his odours were of Punt." The inscription then records in plain terms what occurred, and in due time the divine child was born. It is quite clear that the king, the husband of the queen, was on occasion dressed in the insignia of the god when he visited his wife, and was probably accompanied by priests and priestesses as attendant deities.★ At Abu Simbel the god Ptah is made to address Rameses II and say "I assumed my form as the Ram, Lord of Mendes", and in this guise he visited the mother of Rameses "in order to fashion thy form as the Lord of the Two Lands".†

As the king was the embodiment of fertility, he was also the Divine Victim who might be put to death to ensure fertility, when it was expedient that one man should die for the people. The pyramid Texts show that the sacrifice of the king was well-known in the vi-th dynasty, and they show also that the sacrifice was in the nature of a rain charm. As Osiris was, according to the legend, introduced into Egypt from a northern country, it would seem that his cult even then practised the rite of human sacrifice, the victim being the king. But the Pyramid Texts show that the same rite was used in southern Egypt where Setekh was worshipped. I suggest, therefore, that the cult was indigenous in Egypt, but the reason for practising it, as given in the Pyramid Texts, belongs to the cult of Osiris and was carried into Egypt by the people who brought with them the knowledge of wheat and agriculture.

The text in question begins with a description of falling rain; it then gives as the reason why the king should die, that he had not eaten the "Eye of Horus", which is a synonym for food; this means probably that there was a famine in the land. "The face of the sky is washed,

★ Compare the visit to the prophetess by Isaiah, who took with him two attendants, apparently to bear witness as to the paternity of the child. (Isaiah viii. 2, 3.)
† Cf. the story of Amphitryon,

the vault of heaven shines. Thou hast removed the bareness [literally, nakedness] of the heavens. 'Twice happy art thou,' says his mother. 'My heir,' says Osiris. Pepy Merenrê has not eaten the Eye of Horus. Say the people, 'Let him die for it'. Pepy Merenrê has not eaten the limb of Osiris. Say the gods, 'Let him die for it'. Pepy Merenrê has eaten the bread of Atum. Protect thou him, O Nekhbet! Protect thou Pepy Merenrê, O Nekhbet! Pepy Merenrê has escaped his new moons of death as Setesh escaped his new moons of death, Pepy Merenrê has escaped his full moons of death as Setesh escaped his full moons of death, Pepy Merenrê has escaped his year of death as Setesh escaped his year of death, by ploughing the earth. The hands of Pepy Merenrê raise up the sky like Shu, his bones are of metal, his limbs are an imperishable star. Pepy Merenrê is a Star opening the waters of heaven. Mount up to him, O God, and let him be protected, for Heaven is not dry through Pepy Merenrê, nor is the earth dry through Pepy Merenrê, for ever."★

Another text of the same Pharaoh says that the king was begotten "before heaven or earth existed, before men existed, before the gods were born, before death existed. Pepy escapes his day of death as Setesh escaped his day of death. O ye Gods of the Abyss, who perish not on account of your enemies, Pepy perishes not on account of his enemies; ye who die not on account of the Kingship, Pepy dies not on account of the Kingship; ye who die not on account of any death, Pepy dies not on account of any death, for Pepy is an Imperishable Star."†

Pepy is also said to be within his two limits, meaning the limits of life, between birth and death; therefore he could not die until he reached the farthest limit of his life.‡

It is evident that ploughing the ground was part of the ceremony whereby the Pharaoh preserved his own life when the time came for him to be sacrificed. As late as Rameses III, at least two thousand years after the Pyramid Texts, the king is shown in his temple of Medinet Habu ploughing a field with a yoke of oxen (pl. xi), and later on he is reaping the corn. If the Book of the Dead is to be believed, it was the custom in the xviii-th dynasty for the sacrifice to take place before the ploughing, and the blood of the victims was sprinkled on the field and ploughed in.

The actual method by which the Pharaoh was put to death is never expressed in so many words but may be inferred from the evidence. It seems to have been by snake-bite. Originally the snake in question

★ Sethe, *Pyramidentexte*, Spruch. 570, ll. 1443–55.
† Sethe, op. cit., Spruch. 571, ll. 1468, 1469.
‡ Murray, "The Dying God", *Ancient Egypt* (1928), p. 8.

was the horned viper, known as *fu* (abbreviated to *f*), a word which was used in the names of many of the early kings, *e.g.* Khu-fu, Shepses-ka-f, and was later replaced by the name of the sun-god, Rê, when the solar religion was introduced as the religion of the kings. It was then also that a change was made in the type of snake used for the sacrifice, and the cobra became the royal serpent. When the difference in the type of poison is realised, the explanation of the change becomes reasonable. Viper poison, though slow in action, causes a painful death; whereas cobra poison, by paralysing the nerves, is swift and easy. It was only when the viper disappears from the royal names that the cobra is found as part of the royal insignia. The cobra then became the instrument of death to the enemies of the king, and there is a small amount of evidence of its being also the instrument of death for the king himself, as it certainly was for the last independent monarch of Egypt, Cleopatra.*

If then the king died of snake-bite, the pattern set in the legend must have been followed, and some part of the body must have been buried in the fields before mummification. It is possible that this was the original reason for removing the viscera of the king; in many cases of lesser folk the viscera were not removed. It is at least worth remarking that the heart and lungs are seldom found among the mummified internal organs. As all lands lived by the breath of the king, it may be that the lungs were buried unmummified to give breath, *i.e.* life, to the earth.

A study of the god Anubis shows that he was originally the God of Death for the Pharaoh only. He has four titles: "Leader of the Shrine of the God", "Lord of the Sacred Land" (*i.e.* the cemetery), "Chief of the Hill of the Viper", and "He who is from Ut". Two of these titles show his connection with the king. The *Shrine of the God* is the lattice shrine in the shape of Anubis himself (fig. 11, p. 147) in which the essential parts of the dead king's body were kept; and if, as suggested above, the ritual killing of the king was effected by the bite of the horned viper, the title *Chief of the Hill of the Viper* needs no explanation.

In all countries where the ritual murder of the king was the practice, notice of his imminent death was always conveyed to the victim by some signal. There is evidence in Egypt that this was done by the priest of Anubis presenting himself to the Pharaoh, wearing the jackal

---

* In the Pyramid Texts the uræus, or hooded cobra, is identified with Setekh. "Pepy is the Uræus which came forth from Setekh", and "the Viper is this which came forth from Rê, the Uræus is this which came forth from Setekh". The snake here translated as *viper* is not a viper at all, but the hoodless cobra, which is as deadly as its hooded relative.

mask of his god (pls. xxi. 3; lxxvi. 2),* and it is possible that the priest of Anubis was also the official executioner of the king.

Anubis became in time the god of death for all, and by degrees he lost his close connection with the Pharaoh and became attached to Isis as her protector, so that in the Ptolemaic period he was merely her faithful dog. In the *Golden Ass* of Apuleius, Anubis is described as walking in the procession of Isis: "high he held his dog-like neck" as he marched in front of the other deities.

In magical ceremonies Anubis always played a large part. In the divination by the bowl, the vessel had to be of some material which was dark inside; black bronze, blackened silver† or even blackened pottery. At the bottom of the bowl was painted or engraved the figure of Anubis. The bowl was filled with water over which was floated a film of fine oil; into this the seer gazed while incense was burned and incantations chanted. Visions in the bowl then appeared to the seer; first came Anubis to prepare the way for the great gods who followed and gave the answers to the questions of the seer.‡

Among the earliest deities connected with the Pharaoh were the goddesses of the south and the north, the vulture and the cobra. Nekhebt, the vulture, was the goddess of the south, and was essentially the protector of the king. It was this role of protector that perhaps caused the vulture to be chosen as her emblem (or incarnation), for the vulture having a larger spread of wing than any other Egyptian bird gives a greater sense of protection when seen covering her nestlings. She was the protector of the king only, not of the people in general; and from the time of Narmer onwards she is shown sheltering the Pharaoh with wings outspread over his head.

The cobra goddess, Wazt (Hellenised as Buto), had her chief shrine in the marshes of the Delta. The cult of the cobra was very ancient in Egypt, so much so that in hieroglyphs the correct determinative for the word "goddess", or for the name of a goddess, is the picture of the cobra. Wazt also was the protector of the Pharaoh, but whereas

---

* On a slate palette of the earliest historical period is the figure of a man wearing a jackal mask. An actual mask in the form of a jackal's head to be worn over the priest's head is dated to the xxvi-th dynasty, and in the temple of Dendera there is a representation of a priest wearing such a mask.

† Cf. the silver cup of Joseph "in which my lord drinketh and whereby he divineth". (Gen. xliv. 5.)

‡ The witch of Endor seems to have followed this practice, which may have been derived from Egypt, so closely does it follow the pattern. She first saw gods ascending out of the earth, then "an old man cometh up, and he is covered with a mantle". (1 Sam. xxviii. 13, 14.) Saul saw nothing himself, the figures were visible only to the seer. In modern divination by the ink-pool, servants appear first, then comes the Sultan to answer the questions; and again these figures are visible only to the seer.

Nekhebt was a passive protector, like a bird covering her young, Wazt was aggressive and rushed to the attack on the enemy. The cobra with spread hood ready to strike was worn by all Pharaohs on the forehead as the emblem of royalty. From that position Wazt was said to defend the king from his enemies, either by spitting poison or by a burning flash from her eyes. It was this death-dealing glance which gave rise to the Greek fable of the basilisk, the royal snake.

The crowns of the south and the north appear to have been another form of the two protective goddesses, being in themselves divine. The crown of the south was known as the Lady of Dread, the crown of the north was the Lady of Spells. When the two were united into one headdress, the Double Crown, it was known as the Lady of Power or the Lady of Flame.

Seshat is an early goddess for she had a priest as early as the iii-rd dynasty. She preceded Thoth as the deity of writing and measuring, but she belonged entirely to the Pharaoh and was never one of the deities of the people. One of her chief functions was to take part in the founding of temples, and down to the latest times the "stretching of the cord" for measuring the size of a new temple was performed by the Pharaoh and herself. In these ceremonies Thoth was not included, though he was the god of applied mathematics and geometry; but a temple being a royal building, the royal goddess was always invoked to take part. Another of her functions was to record the name of the king on the leaves of the Tree of Life, so that his name might remain for evermore. But as her earliest known priest, the sinister Kha-bau-Seker of Memphis, was also the priest of Anubis and Setekh and therefore connected with the death of the Incarnate God, it is possible that Seshat was the deity who calculated the length of the king's life.

Though Bes was originally purely a royal god, he became the most popular of all deities from the noble to the peasant. He was a foreign god, first introduced into Egypt in the xii-th dynasty. He was essentially the protector of the new-made mother and the new-born child. In the earliest examples he is represented as a dancer, and in the xviii-th dynasty he is shown dancing round Ta-urt—the goddess of pregnancy and childbirth—slashing with knives and striking a small circular drum (pl. xxv. 1, 2). In Roman times the drum becomes a shield, and he then resembles the Curetes who danced round the infant Zeus, clashing their weapons.

Figures of Bes are unmistakable; he has a small dwarfish figure with bandy legs, a wide face, snub nose, eyebrows meeting in the middle, two short horns growing on the forehead, a beard round the jaw and chin, and is dressed in a lion or leopard skin which is drawn over the head. His hideous and terrifying appearance was intended to frighten away evil spirits from the child and its mother; the knives and drum were for the same purpose.

Bes is the only god who is represented full-face in relief carvings. From the xviii-th dynasty onwards figures of Bes become increasingly common; small objects, such as eye-paint vases, were decorated with his face or figure; amulets of his figure were worn round the neck. So many amulets of Bes of the Ptolemaic period are known that it would seem that every woman or child must have worn at least one. He had become the god of the family, the chief god of the home.

In all primitive societies the mystery of birth impresses the mind, and the event is surrounded with magical ceremonies and strange beliefs. One of these beliefs was that the fate of the placenta would affect the future of the child; it had therefore to be preserved with the utmost care. In Egypt this primitive idea survived long after the country had reached a high state of civilisation, and it survived in a fashion which seems to be unknown elsewhere. The king's placenta was deified and represented as a mummy with the attributes of youth. This deity was called Khe-en-ni-sut, *Placenta of the King*, which was soon contracted to Khensu or Khonsu. In the pantheon he was equated with the moon, perhaps with the idea that the sun being the living child of the Sky-goddess, the moon was the placenta of that child. The royal placenta, wrapped in cloth, was carried on a standard before the Pharaoh on all state occasions.

PRIMITIVE GODDESSES

There are two goddesses whose worship is so universal that it is difficult to place them. The first of these is Hathor, who was one of the earliest goddesses of Egypt (figs. 9, 10 for two methods of writing her name). At the beginning she was a cow, perhaps a buffalo cow;

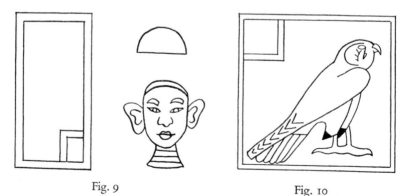

Fig. 9   Fig. 10

later she was a cow of the ordinary species. The main difficulty in the study of Hathor is that she absorbs into herself the identity of many of the other goddesses. She is the Sky-goddess, she is Sekhmet the lioness, and finally she and Isis are so intermingled that it is often impossible to distinguish one from the other. The Greeks, however, regarded these two great goddesses as entirely different; to them Isis was Demeter, and Hathor Aphrodite, but no indication is given as to why they were differentiated.

All cows were originally sacred to Hathor, and it was not until the fusion of Isis and Hathor that the former claimed them. In the temple of Deir el Bahri there was a chapel to Hathor and special reverence was paid in the temple to the sacred cows.

Hathor was also revered as the goddess who received the dead in the Other World. She is then the Lady of the Sycamore Tree, which is depicted as growing on the edge of a stream. The goddess leans out of the tree holding out food and water to the new arrival.

She is the only goddess who is represented full-face in the bas-reliefs; she is there shown as a woman with cow's ears and horns. In many temples the head of Hathor wearing the sistrum or a shrine between the horns was used as the capital of the pillars. The finest example of such capitals is in the temple dedicated to her worship at Dendera (pl. xxxix. 1).

Ta-urt is one of that group of deities worshipped in all parts of Egypt but to whom no separate temple was ever dedicated. She was the goddess of pregnancy and childbirth, and as such she was feared and revered from the queen down to the poorest village woman. She was represented as a hippopotamus standing on its hind-legs (pl. xxv. 2), possibly because the figure of the animal in that position approximates to the figure of a pregnant woman. Votive statues and statuettes of her are common, some dedicated in temples, others for private worship, or for wearing as amulets. These were in all materials, the large ones in stone or bronze, the small ones chiefly in glazed ware. The amulets might represent the whole figure or merely the head of the hippopotamus; in Amratean times these amulets were carved in semi-precious stones, but in Pharaonic times cheaper materials were used, especially for the full-length figures. In the xxvi-th dynasty (680–525 B.C.) small delicately carved figures of Ta-urt were placed on the mummy, which suggested that at that time there was a strong belief that death was but a birth into a new life.

Her name Ta-urt (Hellenised as Thoueris) means "The Great One". The bald simplicity of the name shows that her cult must have descended from an extremely primitive time, when there was but one deity, the Goddess of Birth.

The worship of Rê, the Sun-god, is usually accepted as of paramount importance because, as the god of the Pharaoh, he was more honoured outwardly than any other deity, with the exception of Isis and Osiris. In order to understand almost any aspect of the Egyptian religion the position of the king must be remembered. He was himself God; in one aspect he was Horus, in another aspect he was Osiris. He was the incarnation of every local deity, therefore every temple belonged to him, and he is shown as the equal of every deity for he was himself that deity in human form. There was only one god to whom he owed allegiance, and whom he acknowledged as his superior, and that was the Sun. Until the xviii-th dynasty it seems that no one of inferior rank dared to worship the Pharaoh's god, but a change came over Egypt during the Hyksos occupation, and the warrior-kings of the xviii-th dynasty, who shared the hardships and dangers of a campaign with their soldiers, were more human and broadminded than the aloof divine kings of an earlier age. Divine they still were, but they were human as well.

As the temples were built and endowed by the Pharaohs, it was natural that they should do all in their power to show reverence to their own god, and yet they had to ensure that the local gods were not belittled. A compromise was effected by adding the name of the Sun-god to that of the local god, and therefore in the New Kingdom Amon became Amon-Rê, Sebek the crocodile was Sebek-Rê, and so on. The goddesses retained their own individuality more stoutly, but eventually many of them were absorbed by the royal goddess, Isis. Our knowledge of temple ritual is derived almost entirely from the New Kingdom, when Sun-worship had invaded all the official ritual, changing the special rites as far as possible and bringing the worship into a more or less standard pattern.

According to one of the official legends the Sun was the offspring of Nut, the Sky-goddess, of whom he was born every morning and in whose arms he died every night. But another equally orthodox belief was that he passed over the heavens in a boat sailing on the celestial Nile; the boat was called the Boat-of-Millions-of-Years; in the morning it was the Manzet-boat (i.e. boat of the Dawn), in the evening it was the Mesektet-boat (Evening boat) (pl. xxvi. 1, 2, 3). The journey across the sky during the day was always uneventful, but the journey through the regions of night was full of danger, partly from the darkness and partly from the terrible serpent, Apophis, that lay in wait to destroy the god. The Egyptian idea that the sun was the source of heat but not of light is well exemplified in the account of the sun's journey through the regions of thick darkness. Akhenaten or his advisers were the first who seem to have understood that the sun is also the source of light as well as heat.

Sun-worship was introduced in or about the iii-rd dynasty, and was fully established by the v-th dynasty, when the sons of the High-priestess of Rê became the Pharaohs. The legend states that they were also the sons of the god himself, but there is a strong hint that the High-priest of Rê was the actual father. It was, however, in this dynasty that the Pharaohs took as one of their five titles the words "Son of Rê", which always precedes the personal name of the king, and declares his physical relationship to the Sun.

The principal seat of the cult of the Sun was at Yun, the Heliopolis of the Greeks. The sacred object in the temple which represented the deity was the *Benben*, a pyramidal stone; this, when set on a high stone shaft, became the obelisk. The earliest sun-temple belongs to the v-th dynasty and was built in connection with the royal pyramids at Abusir. In it the chief object of worship was an obelisk with the *Benben* or pyramidion on the summit. The early obelisks were short, set upon a high rectangular base, and in the pyramidion a disc was fixed in a slot; the disc was probably of gilded metal, so set as to reflect the rays of the sun. To the worshippers it would seem that the god was actually in the stone and shining from the disc.

It is strange that the few legends which have survived of this great god of the Pharaohs are all slightly derogatory. In one he is out-witted by Isis, who takes from him all his power; in another he is so old and foolish that he is laughed at by all mankind; in a third, even his curse is made of no effect by the wisdom and cunning of Thoth. In legends of the Late period he is in the background as a sort of last resource if things go wrong with other gods. As a general rule he is rather the otiose high god than an active ruler of the world; and at best he was a Protector of gods rather than a Protector of men.

RITUAL

The daily ritual in a temple varied little from one temple to another, except in the few details which differentiated the lives of gods or goddesses. It was practically the same as that of their fellow-deity, the Pharaoh. The god was roused in the morning by the singing of a hymn of praise; then followed his morning toilet, the perfuming with incense or other scents, the decking with robes and crowns; after which came the first meal of the day, in other words the morning-ing sacrifice. That finished, the god was brought out with chants and hymns into the main part of the temple to transact business by receiving petitions, giving judgment in difficult cases, receiving and acknowledging offerings; in the afternoon he retired to his private apartments, where he either rested or was entertained with music and dancing girls; in the evening he appeared again and had his evening meal (the evening sacrifice), then retired for the night, the robes and crown were removed, incense was burnt before him, the evening hymn was sung, the shrine doors were shut upon him, and he was left to pass the night in peace.

On certain special festivals the god was carried out in procession. On these occasions it was not unusual to carry the image of the god to some place where there was a dispute over land which the deity had been asked to settle. The god could thus have the opportunity of viewing the disputed property and would be enabled to give a more reasoned decision.

One method was that as the shrine was being borne along on the shoulders of the priests, the question was propounded to the god, who at once made the shrine so heavy that the priests could no longer carry it but had to set it down.* This was regarded as giving the god's assent to a simple question such as "Does this land belong to so-and-so?" It was a method much favoured by Christian saints and martyrs in the East, who at their funerals made their corpses too heavy to be borne farther when arriving at the place where they wished to be buried. When the oracle of a god was given in his temple, the case was explained in the presence of the image; then two pieces of papyrus were set before him; on one was written, "So-and-so is guilty", on the other "So-and-so is not guilty". The god is said to have picked up the appropriate piece.

Every temple had its own seasonal festivals, of which the ritual was basically the same, varying only in details according to the sex and character of the deity. The main events were the Appearing of the deity and the sacrifices which accompanied the celebration of the event. A little song commemorates a festival at Thebes: "How glad is the temple of Amon at the New Year at the slaying of the sacrifices, when Amon receives its good things; its oxen are slaughtered by hundreds, its wild game of the mountains by thousands, even for Amon as his due offerings at the festival of the seasons." New Year's Day was kept at Siut "when the temple gave gifts to its lord", but there was also at Siut a peculiar ceremony of kindling fire in the temple when the god went out in procession. Bast had a procession in a barge.

Royal festivals were as numerous and as important as the festivals

* For an example of this form of oracle, see Legrain, *Bulletin de l'Institut francais d'Archéologie Orientale*, 1927.

in the temples. The anniversary of the Appearing (*i.e.* the Coronation) must have had great significance, for the gods promise Pharaoh myriads of Appearings. The Circuit of the Wall was a Memphite rite which took place only in the first year of a reign. But the festival most often mentioned in connection with the Pharaoh was the Tail-festival (*Sed-heb*) (pl. lxx. 2). Though a great deal has been written about this festival no explanation has been given of its meaning or of its strange name. The essential parts of the ceremony were the figure of Osiris enthroned, a royal lady often called the king's daughter, and the four personal standards of the Pharaoh. It has been suggested that it is a marriage festival, which would account for the presence of the lady and for the irregularity of its celebration, but the peculiar name of the festival can only be explained on the supposition that it refers to the giving of the bull's tail to the king as part of his royal and divine insignia.

BURIAL CUSTOMS

Egyptian burial customs have always roused so much attention that there is a very large literature on the subject. But it should always be remembered that the elaborate mummification, the decorated coffins, the painted and sculptured tomb-chapels, belong to the wealthy classes; the poor, if buried at all, were buried in the sand with a few pots of food and drink beside them. It is, however, not certain that the poor were always buried. It is very probable that the peasants were not supposed to have a future life, and their bodies would be cast out either on the desert or into the river. It was not for nothing that the scavenger creatures who live on carrion—the vulture, the crocodile, and the jackal—were all deified.

The elaborate funeral ceremonies and the rich endowments of chapels and priests belonged originally to the Pharaoh alone. It was only when the religion began to be democratised that the great nobles copied the royal funerals and burial customs; after a time, less exalted persons buried their dead with the modifications due to their lesser means; until finally every person who could afford a tomb was identified with Osiris and was buried with all the rites of Osiris that the family could afford.

Mummification was introduced into Egypt in the iii-rd dynasty, the same period that saw the introduction of sun-worship, of the use of stone for large buildings, of the making of pyramids for kings and mastabas for great nobles. Whether all these new ideas were connected is as yet uncertain, and it is also unknown where they came from. There is no gradual development, they arrive complete. But after their first introduction burial customs underwent changes, and it cannot be too strongly emphasised that "changes begin always in the royal tombs and work downwards".*

The methods and details of mummification have been described so many times that a very much abridged account of them will suffice here. The early mummies† had the internal organs (but not the brain) removed, and the cavity filled with spices and resins. The body was then wrapped in fine linen, sometimes with a gilded plaster mask set over the face,‡ and placed in a box-like wooden coffin. After many ceremonies the coffin was deposited in the burial vault, which was hewn in the hard marl underlying the sand of the desert. If a stone sarcophagus was used, it was placed in the burial chamber before the coffin was brought down. The internal organs were embalmed separately and were wrapped in linen and placed either in a box of four compartments or in four jars (now known as Canopic jars). The jars were often enclosed in a box, but whether the viscera were enclosed in a box or in jars they were always set beside the coffin in the burial chamber.

In the Middle Kingdom the method of embalming for persons not of high rank was not so elaborate. The internal organs and the brain were removed, and they, together with the body, were often preserved with quicklime or by soaking in salt.§ The more expensive method of embalming with scented gums, spices, and resins was still used, but was for more exalted personages. The body was laid on the left side, and was enclosed in a coffin carved in human form; this was again enclosed in a box-like wooden coffin, painted inside and out, with prayers and spells and with representations of the personal property of the deceased. In many of the tombs there were wooden models of servants engaged in their different avocations. Though these are roughly made and painted, they have a spirit and vivacity which redeems them from dullness (pls. viii; xiv; xv). In this period there are found statuettes of the deceased represented in mummy form; these are the decadent survival of the fine *ka*-statues of the dead which are such an outstanding feature of the tombs of the Old Kingdom.

The New Kingdom (1738–1102 B.C.) produced a great advance in

* Firth and Gunn, *Teti Pyramid Cemeteries*, i. 43.

† The earliest known mummy is of the iii-rd dynasty. It was found by Petrie at Meydum and was in the museum of the Royal College of Surgeons until destroyed in the bombing of London.

‡ Firth and Gunn, *Teti Pyramid Cemeteries*, i. 22. No mummies of the Kings of the Old Kingdom have been found; but from the fact that lesser people had gilded masks laid on their mummies, it is evident that gold masks, like that of Tut-ankh-Amon, were already in use.

§ Murray, *Tomb of Two Brothers*.

the methods of mummification, and there was a change in the burial customs. "The burials of the New Empire are quite distinct from those of the Middle Kingdom. The Hyksos period had interrupted the even development of Egyptian funerary customs and the objects placed with the dead are for the most part different in form, style, and material from those used in the Middle Kingdom."* Two very important changes are found, one in the Canopic jars, the other in the mummiform statuettes of the dead. In the Old Kingdom the Canopic jars had plain lids; in the Middle Kingdom they had human heads, presumably portraits of the dead; in the New Kingdom the heads represented the four Children of Horus (the four gods of the cardinal points of the compass), and the heads are human, ape, jackal, and falcon.† These are set under the care of the four goddesses who protect the dead, Isis, Nephthys, Neith, and Selket. The statuettes, originally representing the deceased person himself, had now been fused with the servant-figures, and had become the Ushabtis (or Shawabtis).‡ These were always inscribed with the owner's name, and in later times with the sixth chapter of the Book of the Dead, which states that when the deceased is called upon by Osiris to till the fields, to fill the runnels with water, and to carry sand from east to west in the Other World, the figure shall answer in his stead.

In the xxi-st dynasty a new method of treating the mummy came into vogue for persons of high rank; this was an attempt to make the mummy look like a living person by padding the cheeks and other parts of the face and body with clay pushed into place through incisions made in the skin; after which the face of the dead was painted. Amulets on the mummy became common at this time, and the number of ushabtis was greatly increased. At this period the ushabtis are short and stumpy; they are often covered with a beautiful and brilliant blue glaze, and have an inscription in black vertically down the front (pl. lxxxviii. 1).

In Ptolemaic and Roman times mummification was carried out with bitumen, which makes the bodies brittle and black. It was the bitumen from these mummies which was the basis of the pigment called "mummy", used by early European artists for their pictures. It was the same material which medieval physicians used in the unpleasant decoctions which they gave to their patients.

* Firth and Gunn, *Teti Pyramid Cemeteries*, i. 66.
† Of the four "living creatures" of the Book of Revelation, one has the face of a man, and one has the face of a flying eagle.
‡ Ushabti is from *usheb*, "to answer"; shawabti from *shawabt*, "acacia", as many of the early New Kingdom figures were made of acacia-wood. The first gives better sense, the latter is the term favoured at the present day.

Herodotus gives seventy days as the time taken for embalming when he visited Egypt, which was during the Persian regime. This accords with the Biblical account of the embalming of Jacob,* which took forty days† for the actual embalming, but the mourning lasted seventy. The extra thirty days‡ would be required for the bandaging and wrapping of the mummy, as each bandage was put on with appropriate prayers and ceremonies. The two accounts are confirmed by the record of Rameses IV, who was enthroned on the seventy-second day after the death of his father, Rameses III; this gives the regulation seventy days for the embalming and bandaging, one day for the actual funeral, and then came the ceremonies of the accession.

The date of a burial can be judged not only by the type of embalming but by the method of bandaging, by the style and decoration of the coffin, and by the form of the Canopic jars. Royal burials always have fine linen, which was often woven specially for the purpose; lesser people often had old and worn material torn into strips of convenient widths. These are often more instructive for the archæologist than the specially made funerary linen, as they show the materials in common use, the type of yarn, the methods of spinning and weaving, and the dyes. The most beautiful bandaging is found in Roman times, when the relatives kept the mummies in the house.

Coffins were of wood; plain and simple in early periods, but becoming increasingly elaborate later. In the xi-th dynasty the Pharaohs introduced the fashion of portrait coffins; these were coffins shaped like a mummy with the face carved in the likeness of the dead as he was in life (pls. xxvii; xxviii). The fashion soon became general, and was the usual form in all succeeding dynasties till the xxvi-th. Then because wood was scarce, cartonnage came into use. This was a coarse canvas stiffened with stucco, which could be as easily painted as the wooden coffins. The canvas was moulded into the portrait of the deceased, while the stucco was still wet. Under the Ptolemies a still further development was made, and faces were moulded in plaster on the canvas and then coloured. Glass or stone eyes were fixed in the

---

* If this account is true and not part of a folk-tale, there must be, in the Cave of Machpelah at Hebron, an indubitable Egyptian mummy. It would be very interesting if it could be found, as the style of embalming and decoration would give the exact date of a much disputed event.

† The exact number of days for the embalming is given in the stela of the priest Psemtek of the xxvi-th dynasty: "His good life was 65 years, 10 months and 2 days. He was introduced to the Good House and he spent 42 days under the hand of Anubis. He was conducted in peace to the beautiful West in the first month of Shemu, and his life in the necropolis is for ever and ever."

‡ The Israelitish mourning for the dead was thirty days when they first came out of Egypt, for so they mourned for Aaron and Moses.

plaster; and in the case of women, their jewellery was imitated with pieces of glass and gilded plaster. Some of these Ptolemaic heads show a considerable amount of artistic feeling and skill (pl. lxv. 2). The final development of the portrait coffin was under the Romans about the second century A.D. Instead of a modelled face and head, the face was painted on a wooden panel which was held in place by the bandaging (pl. lxvi).

All religions have attempted to specify what part of the human being survives death, and beliefs concerning this spiritual entity are many and various. In Egypt beliefs concerning it and the place to which it would go after death were numerous, having been introduced by the different races who had entered and dwelt in the Nile Valley. In the New Kingdom the theologians tried to bring order into this mass of chaos; they appear to have incorporated at least six ideas into the official religion, for at this period there were six spiritual or imponderable parts of Man to be accounted for:

(1) The Ba (usually translated *Soul*).
(2) The Yakhu (translated *Shining One*, literally, *He of the Horizon*).
(3) The Name.
(4) The Shadow.
(5) The Heart (as the seat of the intellect and emotions).
(6) The Ka.

Each of these was originally a separate entity, and the tribe to which it belonged believed in it as the one essential part of a man which was eternal. The theologians of the New Kingdom combined them together, and taught that each had to be preserved if the man were to live after death. As the beliefs grew more complicated the burial customs became also more complicated, but it is possible to differentiate between some of the beliefs and assign the right future to its appropriate spiritual part. The final official belief appears to have been that when all the parts which had been disintegrated at death were reunited, the dead man became fused with Osiris and was called Osiris. But only the name Osiris was given to him, not the attributes, for he was never regarded as the god.

The earliest and perhaps the most important of the ideas of the Hereafter was the belief in the "ka". No satisfactory explanation of the ka has ever been given, but it was clearly an integral part of gods and human beings. The fundamental meaning of the word is "energy", but it can also mean "food", and with the feminine ending (ka-t) it means "work", usually manual work. When a royal ka is represented pictorially it takes the form of a man rather smaller than the person to whom it belongs; it wears on its head the upraised arms which is the hieroglyphic sign for the syllable ka; the arms hold the rectangle surmounted by a falcon which contains the falcon-name of the king. The connection of the ka with the falcon-totem of the king points to a belief that it was the totem in human form. But whether it belonged to a royal person or to someone of lesser rank, it was certainly the part which was believed to survive death. It could not, however, survive unless it was nourished with material food, hence the offerings to the dead; nor unless it had a habitation, hence the necessity for a tomb. These two necessities, the food offerings and the tomb, are the subjects of the prayers for the dead from the iii-rd dynasty onwards. According to this belief the ka must have remained on earth in or near the tomb, and have consumed the food offerings. In course of time it must have become very clear to the living that the dead are quickly forgotten, and that it was impossible to keep up an adequate supply of food for a long line of ancestors; the custom had then to be modified, and it was dis-covered that it was only necessary to recite the appropriate prayers and the ka would be fed. This is implied in the tomb of Pet-Osiris of the Persian period: "Read the inscriptions, celebrate the rites in my name, pronounce my name in pouring abundant libations, give me food for my mouth, provisions for my lips. This will not tire your mouth to repeat, these are not riches which fall from your hands. As one shall do, so shall one be done by; it is a monument that is left behind to say a good word. God Himself shall requite one according to the way he behaves to my request. Whoever does well by me, so shall it be done to him; he who praises my ka shall have his ka praised; he who does evil to me, so shall it be done to him. Because I am a devotee of God, who will grant that you shall be treated in the same way by those who shall come after you in all time to come."

When the Osiris religion became firmly established, it brought in a new train of ideas. Osiris was the Giver of fertility in the next world as well as in this, and his kingdom in the other world was a glorious place in which hunger was unknown, for the harvests never failed and were a hundredfold more plentiful than in Egypt, where there was always danger of famine, or at least scarcity, if the Nile should be deficient. As it was obvious that it was not possible for everyone to obtain an entrance into that happy kingdom, some sort of test had to be applied to the candidates for admission. How early the idea of the Balance was introduced is uncertain; it is found fully developed in the xviii-th dynasty, when the scene of the weighing is one of the favourite pictures in the religious papyri of that period and later (pl. xxii). In these pictures the confusion of ideas is very marked, for the dead man in person stands beside the balance to watch the weighing. This is possibly the ka of the man and not the corporeal human being. But another confusion occurs when the dead man is called Osiris, for this title originally belonged to the king alone, whether living or dead. The weighing is done by Anubis, the god of death, and Thoth stands beside the balance to record the weights. Somewhere in the scene, usually behind Thoth, is the monster Amemt, ready to devour the heart of the dead man should it be found wanting on the scales. When the weighing is completed, "Thoth says to the Divine Ennead who are in the presence of Osiris: 'Ye hear this sentence. Truly has the heart of Osiris been weighed; his soul stood by as witness against him. His weight is correct upon the Balance. No evil has been found in him; he has not destroyed food-offerings in the temples; he has not done harm; he has not advanced by words any evil thing since he has been on earth!' The Ennead of the Gods say to Thoth, 'That which comes forth from thy mouth is decreed. True and accurate is the scribe Ani. He has not sinned, he has not done evil towards us. Let not Amemt have power over him. Grant that there be given to him the bread which is presented [literally, comes forth] in the presence of Osiris, and a field in the Field of Peace like the Followers of Horus.' " Horus then takes the dead man by the hand and leads him into the presence of Osiris, who is represented seated on a throne set upon water, from which springs a lotus. "Says Horus, the son of Isis: 'I have come to thee. O Unnefer, I bring to thee the Osiris Ani. His heart was true at the coming forth from the Balance. He has not sinned against any god or any goddess. Thoth has weighed it according to the decree recited by the Ennead of the Gods; he is true and righteous. Grant that there may be given to him the bread and beer which are presented in the presence of Osiris. May he be like the Followers of Horus.' " The dead man then makes a speech on his own behalf: "Behold me in thy presence, O Lord of the West! There is no evil in my body; I have not told lies knowingly, nor has there been any duplicity. Grant that I may be like the favoured ones who are in thy train, O Osiris! being greatly favoured by the good God, and beloved of the Lord of the the Two Lands." The speech of welcome from Osiris is never given, but the scenes of the Kingdom of Osiris show the dead man engaged in all the avocations in which he delighted while on earth, besides inspecting the rich harvests and great stores of food which indicated that this was indeed the land of plenty.

The ka figures in another early belief. When the dead man had drawn his last breath, his ka made its way to the borders of the Other World, where a great sycamore tree spread its branches. Half-hidden in the foliage was the great goddess, the Mother of all, waiting to receive and welcome the ka, to whom she gives food and water. In these scenes the ka is represented as a living man, wearing the clothes he wore in life. Consuming the divine food and drink appears to have been the passport into the Realms of Bliss, and this is probably the simplest, as it was the earliest, of all the theories of the Hereafter. It was this view of the ka as the immortal part of Man that inspired many of the chapters of the Book of the Dead, and it is surely this ethereal part which is alluded to in the prayer that for all eternity he may return to earth and "breathe the sweet breezes of the North Wind, and drink water upon the swirl of the New Water".*

The idea of the Journey of the Sun through the Outer World belonged originally to that group of beliefs which clustered round the Sun-god, and was therefore the prerogative of the king only.

The religious beliefs had to be arranged so as to fit the facts of Nature, and as the Sun is always in motion some means had to be contrived to account for the movement. To the Egyptian the highway on earth was a river, and travelling meant a journey in a boat. The Sun was made to conform to these ideas, he crossed the heavens in a boat on a real, though invisible, river, and when he set he passed through the Realm of Night still in a boat and still on a river (pl. xxvi. 1, 2). To accompany the Sun on his night journey was the future that originally the Pharaoh, and later some of his sun-worshipping subjects, hoped for. There are two versions of the Journey; the first, which is painted and inscribed on the walls of royal tombs, was called by the Egyptians "The Book of Him who is in the Other World". The second version, which was inscribed on royal sarcophagi, had no Egyptian name, but is called by modern Egyptologists "The Book of Gates". The versions differ considerably in detail, though the main story is the same. The Other World, known as the Duat, is divided into twelve sections or countries, each section having its own name and being divided from the next by a gate which is guarded by a warden. The sections correspond with the twelve hours of the night. The Boat of the sun is filled with deities who are there to protect the god from all the dangers of the Night, and is piloted through each section by the goddess of that hour, who alone knows the password for the gate at the far end of her domain; without that password even Rê would not be allowed to go through. The Sun dies at sunset, and it is only his corpse that passes into the Realm of Night. Two great events occur during the Journey. The first is the ever–recurring attempt of the terrible and awe-inspiring serpent, Apophis (Aa-pep), to destroy the Sun, an attempt which is always frustrated by the guardian deities; the other is that Khepri, in the form of a scarab,† awaits the coming of the dead Sun,

* See Appendix 4.
† See Appendix 3, p. 230, for scarabs.

"then the soul of Khepri and the soul of Rê are united". *Khepri* means "existence", hence Life. The soul of Rê is thus revivified, and he passes on alive to the sunrise, his dead body being cast out of the Boat before he rises on the land of Egypt. There are, of course, many discrepancies in this journey. Apophis is one of the difficulties; he cannot be destroyed, but awaits Rê in the same place every night, and every night the deities who accompany the dead Sun leap out of the Boat, bind the great Serpent with chains and pierce him with knives. But every night he is loose, strong and well, and ready for the fray in which he always gets the worst of it. In the Book of Gates there is an interesting variant in this scene; the deities are evidently not strong enough to deal with the giant snake, and an enormous hand rises out of the ground and holds the chain firmly. The scenes in the Other World are often inexplicable in our present state of knowledge of Egyptian beliefs, but the punishments of the wicked, "the foes of Rê", are very clearly expressed. The Boiling Lake and the Lake of Fire are plainly depicted. The serpents of the Other World have a peculiar position, being sometimes protective, sometimes hostile. The serpent Mehen throws its coils over the cabin in which the corpse of Rê stands, in order to protect it from the attack of Apophis; another snake, unnamed, spits poison in the faces of an unhappy row of bound captives; and Apophis himself is the most dangerous of all the serpents.

The theologians were hard put to it to reconcile this theory of life after death with other theories. They introduce the Kingdom of Osiris as one of the countries of the Duat; the Kingdom of Sokar, the Memphite god of the dead, was always supposed to be a sandy desert; so when it was included in the night journey of Rê, the Boat had to be turned into a serpent in order to pass over the sand. But the most difficult theories to reconcile with each other were the theory of the Sun arriving in his Boat at the sunrise and the theory of the daily birth of the Sun from the Sky-goddess Nut. The final compromise was a clumsy contrivance; the last hour or country of the Duat was turned into a serpent, through whose body the Sun-boat passed, coming out at its mouth. This symbolised the passage of the infant Sun through the body of his mother and his final birth. Another clumsy contrivance was the appearing of the morning star three times during the night journey.

At first it was the privilege of the Pharaoh alone to accompany the Sun through the Duat and to take part in the nightly defeat of the terrible Apophis, but as the religion became democratised this privilege was extended to great nobles and priests. Their souls went with the Sun from sunset till sunrise, and at sunrise they were at liberty to return to their old homes, where they could sit in the shade of their gardens and enjoy the "sweet breezes of the North Wind". At sunset they gathered together at Abydos, and entered the Sun-boat as it passed through the Gap of Abydos into the Regions of Night and thick Darkness. Whether this monotonous sequence of events was supposed to be repeated throughout all eternity is never mentioned, but it is possible that sufficient variety would be obtained by the daily visits to the earth and its inhabitants.

Another entity that survived death was the *ba*, usually called the Soul by modern Egyptologists. This was represented as a human-headed bird (pl. lxxxviii. 2); the creature being represented as about the size of an ordinary barndoor cock. The belief in it seems to be fairly late, as it is not found before the xviii-th dynasty, but the fact that there is no development of the idea shows either that it was accepted as soon as introduced or that it was an ancient idea of the illiterate people which came into prominence in the nationalistic revival after the expulsion of the Hyksos. The ba was an external entity; it remained near the body of the dead, but no offerings were made to it. It is sometimes shown in the arms of its living owner, it sometimes clings to the breast of the mummy, or is seen winging its way down the tomb-shaft to the burial chamber where it hovers above the dead. Its exact function has never been properly explained, but it is probably some form of the External Soul, which is a common belief of many primitive peoples. It may, however, be merely a modification of the falcon totem of the Pharaoh, altered to suit the more democratic religion of the later dynasties.

Another theory of the Hereafter, one which has received little attention from Egyptologists, is the theory of reincarnation. Herodotus is very definite on this subject: "The Egyptians were the first who asserted that the soul of man is immortal, and that when the body perishes it enters into some other animal, constantly springing into existence; and when it has passed through the different kinds of terrestrial, marine, and aerial beings, it again enters into the body of a man that is born; and that this revolution is made in three thousand years. Some of the Greeks have adopted this opinion, some earlier, others later, as if it were their own; but although I knew their names I do not mention them."★ This statement of Herodotus is fully borne out by the Egyptian evidence. As is usual in all aspects of the religion of Egypt, the faculty of reincarnation was originally inherent in the Pharaoh alone. The ka-names of the first two kings of the xii-th dynasty show this belief clearly; Amonemhat I's name was "He who

★ Herodotus, ii. 123. See footnote to p. 131.

repeats births", and Senusert I's name was "He whose births live". In the xixth dynasty the ka-name of Setekhy I was "Repeater of births", and it was by this epithet that he was addressed by the god Amon at Karnak. Already, however, in the xviii-th dynasty the theory of reincarnation had been so far developed as to include lesser folk, and in that great storehouse of the later religion, the Book of the Dead, there are about a dozen chapters giving the proper spells to be recited in order to incarnate in various forms. The eightieth chapter begins, "The beginning* of the chapters of making existences". Then it goes on to give the spell for "making existence" as a pigeon, and adds in an appendix that if anyone knows this book, "he shall go forth by day from the Other World, and he shall enter after he has come out", and also threatens the careless or ignorant man, "he who does not know this book, he shall not come out from the Other World by day, nor shall he enter after he has come out". The incarnations are very various. Besides the pigeon the dead man can exist as a snake, the god Ptah, the ram of the god Atum, a bennu-bird, a crested heron, a lotus, the god who causes light and darkness, a hawk of gold, a divine hawk, and the crocodile-god Sebek. The spell for this last "existence" is as follows: "I am the crocodile in the midst of terrors! I am the crocodile god! I carry away by force. I am the great Fish in Kenui! I am the Lord of homage [literally bowings] in Sekhem and [the speaker of the spell] is the Lord of homage in Sekhem." There is also one whole chapter devoted to "being in the Ennead of the Gods and existing as a Great One of the Council". How long each incarnation lasted and whether there was a regular cycle through which the soul had to pass, as Herodotus suggests, does not appear, but there is one chapter which, if known, would enable a man to "make existence" in any forms which he desired. Pythagoras is usually credited with having invented the theory of reincarnation, but it was already hoary with age before the Greeks had emerged from barbarism. And as Pythagoras is known to have spent some years in Egypt for the sake of studying under Egyptian philosophers, it is evident that the theory which bears his name was not his originally, but that he, as Herodotus puts it, "adopted this opinion as if it were his own".†

The horror and terror of death is very marked in the religious texts

* The difficulties of translation are very marked. The word translated "beginning" also means "principal" or "chief". In the same way the word translated "chapter" means a fraction, but it can also mean "language"; perhaps "spell" would give a better meaning here.

† As Herodotus lived some centuries before Pythagoras he cannot be referring to that philosopher. The credit of being the first to expound the theory of Metempsychosis to the Greeks and therefore to the world at large may well have been given to Pythagoras by his disciples.

of the Egyptians. In the Pyramid Texts it is the Pharaoh who is encouraged to look beyond into the Other World where he will be the great and supreme God, to whom heaven and earth will be subject. In the Book of the Dead, the spells are for everyone who can learn them by heart and so be able to escape from the darkness of the tomb and "come forth by day". Chapter after chapter gives the means of such an escape. "Death is my abomination," says the man, and he learns with avidity the spells which "cause a man to return to his home on earth". Then there is the "chapter of breathing air and controlling water in the Other World. O Sycamore of the goddess Nut, give to me the water and air which is in thee. I have encircled the throne in Hermopolis, and I guard the egg of the Great Cackler; it grows and I grow; it lives and I live; it breathes the air and I breathe the air." It is the Breath of Life which the Egyptian always craved, for he knew that without breath there is no life; but knowing that death is inevitable he tried to prepare for it by a knowledge of the magic which would enable him to come back to the land and home he loved so well.

RELIGIOUS ENDOWMENTS

The mass of wealth that was spent on the furnishing of the temples was almost fabulous; this was particularly the case in the xviii-th dynasty when riches flowed into Egypt from all parts of the world. Amon and Osiris were the two gods most favoured by the Pharaohs at this period, and their temples must have presented a magnificent spectacle, but the other deities also benefited in large measure.

The Boat of Amon for the festival of the Beginning of the River was an object on which great sums were lavished (pl. xxx. 1). Aahmes I says that he made "a barge for the Beginning of the River called *Mighty is the Prow of Amon*; it was of new cedar of the best of the Terraces, in order that he may make his voyage therein".* Aahmes' grandson, Thothmes I, gave orders to his chief treasurer to make for Osiris a portable shrine (literally, a Bearer of Beauties) "of silver, gold, lapis lazuli, black copper, and every costly stone". The king also announced what he had already done: "I made for him the august barge of new cedar of the best of the Terraces; its bow and stern are of fine gold, in order to make festive the lake that he may make his voyage therein on his feast of the District-of-Peker."† Hatshepsut followed the example of her father: "I led the craftsmen to work on the great barge, *Mighty is the Prow of Amon*, for the Beginning of the River. It was wrought with fine gold of the best of the High-Land; its shrine was of fine gold of the best of the High-Land; it illuminated

* Breasted, *Ancient Records of Egypt*, ii. 24.   † Ibid., ii. 38, 39.

the Two Lands with its rays; its shrine—the horizon of the god and his great seat—was of electrum, a work established for all eternity; and an 'Offering Lifter', whose splendid façade was of electrum."*
But even this description pales before the record of Amonhotep III who was as magnificent in this work as in all that he did: "I made a monument for him who begat me, Amon-Rê, Lord of Thebes, making for him the great barge, *Amon-Rê in the Sacred Barge*, for the Beginning of the River, of new cedar which his Majesty cut in the countries of God's Land; it was dragged over the mountains of Retennu by the princes of all countries. It was made very wide and large, and was adorned with silver and wrought with gold throughout. The great shrine of electrum fills the land with its brightness; its bows repeat the brightness; they bear great crowns, of which the serpents twine along the sides. Flagstaves are set up before it, wrought with electrum; two great obelisks are between them. It is beautiful everywhere."†

The doors of the temples also offered opportunity for a lavish display of wealth. Hatshepsut says of her temple at Deir el Bahri: "Its great doors were fashioned of black bronze, the inlaid figures were of electrum."‡ Thothmes III built "a divine Abode, a monument of fine white sandstone", at Karnak. "I erected the first gate [called] *Men-kheper-Rê is splendid in the Opulence of Amon*; the second [called] *Men-kheper-Rê abides in the Favour of Amon*; the third [called] *Men-kheper-Rê is the greatest of the Souls of Amon*, is wrought with real electrum, through which all offerings are brought for him. My Majesty erected an august pylon of the interior in front of the Holy of Holies. I erected for him a great door fashioned of new cedar, wrought with gold and mounted with real black copper. The great name upon it was of electrum, doubly refined gold and black bronze. It was more beautiful than anything that has ever been."§

Amonhotep III made splendid doors in his temples. At Karnak he erected "a very great portal wrought with gold throughout. The Divine Shadow as a ram is inlaid with real lapis lazuli wrought with gold and many costly stones; there is no other instance of doing the like. Its floor is adorned with silver. Towers are over against it. Stelæ of lapis lazuli are set up, one on each side. Its towers reach the sky like the four pillars of the heavens; its flagstaves shine more than the sky, being wrought with electrum."||

At Soleb he built another temple, which "is finished with fine white sandstone, it is wrought with gold throughout; its floor is adorned with silver, its portals are of gold".¶

* Breasted, *A.R.*, ii. 155. † Ibid., ii. 359. ‡ Ibid., ii. 156.
§ Ibid., ii. 64. || Ibid., ii. 360. ¶ Ibid., ii. 360.

The silver pavement, on which the figure of the deity was set when it was brought out of its shrine, was one of the chief features in all descriptions of the temples in and after the xviii-th dynasty. When Amon was called upon to adjudicate on a matter concerning a certain priest, "the great god appeared upon the pavement of silver in the House of Amon in the morning hour".* The figure of the god was in many cases made of gold, and the shrine was of gold set with "costly stones". This would flash in the sunlight and "illumine the whole land". The ornamentation of the doors with gold is mentioned in the trial of a priest in the xxi-st dynasty, who was enjoined to tell "of all the gold which you stripped, which belonged to the House of Gold of King User-Maot-Rê, and of every man who was with you and who went with you to strip off the gold of the door-jambs".†

Besides the actual building and decoration of the Houses of God, the Pharaohs were equally lavish in the endowments of the priesthoods. Endowments of land and food given to the temples are common from the time of the Old Kingdom. As wealth increased the offerings increased in proportion till in the New Kingdom the priests were the richest class in the land. The list of gifts to the various temples which are recorded by Rameses III shows the wealth that was showered upon them. Land, slaves, animals of all kinds, grain of all kinds, vegetables and fruit, ships and boats, linen in the piece or made up into garments, gold and silver by weight or wrought into vessels, all show that the temples were receiving at least half the income of the kingdom. Even as late as Osorkon I of the xxii-nd dynasty (924–895 B.C.) the temples received from the Pharaoh in silver and gold 2,300,000 *deben* (about 560,297 lb. troy), in silver alone two million *deben* (about 487,180 lb. troy), besides black bronze, lapis lazuli, and wine of the Oases; these last were almost as costly as the precious metals.‡

Even as late as Nectanebo II, the last native Pharaoh of Egypt, the same generosity towards the temples is found. On the day of his coronation,

"His Majesty said: let there be given
The tithe of the gold and silver, of the timber and the worked wood, and of everything which comes from the Greek Sea, and of all the goods which are reckoned to the King's Domain in the city called Henwe.
The tithe of the gold and the silver, and of all things which are produced in Pi-em-roye, called Naukratis, on the bank of the Anu, and which are reckoned to the King's Domain, to be a temple-endowment of my mother Neith for all time, in excess of what existed formerly. And let them be

* *Zeitschrift für Aegyptische Sprache* (1871), p. 85.
† *J.E.A.*, xi (1925), p. 52.
‡ Naville, *Bubastis*, pp. 51, 52.

Cairo Museum

Cairo Museum

1. Ka-aper (Sheikh el Beled). Wood.
Dynasty iv

2. Men-kau-Rê and goddesses. Slate.
Dynasty iv

Photograph by Captain M. M. Barker

3. Statues in a tomb, dynasty iii

4. Amonhotep II,
dynasty xviii

Plate XLIX

Cairo Museum

1. Rahotep and Nefert

British Museum

2. Queen Teta-shery

Cairo Museum

3. Thothmes IV and his mother

Cairo Museum

4. Statuette of a lady, dynasty xix

PLATE L

Head of Nefert.   Painted limestone.   Dynasty iv

PLATE LI

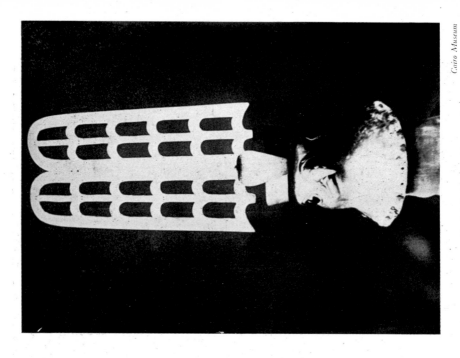

2. Gold falcon, dynasty vi

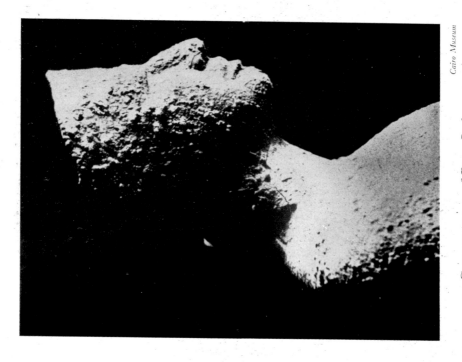

1. Copper statue of Pepy I, dynasty vi

PLATE LII

Cairo Museum

Unfinished statue of Senusert I, dynasty xii

PLATE LIII

Petrie Cell.

1. Head of Khafra.
Limestone. Dynasty iv

Cairo Museum

2. Amonemhat III,
dynasty xii

Cairo Museum

3. King Hor. Wood.
Dynasty xiii

Florence Museum

4. Statue of a lady,
dynasty xix

5. Death-mask of King
Tety, dynasty vi

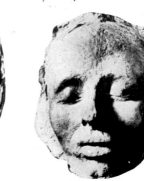

PLATE LIV

Cairo Museum

Obsidian head of unknown king, dynasty xii

PLATE LV

The Great Sphinx

PLATE LVI

Portrait Sphinx.   Dynasty xii, but usurped by later kings

PLATE LVII

Detail of Portrait Sphinx showing cartouche of a king of the xxi-st dynasty

Plate LVIII

1. Statue of Thothmes III

Cairo Museum

2. Statue of Mer-en-Ptah

Cairo Museum

PLATE LIX

Husband and wife, dynasty xviii

PLATE LX

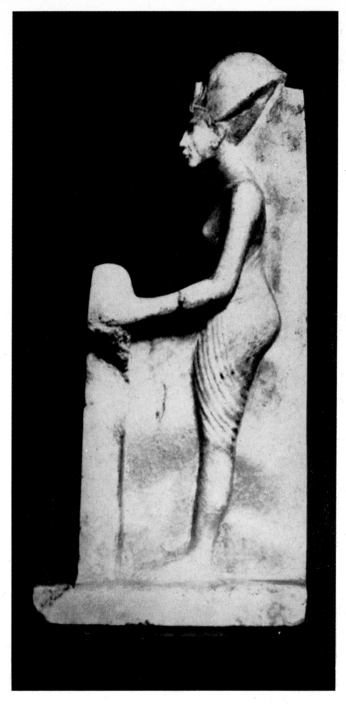

Akhenaten, dynasty xviii

PLATE LXI

Turin Museum

Rameses II

PLATE LXII

Colossal head of Rameses II, dynasty xix

PLATE LXIII

1. Façades of temples of Rameses II and his queen.   Abu Simbel

2. Colossal statues of Rameses II.   Temple of Abu Simbel

PLATE LXIV

converted into one portion of an ox, one fat *ro*-goose, and five measures of wine, as a continual daily offering; the delivery of them to be at the treasury of my mother Neith; for she is the Mistress of the ocean, and it is she who bestows its bounty."*

ETHICS

A great deal has been written on the ethics of the ancient Egyptian. From the earliest times of which we have any knowledge the standard of conduct was very high. The first duty was to God; but, as God and the king were one and the same, a man's duty was to his king. This idea is seen constantly in the inscriptions where the good actions of a man towards his fellows were recorded; intermingled with these acts were the actions towards the king expressed in words which show that they ranked as piety towards God. In a country like Egypt, where famine was an ever threatening possibility, and poverty marked the land, it was accounted an act of mercy to "give bread to the hungry". Then as the highway was the river, full of treacherous sandbanks, where also the current ran strongly and usually against a gusty wind, navigation was often hazardous, and many a boat was lost; therefore a pious and wealthy man gave "a boat to the ship-wrecked sailor". A good ruler prided himself on his non-oppression of his people, and on his care for the helpless. He acted as "the father of the fatherless, the husband to the widow, the protector of the orphan", and was specially careful of "him who has no mother". In times of scarcity he provided for his people, and one proud boast was "there was no one hungry in my time". As a judge the ideal was absolute impartiality, and many judges claimed to have approached that ideal. "Never did I judge two claimants in such a way that a son was deprived of his paternal inheritance", says a judge of the vi-th dynasty. Thothmes III's instructions to his Vizier show this insistence on the impartiality of a judge, emphasising the absolute necessity of treating all men alike, and showing no favouritism to a friend or relative. Haremheb at the end of the xviii-th dynasty went even further and made bribery a capital crime: "As for any official or any priest of whom it shall be said: 'he sits to execute justice against those appointed for trial, and he himself commits a crime against justice', it shall be against him as a great crime of death." Rameses III, when appointing the judges to try the conspirators who had attempted to murder him, enjoined on them to be certain of the guilt of the accused before condemning them, though one might have forgiven him for urging that they should be punished.

* Gunn, *J.E.A.*, xxix (1943), p. 38.

F

Intef, the Royal Herald, in the xviii-th dynasty, makes in his funerary inscription a great point of his impartiality; he was "free from partiality, chastising the guilty for his guilt; servant of the poor, father of the fatherless, guardian of the orphan, mother of the terrified, controller of the turbulent, protector of the weak, advocate of those who have been deprived of their possessions by a stronger adversary, husband of the widow, one for whom the good thank God for the greatness of his worth."*

Sa-Mentu gives the explanation why he was so valued by the Pharaoh, and possibly by others as well: "The King praised me because I was silent, I never repeated any evil word."

A blessing was promised to those who acted righteously: "Any noble who shall do good to the people, who shall surpass the virtue of him who begat him, he shall be blessed in the Hereafter, his son shall abide in his father's house, his memory shall be pleasant in his city, his statue shall be glorified and carried by the children of his house."

A comprehensive list of offences against the ideals of a man's private life is given in Chapter 125 of the Book of the Dead. It is part of the trial of the soul before being admitted into the kingdom of Osiris, when the dead man recites all the sins which he has *not* committed during his time on earth. He denies that he has committed murder, adultery, robbery, false witness, or blasphemy against the gods or the king. He has not defrauded the widow, oppressed the poor, plundered the orphan, nor slandered anyone; he has not spoken words in anger, he has not caused pain nor the shedding of tears. This is a higher ideal than any of the other ancient nations reached, and shows a standard as noble as that of any religion that has ever existed. That these ideals were not a mere outward show of piety is seen occasionally by little human touches in a biography as when a man boasts that "I was beloved by my father, praised by my mother, *and loved by my brothers and sisters*". A man who could so endear himself to his entire family must have had a character of great kindness and uprightness.

In the xii-th dynasty a Pharaoh could boast of what he had done for his people: "I was one who cultivated grain, and worshipped the Harvest-god. The Nile greeted me in every valley. None were hungry in my time, none were thirsty then. All dwelt in content through that which I did."

* Breasted, op. cit., ii. 299.

MAGIC

Egypt is credited with being the home of magic, principally because of the Biblical account of Pharaoh's magicians who were defeated by the superior magic of Moses and Aaron. It is almost impossible to distinguish with any degree of certainty between the practices of magic and the ritual of religion. Some magical practices appear to belong to the ritual of a past, often a forgotten, religion, others are due to a misunderstanding of the laws of Nature, and a certain residue can be attributed to the imagination of untrained minds.

Foretelling events of the future, though now stigmatised as magic, was in origin the attempt to discover the will of God so that the inquirer might act in accordance with that will. Our own word, *divination*, shows the religious origin of the practice. There are many methods of divination; in ancient Egypt the principal method was by dreams. This seems to have been taught in the temples, particularly at Heliopolis, where the High-priest's title was the Great Seer. It may be noted that the most celebrated interpreter of dreams, Joseph, married the daughter of one of the High-priests after having been raised to high rank by the successful interpretation of royal visions.

Another method was by casting lots, though this was practised by the Jews more than by the Egyptians.

One of the chief uses of magic, both in ancient and in modern times, is to induce love. Love potions were probably as common as, or even more common than, at the present day, but few recipes have survived. There are, however, a certain number of spells for the purpose which have been preserved; they were usually to be recited secretly and at night. One of the most curious threatens the god if the lover does not obtain his desire; it dates to the xx-th dynasty (about 1100 B.C.):

Hail to thee, O Rê-Harakhte, Father of the Gods!
Hail to you, O ye seven Hathors,
Who are adorned with strings of red thread!
Hail to you, ye Gods, Lords of heaven and earth!
Cause so-and-so [fem.], born of so-and-so, to come after me
Like an ox after grass,
Like a mother after her children,
Like a drover after his herd!
If you do not make her come after me
I shall set fire to Busiris-city and burn up Osiris!*

Wax images for bewitching an enemy were known at this period, as is seen in the Harem-trial in the reign of Rameses III (p. 46), but

* *J.E.A.*, xxvii (1941), p. 131.

other means of destroying an enemy were used at an earlier date. In the xii-th dynasty (*c.* 2300 B.C.) the names of the king's enemies were written on pottery bowls or platters which were then smashed into hundreds of fragments, thereby destroying the men whose names were written on them: "The prince of Kush, and all his familiars who are with him. All the Nubians of Kush and of Muges, their mighty men, swift runners, allies and associates, who shall rebel, intrigue, fight, or talk of fighting or of intriguing in any part of this land of Egypt." Another curse was even more comprehensive: "Every evil word, evil speech, evil slander, evil thought, evil intrigue, evil fight, evil disturbance, evil plan or other evil thing, evil dream, or evil sleep."★ By the breaking to pieces of this "potter's vessel", all these evil things were magically destroyed, and the person for whom the spell was recited was magically protected.

As there was so much magic which could be performed in secret against a person there had to be counter-magic for protection. For this reason amulets were worn, talismans were hung in the house, especially at the doors and windows to prevent the entrance of evil through those openings, written charms were secreted on the person, and secret practices were common. The vulnerable place to strike a person is the back as he cannot see the coming blow, physical or magical. The *menyt* (pl. x. 1, 2), which hung at the back between the shoulders, gave this protection, for in it the goddess Hathor was immanent.

But occasionally evil magic was too strong for simple amulets or ordinary anti-magic ceremonies to have effect. In such a case it was clear that some dead relative must be appealed to. The relative would be someone who had held a good position in this world and would therefore hold an equally high post in the next and would carry as much influence there as here. The letter was written on a pottery bowl or vase and was placed in or near the grave of the person to whom it was addressed. It was the last desperate remedy to counteract a series of misfortunes, but unfortunately there is no means of knowing how far it was successful. The one which I quote here belongs to the First Intermediate Period, possibly about 2800 B.C. It was written by an unnamed man to his dead father:

> This is an oral reminder of that which I said to thee in reference to myself —Thou knowest that Idu said in reference to his son, "As to whatever may be yonder, I will not allow him to be afflicted of any affliction". Do thou unto me the like thereof. Behold now there is brought to thee this vessel in respect of which thy mother is to make litigation. It were agreeable

---

★ Sethe, *Abhandl. d. Preuss. Akad. Wissen*, 1926.

that thou shouldst support her. Cause thou that there be born to me a healthy male child. Thou art an excellent Spirit. And behold as for those two, the serving maids who have caused Seny to be afflicted, namely Nefertjentet and Itjai, confound them, and destroy for me every affliction which is directed against my wife, for thou knowest that I have need thereof. Destroy it utterly! As thou livest for me, the Great One shall praise thee, and the face of the Great God shall be glad over thee: he shall give thee pure bread with his two hands. Moreover I beg a second healthy male child for thy daughter.*

CURSES

As there is always a certain amount of shuddering interest taken in curses inscribed on Egyptian tombs, I give here some examples of these awe-inspiring threats. It should be noticed, however, that the curses are directed against the violators of the endowment, not against the violators of the tomb itself. In other words, it was a question of property vested in a priesthood, and religious hatred is seldom manifested more spitefully than when exhibited by a priesthood whose estates are sequestered or even threatened. It should be noticed also that as the priesthoods increased in power the curses increased proportionately in virulence.

One of the earliest of these terrible documents is of the v-th dynasty: "As for any people who shall take possession of this tomb as their mortuary property or shall do any evil thing to it, judgment shall be had with them for it by the great God."

Harkhuf, who is well known as the bringer of the dancing dwarf to the little Pharaoh, Pepy II (p. 18), inscribed on his tomb: "As for any man who shall enter into this tomb as his mortuary possession, I will seize him like a wild fowl; he shall be judged for it by the great God."

A curse which was fulfilled is recorded in the temple of Min of Koptos under one of the Yntefs of the xii-th dynasty: "The priesthood of this temple applied to my Majesty saying: 'An evil thing is about to happen in this temple. Hostility has been stirred up by—blasted be his name—Tety son of Minhetep.'" The Pharaoh at once took steps to see that Tety's name should be thoroughly well blasted. "Cause him to be deposed from the temple, cause him to be cast out from his offices, to the son of his son and the heir of his heir. Let him be cast out on the earth; let his bread, his food, his consecrated meat be taken from him. Let his name not be remembered in this temple; let his entries be expunged from the temple of Min, from the treasury, and from every book likewise." This was very severe, for as the name was expunged from the books in the House of Life the wretched man had no further existence in this world or the next. But the Pharaoh had not done with him yet. He goes on: "As for any King or any ruler who shall be merciful to him, he shall not receive the White Crown nor wear the Red Crown; he shall not sit on the Horus-throne of the Living; the two Goddesses shall not be gracious to him. And as for any official who shall apply to the King to be merciful to him [Tety], let his people, his goods and estates be given to the consecrated land of Min. No one of his [Tety's] relations of the family of his father or of his mother, shall hold this office."*

For a really fine curse few can compare with that of Amonhotep son of Hapi, the great Vizier of Amonhotep III, who was deified in Ptolemaic times: "As for any general or scribe of the army who shall follow after men, and shall find this chapel beginning to decay together with the diminishing of the male and female slaves, who cultivate my endowment, and shall take away a man therefrom in order to put him to any business of Pharaoh or any commission, may his body be accursed. And if any others trespass upon them, they shall suffer the destruction of Amon. Amon shall deliver them to the flaming wrath of the King on the day of his anger; his serpent-crown shall spit fire on their heads, and shall consume their limbs, and shall devour their bodies, they shall become like Apophis on New Year's Day. They shall be engulfed in the sea, it shall hide their corpses. They shall not receive the mortuary rites of the good; they shall not eat the food of them that dwell in Keret; the waters of the flood of the river shall not be poured out for them. Their sons shall not succeed them; their wives shall be violated before their eyes. The nobles shall not set foot in their houses, they shall not hear the words of the King in the hour of gladness. They shall belong to the sword on the day of destruction. They shall be called enemies! Their bodies shall be consumed! They shall hunger, without food! Their bodies shall die!"

The curse which Penno in the xx-th dynasty engraved on his rock-cut tomb at Ibrim in Nubia owes its subtly terrifying quality to the vagueness of the threat. He curses the violator of the endowment of his statue: "As for anyone who shall disregard it, Amon King of the Gods shall be after him, Mut shall be after his wife, Khonsu shall be after his children. He shall hunger! He shall thirst! He shall faint! He shall sicken!"

In the xxii-nd dynasty an endowment of five stat (3½ acres) of land was made to a chapel of the goddess Hathor at Per-Sebek in the Delta. The fact was inscribed on a stela, and the inscription ends with a curse and a blessing: "As for any man, or any scribe, who is sent on

* Petrie, *Koptos*, p. 10.

commission to the district of the town of Per-Sebek, who shall injure this stela, they shall come under the blade of Hathor. But the name of him who shall establish it shall remain."

One of the most tremendous curses is the curse pronounced against the enemies of Rê, who is here identified with the Pharaoh. Certain magical ceremonies must be performed, and then come the words: "Burning be on you! They shall have no souls thereby [i.e. by means of the magical ceremonies], nor spirits nor bodies nor shades nor magic nor bones nor hair nor utterances nor words. They shall have no grave thereby, nor house nor hole nor tomb. They shall have no garden thereby, nor tree nor bush. They shall have no water thereby, nor bread nor light nor fire. They shall have no children thereby, nor family nor heirs nor tribe. They shall have no head thereby, nor arms nor legs nor gait nor seed. They shall have no seats on earth thereby. . . . Their souls shall not be permitted to come out of the Netherworld and they shall not be among those who live upon earth, on no day shall they behold Rê, but they shall be bound and fettered in Hell in the lower Netherworld and their souls shall not be permitted to come forth for ever and ever."*

* R. O. Faulkner, *J.E.A.*, xxiii (1937), p. 174.

V

ART AND SCIENCE

MUSIC

COMPARATIVELY little is known of the music, for music is unlike the other arts in that it leaves no concrete traces. A certain amount of information can, however, be gleaned from the instruments themselves and from the representations of the performers although there is no actual record of the sounds.

Secular music seems to have been in the hands of professionals, as no person of rank is represented performing on a musical instrument. The earliest musical instruments were the harp and the flute,* which were used at first only to accompany a singer. It was not until the xviii-th dynasty that they were played as an orchestra; in the scene of the Blind Harper the instruments are the harp, the lute, and two flutes, and there is no singer (pl. lxxiii. 2). Rhythm was as important as melody and clapping was the customary way of emphasising it, for percussion instruments were not popular for vocal music. The Comic Papyrus of the xviii-th dynasty gives a delightful picture of an orchestra; they are led by a donkey playing the harp, followed by a lion who is singing and accompanying himself on the lyre, then comes a crocodile performing on a lily-wreathed lute, and the fourth performer is an ape playing the double flute (pl. lxxix. 1).

Women seem to have been musicians only as accompanists to the dance. They danced to their own playing or as the orchestra for other dancers; their instruments were the harp or a kind of guitar. They also beat time in the dance with instruments of ivory in the shape of a hand and arm, used as a Spanish dancer uses castanets.

For sacred music the chief instrument was the sistrum, which was used chiefly in the ritual of a goddess. The sistrum (pls. x. 2; xc. 2) consists of a long strip of metal bent round to form a loop, the ends being fastened into a handle. In the metal loop loop holes were cut, three on each side, and through each hole a thin metal rod was passed right across the loop from one side to the other; the holes were full large, so that the rods were loose, and the instrument was played by being shaken rhythmically and so making the rods rattle. A percussion instrument was the tambourine; this was also for a "religious" use, for

* For the scales of flutes, pipes, lutes and harps, see Petrie, *Wisdom of the Egyptians*, pp. 3–7.

it is seen in the hands of the god Bes when he dances the protective dance for the new-born child (pl. xxv. 1, 2).

Of wind instruments the flute and pipes appear to have been indigenous in Egypt. Sometimes the flute was short, but there was another kind so long that it rested on the ground when the performer was sitting down. This is found as early as the iv-th dynasty. The double pipe is first depicted in the xii-th dynasty. Trumpets were not known till the xviii-th dynasty and were probably foreign, for they were used only for military purposes; those found in the tomb of Tut-ankh-Amon are of silver.

The earliest stringed instrument represented is the harp. This was at first a simple affair, and in the Old Kingdom was generally played by a female musician as an accompaniment to a male singer. In the later dynasties men are the usual harpers (pl. lxxiii. 2). In the New Kingdom the harps were highly ornamental, very often painted and gilded, and with the Pharaoh's head carved in the round. The lute and the lyre are foreign in origin though they are both found in some of the scenes. The lyre occurs as early as the xii-th dynasty, and at Beni Hasan is shown being played by a man of an immigrant tribe of Bedawin. It occurs occasionally, but never became as popular as the lute, which in the New Kingdom was much used by dancing girls.

ARCHITECTURE

"The art of a country, like the character of the inhabitants, belongs to the nature of the land. It is but a confusion of thought, therefore, to try to pit the art of one country against that of another."[*]

"To understand the mind of the artist we must look to those qualities which in their literature were held up as the ideals of life."[†]

The art of Egypt must be judged in connection with its land, with its people, with their ideals, with the emotions which the artist desired to convey to and arouse in the spectator, and with the reality of those emotions. In the character of the people, conditioned by the rigidity of the landscape and the unchangeability of the seasons—conditions unknown in other countries—lies the explanation of Egyptian art. The high cliffs, marked with horizontal strata and scored with vertical weathering, gave the note for the kind of architecture which had to be displayed against that stern background (pl. xxxi). The fierce sunlight casting deep shadows, the clarity of the atmosphere with no softening misty effects, the sudden contrasts of inundation and dryness, of verdure and sterility, of the teeming life of the habitable land and the lifelessness of the desert, had their effect on the artist's mind and therefore on his

[*] Petrie, *Arts and Crafts*, pp. 1, 2.   [†] Ibid., p. 7.

work. Here were no rounded hills, no forest glades, no gentle stream-lets, no softened outlines, but Nature often at her fiercest, with whirling sandstorms, the great river in spate, the sun burning the whole land to dust. To understand the art of Egypt one must first know the country in all its seasons and aspects.

To the Egyptian the qualities most desired were Stability and Enduringness. His work was made for Eternity, his temples and statues were to last for ever, his name must remain unchanged and enduring like the Imperishable Stars. In dedications of temples, in prayers to the gods, it is this quality of external existence which is the dominant note. It was Life Everlasting for which the Egyptian prayed, with the everlasting hills before his eyes. To ensure this quality in his work, strength was essential, strength in his buildings and his statues to withstand the blast of the sandstorm, the insidious rise of the river, the burning power of the sun, a strength which should connote durability. That he attained his desire is manifest, for his pyramids, his temples, his fortresses, his colossi, still stand to attest the truth and honesty of his work, which for forty, and even fifty, centuries has defied the destroying hand of Time.

As the starkness of the landscape conditioned the architecture, so the architecture conditioned the sculpture, for to the Egyptian artist sculpture was merely an architectural decoration. Not for him, there-fore, an attitude expressing rapid motion, not for him fluttering skirts, streaming hair, muscular arms in action. Against that rigid and for-bidding background such attitudes would have appeared tawdry and frivolous.

Egyptian art, like the art of all other countries, began in the service of religion. The statues in the temples represented God Himself, eternal, majestic, aloof, unapproachable. In the twilight of the colon-naded halls the figures of the King, the God Incarnate, painted in life-like colours, were seen enthroned in majesty or striding forward with eyes fixed above and beyond the worshipper (pls. xlviii. 2; lxii; xxxiii. 3). From the darkness of the Holy Place the great God Himself was borne out on the shoulders of white-robed priests to show his divine countenance to his suppliants. But beyond this rare event there was nothing to break the peace and silence of those shadowed aisles. In such a setting, only simplicity and majestic dignity could be tolerated.

Again, in the tombs the statues were placed for religious purposes and from religious motives. They stood in the tomb-chapel (pl. xlix. 3), of which the architecture, like that of the temples, was con-ditioned by the landscape, and the statues conformed to the architec-ture. As they were for the purpose of religious rites, they were simple and dignified. Made to appear as lifelike as possible, the statues were seen either in the half-light of the tomb-chapel or by the soft white light of little oil lamps. Immanent in each statue was the spirit of the dead person whom it represented, called back from the Realm of the Dead to receive the gifts and remembrances of his descendants. Respect for the dead was a fundamental duty among the Egyptians, and therefore the statues show a simple and quiet dignity in keeping with that feeling.

Within the building, temple or tomb-chapel, with the stern landscape hidden from sight, the artist had in the decoration of the walls more scope to display his innate sense of the beauty of proportion and of colour. In the temples the decoration of painted sculpture consisted of scenes of ritual and figures of the gods; in the tomb-chapels the artist could let his fancy range over the homely scenes of daily life. He was to a certain extent still tied by the architectural scheme, so that he divided the walls into horizontal registers, with here and there a vertical line to divide one scene from another. And in the tomb-chapels there were some religious conventions to be observed, as for instance the representation of the dead man seated before a table of food offerings, for without such a representation he might starve in the next world. With this one exception of a rigidly religious scene, the artist was free to represent what he would, and could vary even the most conventional details. In these scenes the wealth of detail, the accuracy of the draughtsmanship, the beauty of the tool-work, and the brilliancy of the colour, show the love of the craftsman-artist for his work.

As Egypt is a country where sunlight is a glare almost insupportable to the eyes, it was essential to exclude the light from all buildings as much as possible without making the interior completely dark. In stone buildings, whether temple or tomb-chapel, this was done by setting small openings high up on an otherwise blank wall. The early tomb-chapels at Saqqara often have a horizontal slit window just below the stone roof; the sun cannot penetrate but the whole chamber is illumined with a clear cool light. In some of the smaller shrines in a temple, a funnel-shaped opening was made in the roof, through which a pencil of pure light was conveyed into the darkness below, so that the shrine was luminous without any glare. The great temples required stronger illumination; this was provided by building the central nave considerably higher than the side aisles; windows were set in the nave walls above the roofs of the aisles, and made a clerestory like those in our cathedrals. The side aisles had no windows and received light from the clerestory only. The doorways were not used for lighting; they were blocked with mats or curtains or with wooden doors. This matter of lighting must always be remembered when judging the painted wall-sculpture and wall-paintings of the temples and tomb-chapels, especially when they are seen in an unroofed building in the unmitigated glare of an Egyptian sun. But when seen in their proper setting in the soft clear light in which they were intended to be seen, the walls glow like a jewelled mosaic.

In considering the beginnings of architecture in any country it is obvious that the primitive builder must use only the materials most easily available, and that his buildings will be for utility rather than for beauty. In Egypt the most readily accessible building materials were reeds and clay. The climate being practically rainless, these were sufficient to provide all the shelter necessary against the sun in summer and the cold winds in winter. Lattice- or mat-work of reeds was easily made and quickly set up, and when thatched with reeds or straw was quite adequate as a protection against the sun; and when freely daubed with clay was equally adequate as a shelter from wind. Wood fit for building has always been so scarce in Egypt that it had (and still has) to be imported;* and the primitive Egyptian had not learnt the art of quarrying stone. Therefore lattice and clay (Anglice, wattle and daub) must be regarded as the foundation of Egyptian building, and they had their effect on the later architecture. Lattice and clay are used at the present day in Egypt for walls of yards; these are made of interlaced palm sticks covered with clay, the ends of the palm fronds forming a rustling waving coping to the wall. Another use is made of these materials in building the pillars which carry the weight of the *shaduf* buckets and counterpoise; these are made of bundles of palm stalks or durra stalks, covered thickly with clay.

Flimsy structures, such as the primitive Egyptian houses, would soon perish when abandoned, and would leave no trace. But a model house of the Gerzean period, found at Abydos, shows exactly the type. Judged by the objects found with it, it must have belonged to a wealthy owner, yet it is merely a construction of lattice and clay. There was, however, some timber used, for the lintel of the door and the lintels and sills of the two windows were of wood. It was not until the iii-rd dynasty that building-timber was imported into Egypt in any quantity. It then came from Syria, the nearest place from which long coniferous timber could be obtained.

Though no shrines of the early periods have been preserved, there are representations of them in the i-st dynasty. They were light struc-

* A Coptic church built at Naqada during the war of 1914–18, when timber was practically unobtainable in Egypt, was constructed entirely of brick, the door and window frames were of stone; only the door itself and the window shutters were of wood (pl. xliii. 2).

tures of lattice-work, but were not necessarily coated with clay like the houses. The shrines of Anubis (figs. 11, 12) and the shrine of Neith (fig. 13) all show the uncovered lattice. One of the Anubis-shrines is peculiarly interesting on account of its shape, reproducing as it does the very form of the jackal-god; it was a piece of highly skilled work. In later times the Anubis-shrine was still of lattice, but the shape was changed (fig. 12); it was this later shape that was used as a hieroglyph in the title of Anubis, "Chief of the shrine of the God".

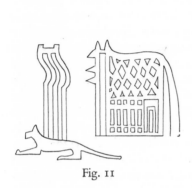

Fig. 11

Fig. 12

The earliest pillars were probably intended to support the light roof of a porch or veranda for a shrine or a dwelling-house, and were made of the same materials that the modern Egyptian uses for cheap structures, but the primitive Egyptian used papyrus stems instead of palm or durra stalks. The flowering stem of the papyrus reed has a triangular section, and ends in a head which is like an untidy mop; though it has a certain amount of strength it would not support much weight. To make a pillar, the ancient Egyptian, who was always highly ingenious, lashed together several bundles of the reeds, tying them firmly with several turns of cord just below the heads, and again at the root ends. To keep the cord taut, he pushed in a short length of papyrus stem between each bundle. He then made a base of solid clay into which he pushed the root ends of his reed bundles so deep that the lashing cord was covered, and the pillar stood upright. He tied the mop-like heads together at the top, and then covered the whole structure with clay from the tied tops of the flowering heads down to the clay base. He would probably make two or three pillars in a row; and would then lay across their tops a lashed bundle of papyrus stems, or a plank if he had one, add a light thatch of palm branches, and his veranda was complete; a shady place in which to sit in the height of summer.

This use of papyrus had an unforeseen result on Egyptian architecture when stone building became possible. The weight of the clay and of the superstructure caused the papyrus stems to bend a little outwards just above the base; but being tightly lashed below, the individual stems could not separate. The weight of the board and thatch had the same effect on the mop-like heads, which took on a gentle curve outwards, slightly overhanging the lashing. When this form of pillar was reproduced in stone, the architect copied the curves and the visible lashing with the utmost fidelity, but found it impossible to copy the innumerable peduncles of the flowering heads which now formed the capital of the pillar. But no Egyptian architect of ancient times was ever daunted by a difficulty; his own ingenuity and artistic sense came to his aid. The curves of the "capital" were reminiscent of an opening lotus-bud, the architect seized on this resemblance and carved his capital as a half-opened bud of the blue lotus just showing the petals inside the calyx. As the short length of papyrus stem which held the lashing taut was not in itself picturesque, he turned that into a small lotus bud with a long stem (pl. xxxiv. 1). In many of the pillars of this type a remembrance of the original papyrus is seen in the ridge down the shaft of the pillar, reproducing the sharp edge of the original triangular papyrus stem. This type of pillar was always the most popular in the great Pharaonic temples. In later times it lost much of its distinctive character, but even to the last the lashing below the capital and the slight overhang of the capital itself were never omitted (pl. xxxviii). So marked was the overhang that it is found in capitals where it is clearly unmeaning, as in the foliage capitals of the Ptolemaic era (pls. xxxv. 2; xxxix. 2) and the Hathor-head capitals where it is superfluous and inartistic (pl. xxxix. 1).

Variants of the capital are found, though they are comparatively rare. The rose lotus with its heavy fleshy calyx is not common (pl. xxxiv. 2); two varieties of the palm-leaf capital are known. With the palm-leaf capital the pillar is cylindrical, without the outward curve at the base (pl. xxxv. 1). The head of the goddess Hathor was used as a capital in the iii-rd dynasty, but did not become popular till the xix-th dynasty. It is seen in its most notable form on the tremendous pillars in the temple of Dendera.

The complete change in Egyptian Art after it had suffered eclipse under the Ptolemies and Romans is clearly seen in the Christian architecture (pl. xliii. 1, 2), more particularly in the columns and capitals (pls. xxxiii. 2; xxxvi, 1, 2. For other forms of Coptic art, see pls. xciii, xciv).

One of the chief difficulties which confronted the Egyptian architect when he began to build in brick and stone was the annual movement of the ground. In the summer, when the Nile is at its lowest, the ground is completely dried up; then comes the inundation, and the seepage of the water into the dry soil will cause the ground to rise as much as twelve to twenty inches; as the inundation subsides, the ground settles down again to its original dry level; but in no case does it rise or fall evenly. It was easy enough if the buildings were erected in the desert near the foot of the cliffs, where neither the seepage nor the surface flood could reach; such buildings were not affected by any ground movement. But it was a different matter when the temple was built near the river, especially when, like Karnak, it stood on the very bank.* Many were the ways by which the Egyptian architect tried to overcome the difficulty, and much of the peculiarity of Egyptian building is due to the natural phenomenon of the movement of the ground. That some of the methods used were brilliantly successful is attested by the temples which have stood the strain for more than three thousand years.

Though the prehistoric people erected little hovels of mud-brick, real building does not appear till the i-st dynasty. The great royal tombs of that period show that the knowledge of such building was well advanced. The bricks were made in moulds of a standard size, and were dried in the sun; they were laid in what is now known as "English bond" in a mortar of clay. The bricks are as well and truly

* I have myself seen floods in the temple of Karnak due entirely to seepage, for though the river was running bank-high it had not overflowed. And there is always the danger that the river may rise above its banks, then "the emboldened floods link arms and flashing forward drown" whole villages. Two records of such an event are found. The first is the inscription of Smendes of the xxi-st dynasty, engraved in the quarry at Gebelên: "His Majesty sat in the hall of his palace in the city of Memphis, when there came messengers to inform his Majesty that the canal work, which forms the boundary of Thothmes III's temple at Luxor, had begun to go to ruin, [on account of the waters] making a great flood and a mighty current therein on the great pavement of the house of the temple, it encircled the façade. His Majesty said, 'There has been nothing like this in the time of my Majesty, or from of old'. His Majesty sent master-builders and three thousand men with them of the choicest of the people." The rest of the inscription is broken away. The other record is of the reign of Osorkon II of the xxii-nd dynasty, and narrates not only the effect of the flood but the carrying out of the image of Amon by the priests to quell the rise of the waters: "The flood came on in the whole land, it invaded the two shores as in the beginning; the land was in its power like the sea; there was no dyke of the people to withstand its fury. All the people were like birds, all the temples of Thebes were like marshes." The resemblance of the people to birds was because they had to take refuge from the flood on the branches of trees. The height of this inundation is recorded in the Nile levels marked on the quay at Karnak, and they show that the water must have risen and flooded the temples to the depth of two feet above the pavement.

laid as any modern bricklayer could lay them, showing that the Egyptian builders had a complete mastery of material and method. Not only did they erect walls ten feet high and over four feet thick, but in the tomb of King Udy-mu they built a staircase of seventy steps of sun-dried brick, evenly laid and still usable. In that dry climate and buried in the sand, these early brick buildings are still strong and sound, except for the destruction wrought by the hand of man.

For brick buildings on the surface the walls were built with a batter on one side, vertical on the other, so that the base was considerably wider than the top of the wall. This was to counteract the movement of the ground. When building in stone was introduced this method of building high walls was followed (pls. xl. 2; xlii. 2). Another device to counteract ground movement was to build a wall in sections, without bonding the sections together. Such a wall, though apparently all in one piece, would give easily to the uneven rise and fall of the ground and yet remain standing. Still another method was by "pan-bedding", with curved courses of bricks (pl. xli. 2). Buttressed walls were for the same purpose, and of this type the gigantic wall of the enclosure known as the Shuneh at Abydos is a good example. At Abydos were found two other methods which do not seem to have been very successful; one is the bastion wall and the other was a wavy wall, of which only the foundations remain (pl. xlii. 1). Wide spacing of the bricks was yet another method of overcoming the difficulty.

The Egyptian architect evolved the round arch as early as the iii-rd dynasty. This was always of brick, and was used very sparingly and only where it could not be seen from the outside. It is the true arch made by setting the voussoirs correctly. The bricks were not shaped, but the intervals between them were filled with mud-mortar. The corbelled arch is not known in Egyptian brickwork; in stone, a kind of false arch was used, as at Abydos, where a flat block of stone, which forms the roof of a stairway, has been cut into the shape of a round arch. Barrel-roof valuting in brick does not appear until large buildings came into existence (pl. xli. 1). The method of making them is interesting, and is thus described by Petrie: "Barrel-roof vaulting was constructed by very tilted arching, so sloped that each course could be built on the sloping surface, and held in place by the mud-mortar till the course was completed. Each superimposed ring of arch was tilted in an opposite direction, so that the bricks crossed joint, and thus each ring held those above and those below it in place, and prevented splitting."*

All brickwork of ancient Egypt was of sun-dried clay. The bricks were made in moulds, and were exposed to the sun for a few days.

* Petrie, *Wisdom of the Egyptians*, p. 83.

They varied in size according to the period, and in excavating it is necessary to know the dimensions of the bricks before giving an opinion on the date of a brick building. The bricks were laid with clay-mortar, and when the whole structure is consolidated it is very firm. It was not until Roman times that burnt bricks became common.

The use of stone in buildings began as early as the i-st dynasty, when so many new ideas were introduced. In the tomb of King Udy-mu at Abydos the floor was made of large blocks of granite. These had been slightly squared to make them fit into the space, but it was not until the ii-nd dynasty that the first tentative use of stone in actual building was made. In the iii-rd dynasty King Zoser constructed the Step-pyramid and the amazing series of temples round it, all of stone (pls. xlv; xli. 3). So far no development of stone building has been found; the art springs into existence full-blown without any apparent origin, for the ii-nd dynasty work can hardly be regarded as leading up to the magnificent buildings of Zoser. Yet there must have been some connecting links between the poor little beginning in the ii-nd dynasty and the full flowering in the iii-rd.

The builder in stone had to contend with the same difficulty as the builder in brick, for the movement of the ground would bring down a stone temple as certainly as a brick building. The pyramids, being built at a distance from the river, were not affected by either seepage or flood, and consequently were secure; so also were the mortuary temples, which were erected near the entrance to the tombs beyond reach of the water. But the god-temples, where the people went to worship, were necessarily in the habitable part of the Nile Valley, which meant being near the river. Special methods were required for such buildings. It was for this reason that in a stone wall the blocks were cut so as to "break bond", i.e. the junctions, both vertical and horizontal, are not continuous. A curious method of stone building for which there is no apparent reason was to build a hall or chamber smaller than was intended, then to cut away from the inner surface the excess of stone. By doing this, the corners of the chamber are actually cut out of the stone, and are not made by the junction of two blocks.

From the iii-rd dynasty onward the use of stone in building became general for pyramids and temples, and by the time of the iv-th dynasty the Egyptian was able to build a temple in that intractable material, granite. Khafra's granite temple is made of large monolithic blocks of granite, squared with great precision (pl. xxxiii. 1). Its only decoration was the lining of some of the less important chambers with slabs of veined alabaster. But in its simplicity and dignity there is no temple of Egypt that can compare with it.

With the exception of Khafra's temple the buildings of ancient Egypt were of limestone or sandstone. These two kinds of stone were quarried in the same way by cutting into the face of the cliff and hollowing out large chambers in which pillars of the rock were left to support the superincumbent weight. The quarrying began at the top, and the blocks were cut out by making a trench all round the piece that had been marked out. When it became the fashion to convert such quarry-chambers into tomb-chapels or temples, the same plan of beginning at the top was followed. Thus the ceiling was finished first, then the pillars had the abacus cut, afterwards the capital and the shaft, and it was not until the floor was almost reached that the bases of the pillars were shaped. This process is the reverse of building.

Granite required different treatment from the softer limestone. The exact method of quarrying large blocks for building is not certain. It was possibly done by two methods, of which one was by cutting a groove along the line where the block was to be split off, then driving in wedges of dry wood, which were wetted, and the force of the swelling wood would split the block off. The other method is somewhat similar: a fire would be lighted all along the groove, then when the stone was very hot, water would be poured over it, with the same result that the block would split away from the main rock. In the xviii-th dynasty there was yet another method of quarrying granite, which was used for the obelisks which Queen Hatshepsut set up at Karnak. This was by the arduous method of making a trench by pounding with stone pounders all round the embryo obelisk. Pounding with stone was the customary method of rough-dressing stone in the quarry; the hammer-stones were made of a quartzose rock and were usually about two pounds in weight. A building was erected with stones which were only rough-dressed; when in position each stone had a true drafting cut round the edge, and the excess was then cut away with metal adzes. The face of the stone was then tested with a "facing-plate" smeared with red ochre.

The founding of a temple was a religious ceremony, performed by the Pharaoh in person assisted by the goddess Seshat, who was probably represented by the Queen. Each of them held an end of the measuring-cord and marked on the ground the dimensions of the temple. After the measurements had been traced out a sand-bed was made, and on this rough stone blocks were laid to form the foundations. At each corner of the building, and wherever an internal wall touched the outside wall, foundation deposits were placed under the blocks. These deposits consisted of models of all the tools and implements used in the building of the temple, models of offerings, and scarabs or plaques bearing the name of the royal founder. Even when a temple has been completely destroyed and the foundation blocks removed, it is possible to recover the plan and the name of the founder by means of the foundation deposits. The foundation blocks were scored with lines on the upper surface, which had been smoothed, and on these lines the walls were built. As the walls rose in height earth ramps were built against them, up which the stones were dragged on rollers. Pillars were built in the same way with ramps. This method of raising blocks of stone to the desired level is as early as the pyramids. It is uncertain whether a temple was built from a plan drawn out by the architect before beginning the work; if so, all such plans have perished. If not, then one is confronted with the fact that the architects of those early days were capable of planning a temple or pyramid completely, including the length of ramps required, and carrying it through to completion without even a note.

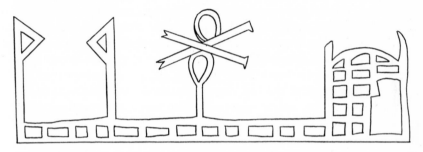

Fig. 13

The roofs of temples were made of slabs of stone (pl. xl. 1). As these were laid flat they needed a considerable amount of support, consequently a pillared hall became a forest of columns (pl. xxxvii). In side-colonnades one end of each roofing stone rested on the side wall and so was held safely; this can be seen in all temples which have side aisles or colonnades round a courtyard.

The primitive temple was enclosed with a lattice palisade to exclude unauthorised persons. When brick-building replaced lattice, the sacred precincts were enclosed with a high brick wall, so high that nothing could be seen from the outside but the twin towers of a pylon, the pointed tip of an obelisk, or in early times the soaring grandeur of a pyramid.

There were in Egypt, from the earliest historic times, two types of shrine or temple; the one was dedicated to the worship of the local deity, the other was the shrine of the dead king.

The representations of the god-shrines of the i-st dynasty show that they were of lattice- or mat-work (figs. 11, 12, 13), light structures which would perish quickly if neglected. In front of the shrine was a courtyard surrounded by a latticed palisade, the entrance to which was marked by a pair of poles with streamers attached. In the centre of the courtyard was a pole bearing the emblem of the deity to whom the shrine was consecrated.

Fig. 14

The use of poles in front of a shrine, and later in front of a temple, is, as is seen here, very early. The pole with streamers derives from the Gerzean period, when ships carried their divine emblem on a pole set amidships; and, in order to call the attention of the god to those under his care, pieces of cloth—originally fragments of the suppliants' garments—were fastened to the pole. In artistic representation these were stylised into streamers. When, in dynasty 0, writing first began, a picture of the pole with streamers stood for the word "God", reading Ni-ther, "He of the tree". The Egyptian artist-scribe, however, disliked loose ends; he made the two streamers horizontal and then joined them together (fig. 14). Though the written form changed, the poles themselves and their streamers remained unchanged, and were an integral part of the entrance of an Egyptian temple down to the latest period. There are many references to them in accounts of the building of temples, and they are often shown in representations of the entrance façade of a temple (fig. 15). Akhenaten was peculiarly addicted to streamers, for he not only had ten streamer-poles in front of his Sun-temple (the usual number being two or four), but he and his

Fig. 15   queen wore them, presumably to emphasise the idea of their divinity (fig. 16). As the poles were always of wood and the streamers of cloth, none have survived, but the grooves in which the poles stood are seen on several pylons (pl. xl. 2).

Egyptian god-temples are built on a simple plan, which is recognisable even when overlaid with superfluous buildings. The plan consists of four parts: an outer court, an inner court, a vestibule, and a shrine (fig. 17); the shrine being always in the axis of the temple opposite the main entrance. The outer court appears to have been for the general

Fig. 16

public, the inner court for the devotees and the partly initiated, the vestibule and sanctuary for the fully initiated and the priests. The shrine was screened from public view by hangings or by wooden doors.

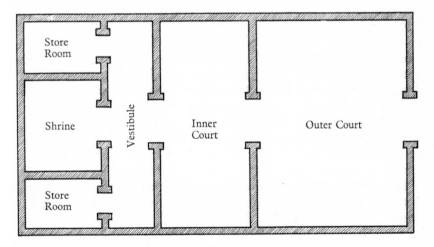

Fig. 17

As all the stone temples of the early periods suffered more or less complete destruction at the iconoclastic hands of the Hyksos, it is only on the analogy of the changes in the mortuary shrines of the kings that the changes in the god-temples can be followed. The simple plan was altered by degrees, beginning with a few store-chambers at the sides and perhaps a room for the priest. The sanctuary gradually became more difficult of access by the addition of vestibules and antechambers, and roofing of the inner court caused the darkness so desirable for the celebration of mysteries. The outer court remained open to the sky, with sometimes a roofed colonnade round the sides. Hatshepsut's temple at Deir el Bahri is a good example of this transitional form, with an open colonnaded outer court (pl. xxxii), a pillared inner court (now a ruin), a vestibule, and a rock-cut shrine in the axis of the temple. Amonhotep III's temple at Luxor is a typical god-temple. Like all Egyptian temples it is orientated by the river, which here runs rather to the east of north, and it was built on the site of an early shrine, probably one of the many temples of the xii-th dynasty which the Hyksos destroyed. The plan of Amonhotep's building was the usual one; the outer court originally was enclosed with a wall and had a roofed colonnade at the sides (pl. xxxviii); but the inner court was the glory of the temple with its forest of pillars. The vestibules and shrine have suffered much at the hands, first of the Romans, then of the Christians, who altered the buildings and covered the ancient sculptures with figures of saints. All the walls of the temple were once richly sculptured and painted. Though the temple was very splendid and glorious the early plan is clearly visible. Later kings, however, added to it but without altering the fundamental design. Haremheb built a processional colonnade with seven pillars on each side and enclosed with a wall and roofed. This led from Amonhotep's outer court into a much larger enclosure which appears to be later in date. The walls and pillars of this great court were once brilliantly painted, and it was here that the festivals of the god were celebrated.

In some of the later temples, especially in those of Ptolemaic date, when splendid pageants were staged for the greater glory of the god, an ambulatory was made round the shrine; but this did not alter the relative positions of the sanctuary and the entrance.

The temples of Dendera are fine examples of Ptolemaic buildings. A temple must have stood on the site from an early period, for the Ptolemies built only on sites that were already holy and sanctified by shrines. The dedication was to the goddess Hathor, who in the time in which the temple was erected was identified with two other goddesses, Isis and Nut. Like Karnak, the great temple of Dendera is the largest of a group of temples which cover a considerable area and are enclosed with a brick wall. It is one of the most stately and dignified of all the temples of Egypt. The entrance portico with its gigantic pillars has an impressiveness and glory beyond almost any other religious building. The number of little chapels and shrines on the roof and underground show that it was a temple for the cele-

ART AND SCIENCE
157

bration of mysteries; and as it was a goddess-temple those mysteries
were of the greatest of all mysteries, Life. Every part of the temple is
decorated with sculpture which, though it cannot compare with any
earlier work for beauty or technique, has the effect of great richness,
and is in keeping with the general scheme of the building.

Within the sacred precincts is the Birth House, without which no
Ptolemaic temple was complete. This is merely an extension of the
Birth Colonnade of Hatshepsut's temple at Deir el Bahri, and was
built to emphasise the divine birth of the Pharaoh. Another important
site within the enclosing wall was the sacred lake (pl. xliv). This was
a large rectangular structure, stone-walled, with a stair at each corner
leading down to the water. It was probably filled with seepage from
the Nile, and was used for the sacred voyages of the goddess and for
the midnight ceremonies which seem to have formed part of the ritual
of many of the Egyptian deities.

Rock-cut temples began as natural caves, but grotto worship was
never so common in Egypt as in the neighbouring country of Palestine.
This was perhaps for the simple reason that in Egypt the highway, and
therefore the traffic, was on and by the river, the cliffs were far off
and separated from the habitable part of the country by a strip of desert,
so that they were not part of the daily life of the people as in Palestine.
When rock-cut temples first began, it was only the shrine which was
hollowed out of the cliff, as at Deir el Bahri; later, the complete temple
was cut in the rock, as at Abu Simbel.

The rock-cut temples and tombs of Egypt are unsurpassed in size
and beauty of decoration, the most magnificent being the great temple
of Rameses II at Abu Simbel in Nubia. This is not a mere straight-
forward excavation or quarrying, but the colossal figures both inside
and out are carved in the rock itself.

The temple of Abu Simbel was designed to face the sunrise, and
above the main entrance between the colossi is the figure of the falcon-
headed Sun-god himself, stepping forward to greet the rising sun. The
temple has the usual form of an outer court, an inner court, a vestibule,
and a shrine, all hewn in the solid rock. The shrine contains the four
deities to whom the temple was dedicated, Amon-Rê of Thebes, Ptah
of Memphis, Rê-Harakhti of Heliopolis, and Rameses himself. When
the sun rises the rays strike right through the temple and fall on the
four enthroned figures in the shrine. During that short time the
figures are brilliantly illuminated, then as the sun rises higher they are
gradually shrouded in twilight and gloom till again the sun sends his
beams to "lighten the thick darkness". The inner court is remarkable
for the colossal standing figures of Rameses as Osiris; there are four
on each side, thirty feet high, carved from the rock which was left

when the court was hewn out. The temple itself is dwarfed by the magnificence of the façade with its four gigantic enthroned figures of the Pharaoh (pl. lxiv. 1, 2). The face of the rock behind these colossi is carved in the form of a temple-pylon, with cavetto cornice and astragal moulding, the cornice being surmounted with a cresting of dog-headed baboons. These figures face to the east, for baboons were credited by the Egyptians with worshipping the sun at its rising. The colossi are sixty feet high, and the architect of the temple showed his amazing faculty for dramatic effect by sculpturing them in a stratum of rock which is lighter in colour than the background, so that whether the figures are in sunshine or shadow they stand out in bold relief against the darker colour of the rock behind them.

The great outburst of building in Egypt began after the expulsion of the Hyksos and ended with Rameses III of the xx-th dynasty, and it was at this time that the mortuary-temples were built. They were always royal and were built by the Pharaohs for the worship of them-selves, living or dead. Like the god-temples the place for worship was only part of a vast enclosure, which included the *âhâ* or palace for the divine king when, as "Horus in the âhâ", he showed himself to his worshippers.

Mortuary-temples, like the god-temples, began as lattice-work shrines, but they have this peculiarity that the earliest form of which there are any representations was made in the likeness of a couchant jackal, *i.e.* of Anubis, the god of death. Such a shrine was presumably the place in which the whole body, or the essential parts of the body, of the king were preserved. These representations date to the i-st dynasty, and are contemporary with the royal tombs in which they were found. The royal tombs were marked by stelæ sculptured with the king's name, and were the places at which the offerings to the dead monarch were made. In the underground burial chambers, which surrounded the actual burial of the king, was stored the stock of food needed by him in his journey to the Other World; the offerings at his stela were the daily provisions which came fresh and fresh every day. It seems likely that the Anubis-shrine was erected over the stelæ, and served the double purpose of sheltering the special relics of the royal corpse and providing a convenient place for presenting the offerings. The combination of shrine and stela is clearly the origin of the mortuary-temple.

The development can be traced. Beginning with the Anubis-shrine and the stone stelæ, it seems that the shrine perished, being made of unsubstantial materials, yet the idea of a building round the durable stela remained; and when the next great innovation of the dynastic Egyptians occurred—the introduction of building in stone—the lattice-shrine was reproduced in a stone building. Snefru's pyramid temple at Meydrum is in the direct line of development;* two stelæ were set up at the east side of his splendid pyramid; in front of them was a small courtyard enclosed with a wall, and within the enclosure were small store-rooms. All through the Old Kingdom each pyramid had its own temple, varying in size and splendour according to the wealth and importance of the king who built it.

After the blank of the First Intermediate Period the Pharaohs of the xii-th dynasty revived the custom of building a pyramid with a temple attached. The most remarkable of all the mortuary-temples erected in Egypt was undoubtedly the Labyrinth, that vast edifice which so excited the Greek authors who visited it. Herodotus is enthusiastic in his account: "The pyramids were beyond description, and each of them comparable to many of the great Greek structures. Yet the Labyrinth surpasses even the pyramids. . . . The upper rooms, which surpass all human works, I myself saw; for the passages through the corridors, and the windings through the courts, from their great variety, presented a thousand occasions of wonder, as I passed from a court to the rooms, and from the rooms to the halls, and to other corridors from the halls, and to other courts from the rooms."†

The mortuary-temples of the New Kingdom were built at the edge of the desert at Thebes on the west side of the river. The greater number have perished, but the few that remain bear witness to the splendour that was Egypt. One of the finest is the mortuary-temple of Rameses II, now known as the Ramesseum. Diodorus gives a fairly clear account of it, in which he says that in front there were "three great monolithic statues, the workmanship of Memmon; one of them, representing the King seated, surpassed in size all the statues of Egypt. The work was wonderful, not only for its size but for the art, and also for the excellence of the stone in which, huge though it was, there was neither crack nor blemish." The stone has disintegrated since then, and the whole upper part of the statue has fallen to ruin, so that now Shelley's "vast and trunkless legs of stone" is a more accurate description. Diodorus also speaks of the library attached to the temple, which he says was called "The Medicine of the Mind". This was at the back of the temple and formed one of the immense

---

* Zoser's temples at the Step-pyramid, though intermediate between the lattice shrine over a stela and the built temple at Meydum, appear to have been built without plan and to be entirely experimental. They are not derived from any known Egyptian source, and had no effect on the plan or arrangement of later mortuary- or god-temples.

† Herodotus, ii. 148.

number of buildings which, including the temple, were enclosed within a high brick wall.

The ritual in a mortuary-temple seems to have differed very little from the worship of any other deity. The statue was carried in procession on certain festival days, there were offerings of food and drink, of incense and flowers, of fire and water; prayers and chants were a necessary part of the ceremonies in god-temples and mortuary-temples alike; it was only in the number of priests and the size of the endowments that there was any real difference. This was particularly noticeable when there was a change of dynasty, for then the priests of the mortuary-temples of earlier date were apt to suffer.

Cenotaph shrines and temples were known in Egypt; of these the most splendid is the temple built by Setekhy I at Abydos. It is unique in plan for it is dedicated to more than one deity, having seven chapels in a row, each for the separate worship of a different god. The dedications of the seven chapels are, starting from the east, the King, Ptah, Harakhti, Amon, Osiris, Isis, and Horus. The central chapel, which is in the axis of the temple, is the chapel of Amon. The pillars of the two hypostyle courts are arranged in pairs so as to form aisles leading to each of the chapels. Six of the chapels end in a stone wall which has been carved to represent a wooden door, but the Osiris-chapel leads to an inner chamber behind the Amon-chapel and in the axis of the temple. A line drawn through the axis passes through the Amon-chapel, the inner chamber, the desert pylon, straight to the group of royal tombs three miles away across the desert. The tombs are of the kings of the i-st and ii-nd dynasties, whose names are in the list of kings inscribed on the wall of the temple. Clearly the temple was designed for the worship of the dead divine kings.

Rameses II built a small temple by the side of his father's; it was almost completely destroyed at the end of the nineteenth century by the local inhabitants who wanted stone to build their houses. The plan shows that there were three chapels, but the sculptures give no indication of the true purpose of this temple.*

In the axis of the Setekhy temple is an underground building, which was first published under the name of the Osireion. It was made for the celebration of the mysteries of Osiris, and so far is unique among all the surviving buildings of Egypt. It is clearly early, for the great blocks of which it is built are of the style of the Old Kingdom; the simplicity of the actual building also points to its being of that early date. The decoration was added by Setekhy I, who in that way laid claim to the building, but seeing how often a Pharaoh claimed the work of his predecessors by putting his name on it, this fact does not

* *Ancient Egypt* (1916), p. 121 *seq.*

carry much weight. It is the style of the building, the type of the masonry, the tooling of the stone, and not the name of a king, which date a building in Egypt.*

PYRAMIDS

The pyramid is so essentially Egyptian that the mere mention of the word calls up a mental picture of the great structures in their surroundings of desert sand. The form reproduces in stone a sand-heap where the sand has run down to the angle of rest.†

The earliest is the Step-pyramid at Saqqara (pl. xlv. 1). It stands on high ground six miles from the river and was therefore safe from seepage and flood. It dates to the time of King Zoser of the iii-rd dynasty, and like all his work is tentative in design. The architect was clearly trying to produce a form which he had not mastered entirely, and he was also unsure as to the method of building, for the pyramid is not only built in steps but the stones are laid in successive coatings at the sides. The blocks of stone are so small that at a distance the pyramid looks as though built of brick (pl. xli. 3). The smallness of the stones may perhaps account for the insurmountable difficulty of making a continuous outline to the pyramid, and as the architect was making the first experiment in a pyramidal building—not to speak of its being the largest building then ever erected—he seems to have taken "Safety first" as his motto, and built his pyramid in a series of seven steps, each step being flat-topped and forming a platform on which to build the next. The pyramid may be described as a series of seven separate buildings, one above another, decreasing in size to the top. Like all other pyramids the Step-pyramid is part of a group of buildings within an enclosing wall. Zoser's pyramid stands at one end of the enclosure, and the rest of the area is filled with a number of magnificent religious buildings, unsymmetrical, almost haphazard, in arrangement. There

---

* Though Sir Flinders Petrie was not altogether prepared to agree with me as to the site where the pyramid-kings were buried, he pointed out to me the place where another Osireion is perhaps waiting to be unearthed.

† Though it is merely a theory without any proof, I cannot help suggesting here that the early royal tombs were originally distinguished by having the sand, which had been excavated to make the underground chambers, piled over the top. The sites were thus marked by a row of little sandhills. This would account for the use of the three-hill hieroglyph as the determinative for a cemetery, and also for the sudden appearance of pyramids as soon as the Egyptian learnt how to build in stone. In the course of centuries the wind, aided by plunderers, would disperse the sandhills over the royal burial-places. This theory, however, is in flat contradiction of Petrie's con-clusions when he carefully studied the royal tombs. (*Royal Tombs*, i. 6.)

is also a vast series of underground chambers, whose use is conjectural; the space is too great for the ordinary offerings, even for a dead king, and the wall decorations suggest that religious ceremonies were performed in the darkness and silence of these underground halls.

Snefru of the iii-rd dynasty had two pyramids; one probably at Dahshur, the other at Meydum. The latter is the most magnificent of all the pyramids of Egypt (pl. xlvi). In the rosy glow of the dawn it towers majestically against the sky, the vastest and most impressive building that the hand of man has ever raised. Its very faults as a pyramid, for it is built in three tiers, enhance its massive grandeur. The Great Pyramid itself sinks into insignificance beside it; the temples with their solid stone pillars and roofs are like cardboard structures in comparison. In its lonely glory it is the finest of all the great architectural achievements of Egypt.

The Meydum pyramid is the connecting link between the stepped and the smooth outline of a pyramid. The architects of the time of Snefru had mastered the problem of the smooth sloping surface, but were still tied by the convention of steps, and combined the two forms together. It was not until the iv-th dynasty that a complete pyramid was evolved. By that time two other problems had also been solved, the expert quarrying of large blocks of stone and the expert handling of such blocks.*

Pyramids were built in groups (pl. xlvii). The group of nine pyramids at Gizeh is the most celebrated, partly because they have always been easily accessible to visitors to Egypt and partly because being a group they appear important. The building of them was very simple; the great blocks were brought up a ramp on rollers,† and with the help of rollers and levers were put in their allotted place. Each layer of blocks was built so as to form a level floor, and each block was keyed into the one below it. The sides of the pyramid were built as a series of small steps until the top of the pyramid was reached, when the casing was put on. The casing was composed of blocks, which were fitted into the steps and were then cut on the outside to the correct angle to form a smooth slope. In the Great Pyramid relieving arches were left above the so-called King's Chamber to resist the weight, and air-passages were also made communicating with the King's Chamber.‡ The ascending passage from the entrance to the King's Chamber is a marvel of ashlar masonry, and in marked contrast with the descending passage which is rough-hewn in the rock. It is, however, this descend-

---

* This was effected by the use of wooden levers and rollers, earth-ramps and well-directed human labour.

† Herodotus, ii. 124, 125.

‡ The names, *King's Chamber* and *Queen's Chamber*, are modern.

ing passage which has given rise to the idea that the pyramid was built for astronomical purposes. The pyramid is set square so that the sides face to the cardinal points of the compass, because like all great buildings in Egypt it is orientated by the Nile which here runs due north. The entrance of the pyramid is on the northern face, and therefore the passage looks also due north; but there is no proof that this was done for astronomical observations, or in honour of the Imperishable Stars which circle round the Pole.

Pyramids are invariably royal, and it would seem that every king of any importance from the iii-rd till the xii-th dynasty built his own pyramid. Many of these structures have perished by being torn to pieces, partly by tomb-robbers, but more frequently by lime-burners, who found it easier to prize the blocks out of a building than to quarry the limestone in the Mokattam hills. In this way the pyramid of Dad-ef-Rê has disappeared, so also has that of an unknown king at Gizeh; both of the iv-th dynasty. The pyramids of the Middle Kingdom have suffered more than the earlier buildings for they were built of mud-brick and merely cased with limestone; when the limestone was ripped off the mud-brick was the prey of the sebakh-digger, and thus the pyramids of the xi-th dynasty kings at Thebes have vanished.

The Hyksos occupation made great changes, and after their expulsion pyramids are no longer found in Egypt, and rock-cut tombs became the custom for the Pharaohs. But curiously enough, the royal pyramid was introduced with other Egyptian religious ideas into the south, and pyramids were built as royal tombs at Meroë as late as the time of Piankhy (xxiii-rd dynasty), though in Egypt itself there was nothing later than the false pyramids of Aahmes I of the xviii-th dynasty at Abydos.

The question as to the use of the early pyramids has never been satisfactorily answered. It is usually stated that they were burial-places; this may be true of the later ones, but there is no proof that this was their original purpose. But there is evidence that they were used for some special religious ceremonies in connection with the Divine King, though whether he was alive or dead is uncertain. It must also be remembered that many Pharaohs had both a burial-place and a cenotaph, and it is possible that the pyramid was the cenotaph. In the cenotaph-temple of Setekhy I at Abydos there is a list of kings to whom offerings are being made. This is usually regarded as an official list of the rulers of Egypt, but it appears more likely that it records only those kings who were buried or had cenotaphs in the holy ground of Osiris. Many a royal tomb and cenotaph still lie undiscovered under the sands of Abydos.

SCULPTURE AND PAINTING

Egyptian art, like the art of all countries, was subject to fluctuation. Great artists did not arise in every period and types of art changed, so that it becomes necessary to recognise the typical forms of art in each period. There were also in Egypt, as in all other countries, "the vulgar replicas made by second-class workmen", which have to be ignored, for it is only by the study of the best that a true knowledge of a national art can be obtained. The appreciation of the art of any country arises from an understanding of the ideals which the artist is trying to express. In Egypt, until the national art was contaminated by the attempt to copy slavishly the ideals of a foreign country, the three ideals were dignity, simplicity, and durability. Even at the worst period of its long history Egyptian art, as expressed in its sculpture, is always simple in line and in attitude, is never overloaded with detail, is never undignified, and always gives the impression of firmness and force. To the Egyptian, sculpture was an architectural decoration which had to conform to the conditions which governed architecture. The lines of the architecture being vertical and horizontal, the statues which decorated the building were made as vertical and horizontal as is consistent with the human form. All Egyptian art was in the service of religion; and as in these matters religion is conservative, the art retained to the end many primitive characters.

STATUES

The style of Egyptian art depends not only on the period but also on the material of the statues. Red granite, being very coarse in grain, never shows fine work, and is tolerable only for large figures to be seen at a distance. As a building stone it is admirable, but is not satisfactory for good artistic work. Black granite, on the other hand, has a fine grain, and much of the best work of the Middle and New Kingdoms was done in this stone. Basalt is another stone which gives good results for the sculptor. Green basalt was used in the xviii-th dynasty, and black basalt was one of the favourite stones in xxvi-th dynasty, when it was always very highly polished. Slate, diorite, obsidian, and schist were also used for statues, but the most usual stone and one from which the finest and most delicate results could be obtained was limestone, which is not only fine in grain but fairly soft. Alabaster was little used till the xviii-th dynasty, when the sculptors were beginning to prefer soft stones, but it is so soft that much slovenly work was done in this stone. Wood was sometimes used for life-sized statues, but as large timber was rare in Egypt, wood was more common for small figures.

Metal was rare in the early times but came increasingly into use. The great figures of Pepy I and his son are of copper; the king's figure stands 69½ inches high (approximately), and measures 40½ inches round the chest.* But usually metal was not used for large statues. Statuettes of deities cast in bronze are frequent from the xviii-th dynasty onwards, and were made in large quantities in the xxvi-th dynasty. At this late date they were mass-produced and are seldom of any artistic merit, though often archæologically interesting.

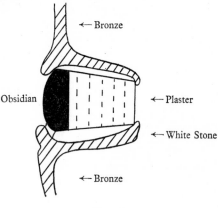

Fig. 18

Gold was not rare for statuettes, and for tiny figures of gods to be worn as amulets; these were cast in moulds, and much of the detail put in with a graving tool later. They are usually of delicate and beautiful workmanship. Large pieces in gold are rare, but this is perhaps due to the activities of tomb-robbers rather than to want of the metal. The head of the sacred falcon of Hierakonpolis (pl. lii. 2) is about four inches high; with the plumes, 14 inches. The plumes, which were detachable, were cast flat, but the head was cast by the *cire-perdue* process and finished with graving tools; the eye is a bar of obsidian, rounded and polished at both ends and fitted across the inside of the head; the brilliant black of the obsidian gives a remarkable resemblance to a bird's eyes.† Gold coffins and masks are recorded from early times; the tomb-robbers, who were tried in the xix-th

* As was common in most statues, the eyes were inset, being made of a different material. Great care had been taken that the eyes should be so firmly fixed that they could not fall out (fig. 18).

† The body of the falcon was of thin sheet copper nailed on a wooden core with copper or gold nails. The total weight of gold of head and plumes together is 199 ounces.

dynasty, acknowledged having found and carried off the gold coffin of an xi-th dynasty king and queen; Sinuhé (p. 212) was promised a "mummy-shell", *i.e.* an inner coffin, of gold if he returned to Egypt. But the only gold coffin yet found is of Tut-ankh-Amon of the xviii-th dynasty (Frontispiece). With it was a gold mask of the same beautiful workmanship. Another large piece of sculpture in gold found in the same tomb was the head of the sacred cow. Gold and silver masks have been found of the xxi-ist dynasty, when non-royal persons also were so honoured; and as late as the xxvi-th dynasty a rich man of no special rank could have a mask of sheet gold, with the wig of silver with gilded stripes, fastened on the bandages of his mummy.*

The amount of gold that was buried as the adornment of the dead was extravagantly great, and has been a temptation to tomb-robbers ever since there have been tombs in Egypt.

The prehistoric peoples of Egypt produced only small statuettes in ivory and pottery; in the i-st dynasty life-sized statues of stone appeared; of these the noble head of Narmer (pl. v) is the finest example. But it was not until architecture in stone was fully developed in the late iii-rd and early iv-th dynasties that fine sculpture is found. The iv-th dynasty is perhaps the best period for portrait statues and statuettes. The little ivory statuette of Khufu (pl. xlviii. 1), though less than five inches high, shows the ideals of Egyptian art as clearly as the life-sized statue of Khafra. Khufu sits enthroned, crowned with the Red Crown of the North and holding the emblems of sovereignty in his hands. Simple and dignified as is the attitude, the sculptor has conveyed into the face and figure something of that tremendous character who braved the wrath of the whole priesthood, who organised the labour of the entire country, and who produced that great monument which rightly ranks as one of the Seven Wonders of the World. In that small statuette the dominating personality of one of the greatest rulers of all time is clearly seen; it is Energy and Power personified. The great diorite statue of Khafra is entirely different (pl. xlviii. 2); the splendid strength, the majestic pose, the serenity of expression indicate the Divine King; it is a God rather than a Pharaoh who sits enthroned above his worshippers. In his statues of women the artist of the Old Kingdom had more freedom to express his ideals of beauty as well as of character. In the seated statue of Nefert (pl. l. 1), the figure of the lady, half-hidden, half-revealed under the diaphanous robe and cloak, shows the delight the artist took in the lovely curves of a woman's body.

* Petrie, *K.G.H.*, p. 19. The gilded or yellow-painted faces carved in wood, which are common on mummy-cases from the xii-th dynasty onwards, are imitations of the gold masks of royalty and personages of high rank.

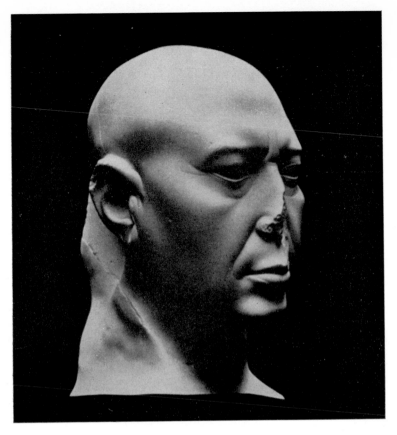

Berlin Museum

1. Head of unknown man

Photograph by Dr. S. Pritchard   *Fitzwilliam Museum*

2. Head. Painted plaster.   Ptolemaic

PLATE LXV

Painted portrait

PLATE LXVI

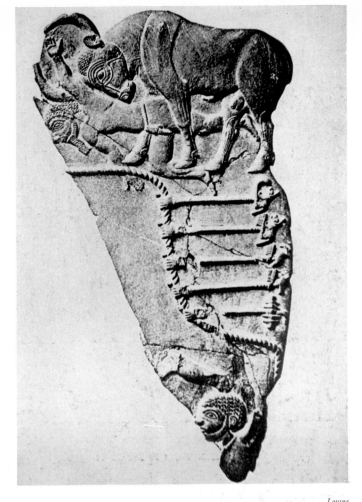

Louvre

1. Slate palette.   King as a buffalo destroying his enemy

Cairo Museum

2. Slate palette, commemorating
victory over Libya

Petrie Coll.

3. Great mace-head.   Pig-tailed
man dancing

PLATE LXVII

Slate palette of Narmer

PLATE LXVIII

1. Flock of cranes, dynasty v

2. Setekhy I offering to Isis.   Temple of Abydos

PLATE LXIX

1. Akhenaten and Nefert-yty worshipping

2. Akhenaten celebrating the Sed-festival

PLATE LXX

1. Sketch of a head

2. Sketch of Akhenaten   PLATE LXXI

Nefert-yty, dynasty xviii

PLATE LXXII

1. Slave market

Bologna Museum

2. Blind harper

Leyden Museum

PLATE LXXIII

Setekhy I.   Temple of Abydos.   Dynasty xix

Plate LXXIV

Rameses II. Temple of Abydos. Dynasty xix

Plate LXXV

Berlin Museum

1. Kha-em-het

2. Neuserre and Anubis

Cairo Museum

3. Procession of offerers.   Tomb of Zanefer

PLATE LXXVI

1. Bint-Anath, daughter of
Rameses II

2. Cleopatra the Great

PLATE LXXVII

Plate LXXVIII

Turin Museum

1. Comic scenes on a papyrus. Above,
musician; below, farm scenes

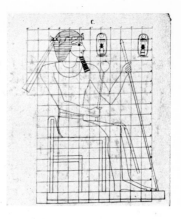

3. Canon of proportion,
dynasty xviii

Turin Museum

4. Sketch on papyrus.
Lady using lipstick

Turin Museum

2. Comic scenes. Above, administration of
justice; below, battles

Tomb of Ramose

5. Sketch.
Four foreigners

PLATE LXXIX

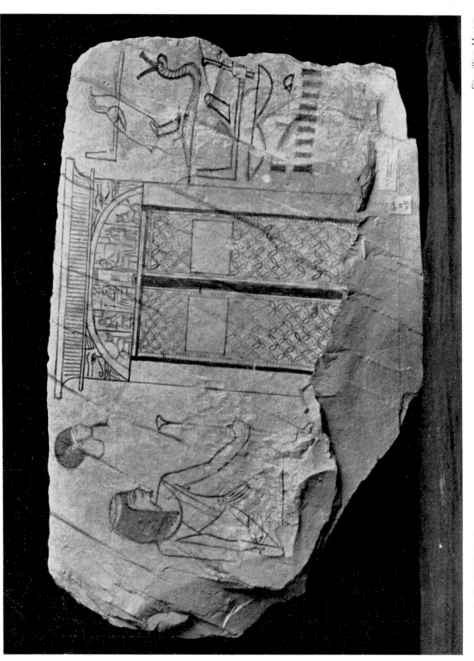

PLATE LXXX

The art of the iv-th and v-th dynasties shows the Egyptian artist at his best. Though he was hampered by conventions, especially in the pose of the figures, he never loses his sense of the dignity of the human beings (pls. xlix. 1, 2; l. 1). In the standing figures the man is moving forward towards the spectator; in the seated figures he is essentially the master of the house or estate (pl. lx); in the squatting figures he is the scribe engaged in the noblest of all occupations. In each figure there is a simple but convincing dignity, which is emphasised by the calm and serene expression of the face. Yet in every instance the face is obviously a portrait.

Another great period of Egyptian art was the Middle Kingdom. There is a life and vigour about the statues as great as in the Old Kingdom, though differently expressed (pls. liii; liv. 2, 3); this is seen in the figures of lesser folk as well as in the portraits of the Pharaohs. During this period the sculptors showed a preference for portraits of men in middle life, and there are many statues of men of at least fifty, which is in contrast with the Old Kingdom when everyone was young. The beautiful standing figure of Mentu-hotep III is remarkable for its firm and easy carriage and regal dignity. The magnificent black granite torso of Senusert I, battered though it is, shows that king as he was; the broad face, the level brows, the firm lips indicate the splendid character of the man. One of the masterpieces of ancient art belongs to the xii-th or beginning of the xiii-th dynasty. This is the head of a small statue carved in obsidian. The accuracy and delicacy of the modelling are superb, and the artist has clearly revelled in depicting the strong features and lined face of a great ruler (pl. lv).

The sphinx as a portrait statue becomes common in the Middle Kingdom. Though known before as a composite animal with a lion's body and a falcon's or a ram's head (pl. xxxiii. 4), it is only in this period that it first becomes a portrait of the monarch (pls. lvi; lvii; lviii). The lion's body is still retained, but the face is human with the lion's mane surrounding it. Rather later, the whole head is represented as human (pl. vii. 3), though in every instance the portrait is that of a king or queen.

The great influx of foreign elements into Egypt, due to the invasion of the Hyksos and afterwards to the conquests of Thothmes I and Thothmes III, brought changes in the art in the New Kingdom. Instead of the force and vitality of the earlier periods there was now an appreciation of gentleness and beauty which in the hands of a great sculptor produced fine work, but in lesser hands was apt to degenerate into weakness by the smoothing out of any harsh lines. As the power of Egypt was at its height at this time, it was a period of cheap luxury, and undistinguished but wealthy people desired to perpetuate their

G

personalities in stone. Statues and statuettes were produced by second-rate and even third-rate sculptors for the benefit of wealthy patrons who had no knowledge of art. Portrait statues therefore abound, some of them fine works of art (pl. liv. 4), but the greater number of interest for archæological reasons only. At all periods the Egyptian artist excelled in portraiture, and to ensure an exact likeness death-masks were often made (pl. liv. 5).

The finest of all the statues of the New Kingdom is the green basalt figure of Thothmes III (pl. lix. 1). It is clearly a likeness, for the big nose was a family characteristic, and the mouth is like that of the portraits of his sister Hatshepsut. In spite of the formality of the raised bands to represent the eyebrows as well as the streak of paint round the eyes, the face is full of expression, and it is possible to see in that expression the reason why the great conqueror was so much beloved by his people.

The art of Tell el Amarna is better known than that of any other period of Egyptian history. This is partly due to the fact that it is an episode complete in itself, without previous development and without after-effect; it can therefore be studied in its entirety and without reference to anything beyond. The whole of that artistic period lasted something under twenty years; it produced one great artistic genius, the sculptor of the head of Nefert-yty,* but the general level of Tell el Amarna art is not high. There is no doubt that Akhenaten attempted to introduce a new type of art which the Egyptian artist could not grasp, and on the death of the royal patron, who was at the same time a tyrant in the realm of art, the artist could return thankfully to the conventions he understood and in which he could produce good work.

As Akhenaten rewarded his officials with sculptured tombs and with portraits of himself, besides having his temples and palaces at Tell el Amarna decorated elaborately, the number of artists employed must have been considerable. Yet it is remarkable how little really first-rate work was produced. The best is the sculpture in the round, but the ungainly appearance of Akhenaten himself makes even a good statue of him unpleasing, though possibly truthful (pl. lxi). The beauty of Nefert-yty, however, must have been an inspiration to the royal artist, who seems never to have tired of reproducing it. The complete destruction of Akhenaten's city has resulted in the mutilation of many

* This celebrated head is part of a composite statue. The figure may have been of some other material so carved that the head would be slipped into place. The proof that the head belongs to a composite statue lies in the way that the shoulders are cut, and from the fact that the eyes were inlaid. (Pieces of a composite statue from Tell el Amarna are in the Petrie Collection at University College, London.)

of the figures of her, but the heads which have survived show what she was like.

The art of Egypt never recovered completely from the fatal habit introduced by Akhenaten of copying the ideals of another nation. This, coupled with the slow but steady decline of the whole civilisation, resulted in an equally steady decline in artistic work. The statues of the xix-th dynasty are, with two notable exceptions, inferior to those of the xviii-th, and the xx-th dynasty falls lower still. The two exceptions are statues, both of Rameses II. The first shows him as the Pharaoh, the great Divine King, enthroned, crowned, and holding the emblems of sovereignty (pl. lxii). Another statue is of the king offering to a god. Here he is the human suppliant; the attitude shows that he has run forward and thrown himself on his knees in a passion of adoration. The sculptor has caught the moment when the forward movement is just arrested, when the whole of the youthful body is still quivering with rapid motion.

The portrait of Mer-en-Ptah, Rameses' son and successor, is clearly a likeness, and is of interest as showing the degeneration of the artist's observation and the consequent deterioration of his work (pl. lix. 2). One sign of the decadence of art in Egypt is the want of observation in the delineation of the ear. Towards the close of the great periods of art in Egypt the sculptors invariably exaggerated the size of the ears, making them about twice the natural size. This defect is very marked at the end of the xii-th dynasty, under Akhenaten at the end of the xviii-th dynasty, and again in the xix-th dynasty.

The statues of the Late Period became increasingly stylised, and even the portraiture can hardly be called truthful. In more than one instance the sculptor cared so little for his own work that he has cut the inscription upon the figure itself; a piece of barbarism otherwise found only among the brutal Assyrians. The light, however, was not completely extinguished, for the gold masks found on the mummies of King Psusennes and the captain of his archer-guard show that much of the old splendid tradition still remained among the workers in metal, though it was rapidly decaying among the sculptors in stone.

In the xxv-th dynasty there was a sudden rise in Egyptian art, due perhaps to Ethiopian influence. The sleek style with smoothed surfaces and no angles became outmoded; the artist was feeling for a means of expressing what he felt to be the truth. The alabaster statue of Queen Amenardus is a notable example, though the sculptor was not altogether successful in the modelling of the figure; there are faults also in the modelling of the face. But in spite of all these faults, the sculptor has managed to convey much of the beauty and charm of the royal lady. The portraits of the men of this period are remarkable. The fine head of Mentu-em-hat shows the noble governor of Thebes, who restored some of the splendour of that ruined city after its sack by the ruthless Assyrians. Another fine head is that of Taharka, the Ethiopian King of Egypt; it is in black granite, an appropriate colour in which to represent a negro. To this period belongs probably the remarkable head of an unknown man (pl. lxv. 1). But for the almost complete ruin of the country by the Assyrians, it would seem that Egyptian art was about to enjoy another and magnificent flowering period, but the disaster had been too great for any recrudescence to be possible.

The artists of the xxvi-th dynasty, having lost the means and desire to express themselves, were reduced to copying the fine work of earlier times. The sculpture of the Old Kingdom was the favourite, and much archaistic work was produced. The technique is good, but there is no vitality, no spontaneity, no real observation; it is all flat and expressionless. Life-sized statues are rare at this period; but small bronze statuettes, chiefly of deities, are common. Few of these are of any merit artistically, as they are entirely conventional. The stone statues show the same conventions as the bronze; they are often of black basalt, polished to an almost mirror-like brilliance. All the small details of ornaments or clothing are worked with meticulous care, the sculptor trying to cover up bad work by attention to unimportant detail. It is the work of this period that is so often regarded by visitors to Egyptian collections as "typically Egyptian", whereas it is typical of one period only, and that not the best. There is much delicate and careful work on statues and statuettes, but there is no real feeling in the modelling of the figures or faces. The best work of the period, from the end of the New Kingdom till the Romans destroyed the last remains of the indigenous art of Egypt, was in the portrait coffins.

As the Ptolemies were Greek in origin there was some attempt at the beginning of the period to imitate Greek art, with the usual result of copying. The attempt to reconstitute Egyptian art on Greek lines was foredoomed to failure, and the Egyptians reverted to their own conventions. Unfortunately they not only retained the faults of those conventions but exaggerated them. But even at its worst it is still possible to trace the ideals of the splendid periods; for Egyptian art never degenerated into the pretty-pretty, it was always dignified, simple, and, when not a copy of another ideal, it was sincere.

PORTRAIT COFFINS

The portrait coffins form an interesting chapter in the history of Egyptian art. The earliest coffins are merely plain boxes, but in the xii-th dynasty, when so many new ideas came in (due to continuous intercourse with foreign countries), the coffin was carved in the semblance of a mummy with the face exposed. It is possible that this took the place of the portrait statue, for in many cases there is an attempt—not always successful—to represent the features of the dead. This fashion increased in popularity as time went on, and in the xviii-th dynasty royalty as well as lesser folk had their portraits carved in wood, and the face was affixed to the mummy-shaped coffin when the time came (see also pl. xxix. 2 for a statuette with face pegged on). It would seem that the undertakers kept types of coffins in stock to which the portrait face could be fastened. The face was painted to represent life, and often eyes of white limestone and black obsidian were inserted, as in so many statues (pls. xxviii. 1, 4; li; liv. 3; lxxxv. 3; fig. 18). When carefully fixed to the coffin and the junction masked with stucco and paint, the whole appears as if carved in one piece. Many of these faces were carved by good artists, and the different characters are often carefully represented (pls. xxvii; xxviii). In the xxvi-th dynasty wood became too expensive for ordinary people, and a cheaper material was used for the inner coffin. This was the material now called *cartonnage*, which consists of stout canvas stiffened with plaster or stucco, moulded into shape while still pliable, and then painted. With these materials it was almost impossible to get a real portrait, in spite of many a gallant attempt in that direction. Under Greek influence in the Ptolemaic period the face was modelled in plaster and was held in place by bandages round the head of the mummy. This method developed into modelling the whole of the upper part of the body in plaster, sometimes with the bandaging imitated in plaster, sometimes with the head and shoulders free. This gave the artist scope to produce a fine portrait of the dead person (pl. lxv. 2).

During the Roman occupation there was a new development; instead of the modelled face it became the custom (chiefly in the Fayum) to have the face painted in panel and inserted in the bandages, as had been done with the plaster faces (pl. lxvi). These painted panels which are the earliest painted portraits in the world, are thus the direct descendants of the carved wooden portrait coffins. The style of the painting and the types of the faces show that these portraits are not truly Egyptian, though many of the originals may have had Egyptian blood. The artistic feeling, the technique, the brushwork, and the materials are not only un-Egyptian, but the style is obviously the precursor of European art. The medium used was beeswax, laid on with a brush, and the artists were accustomed to indicate light and shade. The range of time in which these portraits were painted was short, covering not more than 150 years, from about A.D. 100 to A.D. 250. Though the reason for the use of these portraits was certainly Egyptian, and the portraits themselves were the direct descendants of the portrait coffins, the art itself was foreign and died out leaving no trace.

RELIEF SCULPTURE

One of the problems of relief sculpture is the same as in drawing, which is how to represent a solid object on a plane surface. When there is no knowledge of foreshortening, this problem is insoluble and a compromise has to be effected. Animals are easily drawn in, side-view, but the real difficulty arises in portraying a human being. The primitive artist had also to satisfy his clients that a man had two arms, two reasonably sized feet, and that the nose projected from the face. He therefore represented the man as walking, the legs being in

Fig. 19

profile so as to show them and the feet as well; the body was drawn as seen from the front, which gave a view of both arms; the head was in profile, but in order to overcome the difficulty of the fore-shortened eye, it was drawn as if from the front.★ In ancient Egypt all art was religious and consequently was intensely conservative. The primitive conventions had to remain in all temples and tomb-chapels, though it is clear that the artists were capable of drawing the human figure and face as freely as any artist of any period had not priestly rigidity forbidden any change. For every sculptor and every draughtsman could delineate the goddess Hathor, whose face was never drawn in profile,

★ In Greece the front-view eye in a profile face is found till the time of the Parthenon sculptures. In Crete it was common practice, but no Egyptian artists ever sank to the level of putting the eye in the middle of the cheek, as in the Cretan painting of a fisherman.

and could draw the hieroglyphic sign *hr* (figs. 9, 19), which is a face seen from the front. In ancient Egypt art moved in the fetters of religion and never broke free. But in spite of his limitations the Egyptian artist achieved some of the masterpieces of the world. His portrait sculpture has never been surpassed, and in the decorative effect of his bas-reliefs there are few, if any, examples from other countries which can compare with his for beauty and harmony of design and for appropriateness for the spaces and purposes which they were intended to fulfil.

The earliest relief sculpture is found on the sculptured stone mace-heads and slate palettes, which belong to the very dawn of history, for the latest of them dates to the i-st dynasty (pls. lxvii; lxviii). Most of the scenes record historical events, though a few may be religious or even purely ornamental. The style shows that many of the artistic conventions of the later periods were already fixed; the profile face, front-view torso, and profile legs and feet are invariable, as is also the front-view eye. The technique is skilful, and indicates a long tradition of such sculpture. One of the earliest examples is the palette which depicts a bull trampling on a human enemy (pl. lxvii. 1). The outlines are rounded and the surfaces of the figures modelled, the muscles being strongly indicated. The helpless pose of the man's hand is worth noting, and the menacing attitude of the bull, as it lowers its head preparatory to goring its victim, is full of careful observation. The conventionalised form of the same scene on the palette of Narmer (pl. lxviii. 1) shows that the art of that early time was not static. The mace-heads, three in number, are of the shape of the Gerzean maces though enormously exaggerated in size. Two are carved with representations of the most important festival, the Sed-heb; the third depicts the Pharaoh cutting the dyke on the festival of High Nile.

Reliefs are rare in the i-st and ii-nd dynasties, but in the iii-rd dynasty the reliefs in the underground chambers of the Step-pyramid are distinguished by their delicacy of workmanship and vividness of treatment. They are among the finest examples of Egyptian art. Throughout the Old Kingdom relief sculpture was the chief decoration of the walls of tomb-chapels (pl. lxix. 1). The tomb-chapels of Saqqara have the finest work, which is not surprising, for it was the burial-place for the nobles of Memphis whose god was Ptah, the god of Art. In many of the scenes the figures are full of action, and the energetic movement depicted in the reliefs is in strong contrast with the calm dignity of the statues.

Hollow or sunk relief began in the Old Kingdom as a cheaper form of decoration than the bas-relief. In hollow relief the background is not touched, the figures being sunk below the surface; this is in contradistinction to the bas-relief, where the background is removed leaving the figures standing higher than the ground. In both methods the figures are carefully modelled, but the amount of labour saved by leaving the background untouched was considerable.

In the Middle Kingdom hollow relief became increasingly popular. The figure of Senusert in the running dance shows what could be done in this medium. The work is strong and virile, but without the delicate beauty of technique seen in the low reliefs of the earlier period. As the centre of civilisation had moved from Memphis to Thebes, the worship of the god of Art was not so ardent as it had been in the Old Kingdom. The Theban god and his votaries were more interested in material things than in the arts, and this outlook on life affects the expression of ideas in art. This is seen in the reliefs more than in the statues in the round. Very little relief sculpture of this period has survived, as the temples were ruthlessly destroyed by the Hyksos, and the tomb-chapels of the nobles were not so common nor so highly decorated as in the Old Kingdom.

With the expulsion of the Hyksos there arose a new desire for decoration of temples and tombs. Like the statues the reliefs show an increase of beauty and grace with a loss of vitality and strength (pl. lxxvi. 1). Hatshepsut's temple at Deir el Bahri is richly decorated with reliefs, all of which are worth studying. Conventional though they are, the grouping of the figures, the gracefulness of the drawing, and the harmoniousness of the whole effect show that the artists of the xviii-th dynasty were inspired with a true love of beauty. The splendid temples of Karnak and Luxor, and the smaller temples built by the xviii-th dynasty Pharaohs, show the same feeling for beauty of design. Egypt was recovering from the effect of the Hyksos, and if left alone might have produced another magnificent blossoming time. But disaster fell upon the promise of May and withered the blossom while still in bud. Akhenaten started to reform the art as well as the religion; everything had to be new, everything had to be different. All old ideals and methods were cast aside with contempt, and the New Art was exalted. "The natural but ungainly attitudes, the flourishing ribands, the heavy collars and kilts, the ungraceful realism of the figures, the loss of all expression and detail of structure—all these show the death of a permanent art in the fever of novelty and vociferation."* The result was terrible in the relief sculpture (pls. lxx. 1; lxxii), of which there are but few examples that can be regarded without a shudder, but those few are among the finest in the range of Egyptian art (pls. lxxi. 1; lxxiii. 1, 2).

* Petrie, *Arts and Crafts*, p. 53.

Though Akhenaten's artistic "reforms" had as little effect in altering the art of Egypt as his religious reforms on the Egyptian religion, their real effect was the killing of all individuality in the art. Copying became the rule and not the exception, and in the xix-th dynasty technique was the end and aim of all sculptors. One of the outstanding examples of this period is the portrait of Bint-Anath, daughter of Rameses II (pl. lxxvii. 1); though for sheer beauty of technique nothing can equal the soulless sculptures of the temple of Setekhy I at Abydos (pls. lxix. 2; lxxiv). The faultless tool-work is a delight to the craftsman's eye, but the conventional scenes and the stylised figures show that there was no life in the art. Akhenaten had much to answer for, but one of his worst crimes was the slaughter of Egyptian art.

From this time onwards the relief sculptures in the temples were usually conventional religious scenes (pl. lxxv) and figures of gods, with the exception of battle scenes in the temples of Rameses II and Rameses III. Rameses III also struck out a new line in his temple at Medinet Habu by recording scenes of the chase. In the scene of hunting wild cattle in the marshes the sculptor has provided a background; the wounded bull is seen crashing through the reeds, while a rampart of flowering seeds is seen beyond the dead bull. This is so long after the time of Akhenaten that it cannot be a reminiscence of the Tell el Amarna art, but must be due to the foreign influence brought in by the captives taken in the great battle against the Sea Peoples.

In the xxvi-th dynasty there is the same deliberate copying of ancient models as is seen in the statues. The favourite scene in tomb sculpture is a procession of bearers of offerings; this often has rather a charming effect if not criticised too closely. But if compared with the same scenes in the tombs of the Old Kingdom, which served as the models for the xxvi-th dynasty artists, the degeneration of style is seen at once. But taken as a whole the work of the xxvi-th dynasty is careful and often pleasing (pl. lxxvi. 3).

The Ptolemies showed the boastfulness of their characters in the sculptures which decorated the outside of their temples. Across the pylons sprawl gigantic figures representing the king smiting his enemy (pl. xl. 2), or being cordially welcomed by the gods. Ptolemaic relief sculpture is easily recognised; the faces are extremely fat, with lumpy cheeks; the women's figures are absurdly narrow, with every curve of the body exaggerated; the hands are coarsely formed, all the fingers being of the same width, and both thumbs on the same side as the spectator; the feet are too large and are only recognisable as feet from their position at the end of the legs; all the muscles of the body are indicated as rounded lumps. The details of the ornaments and the hair is elaborately represented, but this does not hide the essential badness of the work (pl. lxxvii. 2).

PAINTING

Painting in Egypt was always a cheap substitute for relief sculpture, and was never an art in itself. All sculpture, whether in relief or in the round, was painted in flat colour without any attempt at shading, the shadows being given by the modelled surface under the coat of paint. When painting was applied to a flat surface, the same method was used, so that Egyptian painting is merely outlines filled in with a flat tint; any details are painted over this in lines of a darker or a different colour.

The earliest example of Egyptian painting is the painted tomb at Hierakonpolis,* which dates to the late prehistoric period. Though extremely interesting archæologically it is so primitive as hardly to be reckoned as Art. It is mentioned here only as the earliest known example of painting in Egypt, and therefore probably the earliest in that cradle of civilisation, the eastern Mediterranean.

No paintings of the first two dynasties have survived, but in the iii-rd dynasty the tomb of Nefer-maot has revealed what the Egyptian artist could do with the very limited means at his disposal. The flock of geese is painted in natural colours; and though the technique is of the simplest, merely outline filled with colour and with details lined in, the whole scene is most effective. The artist was far beyond his time in attempting to indicate a background by the little tufts of herbage between the birds. Another tomb-chapel of the same period in which paintings still exist is that of Ra-hesy, but as these represent various household objects, chiefly of wood, the interest is archæological only. Throughout the Old Kingdom painting was used in the tomb-chapels, but only for the less important figures or scenes; the colour is often pleasing, but they are not interesting artistically.

In the Middle Kingdom, there are no fine examples of painting, but a great deal of work survives in the tomb-chapels of the princes of Menat-Khufu (Beni Hasan). These were the work of provincial artists, whose attainments cannot compare with the artists of Memphis. Their attempts to represent a body in profile were disastrous, but they excelled in painting gaily coloured and patterned dresses. Painting in this period was beginning to take the place of relief sculpture, per-haps because of its cheapness, for the saving of time and labour was very great.

* Quibell and Green, *Hierakonpolis*, ii. pls. lxxv–lxxix.

In the xviii-th dynasty painting had become the favourite method
of decoration. That great series of tomb-chapels of nobles and officials
at Thebes was decorated entirely with paintings. Amonhotep II
began the fashion of painting the walls of his tomb, a fashion which
continued till the end of the xx-th dynasty. Amonhotep's decoration
was severely simple, and consisted in painting the walls the colour of
papyrus inscribed with religious texts in dark green. Later Pharaohs
improved on this, and religious scenes were introduced, giving opportunities to the artist to use the most glowing colours on his palette.
The tomb of Setekhy I is the finest example of this kind of decoration,
for it sets out with great wealth of detail the whole journey of the Sun
through the World of Night and Thick Darkness. Some of the paintings in the Theban tombs show a freedom of drawing and a charm of
composition that make them outstanding examples of Egyptian art.

At Tell el Amarna, as might be expected, there was a complete
alteration in the art of painting, and here Akhenaten's influence was
for good. The painters were able to absorb the new ideas in a way
that the sculptors could not, and some of the results are amazing.
Animals in rapid motion, flowers painted for their beauty and not as
mere accessories to figures, backgrounds of plants, all these were freely
used to beautify every part of the temples and palaces of Akhenaten's
city (pl. lxxviii). An outstanding piece of painting from Tell el
Amarna is the scene of two little princesses sitting at their mother's
feet. In this the artist has tried to overcome the then insuperable
difficulty of representing a rounded object on a flat surface, a three-
dimensional object on a two-dimensional plane. He has done this by
putting a shadow in darker paint along the backs of the figures and a
high light on the legs. Such an innovation is not seen again in Egypt
till the Greeks introduced their own conception of art.

In the Late Period painting was greatly used for small wooden
stelæ, usually representing a worshipper making offerings to some
deity or to an ancestor. Many of these are beautiful examples of
colour though the arrangement and drawing are extremely formal.
Specially noticeable in many cases is the winged sun at the top of the
stela, the lovely wings drooping protectively over the figures below.
The only example known of the drawing of a landscape is of this period.
It commemorates a lady called Zed-Amon-auf-ankh, and shows her
tomb at the edge of the desert, with date-palms and a sycamore in the
foreground and the cliffs of the valley rising behind the tomb. A
mourner, drawn much too large, is introduced to lend a touch of grief
to what would otherwise have been a scene meaningless to Egyptian
eyes.

From the xviii-th dynasty onwards, but more numerous in the Late

Period than at any other, are the paintings on papyrus (pls. xxii; xxiii). These are always illustrations of religious subjects; the favourite is perhaps the weighing of the heart before the dead person is admitted into the Kingdom of Osiris. These illustrations, chiefly as vignettes in the copies of the Book of the Dead, are often exquisitely painted, and show the most delicate craftsmanship, but being for religious purposes they are entirely conventional in subject and treatment.

Greek art, which came into Egypt with Greek trade, had little effect at first on the indigenous art of Egypt. When it did take effect it was on the sculpture, for under the Ptolemies painting as painting is unknown. It must have existed but none has survived, and for several centuries there is a complete blank. It was not until the Romans had occupied the country for more than a hundred years that painting became common again. Even then it was only in one part of the country, the Fayum, that tract of land where foreign mercenaries had been settled by the Ptolemaic rulers. These paintings are a combination of Egyptian and Greek ideas, for they were for the use of the dead and took the place of the portrait coffins of the earlier Egyptians (pl. lxvi), but they are Greek in style, feeling, and probably in technique.*

Under the Romans the indigenous art of Egypt appears to have died out completely, as did her ancient religion and ancient writing. The striving after foreign artistic ideals and methods was fatal, for it forced the artist to copy instead of creating. When, however, the new religion of Christianity was introduced, a religion which appealed at once to the Egyptian mind, a new type of art sprang up, so nearly allied to the ancient as to raise the question whether it was really new or actually an ancient art revived. The Coptic artist had learned by this time— perhaps from a foreign portrait painter—to draw the whole human figure as seen from the front, and he made full use of his new-found ability. But the beautiful austere figures, the firm line and the general aspect, whether of single figures or of groups, bear too close a resemblance to the ancient work to be disregarded. That these figures resemble Byzantine art, which flourished at a considerably later date, suggests very strongly that the Byzantine artists drew their inspiration from Egypt. Byzantine art was introduced into Europe, and throughout the centuries exercised great influence on European art, but like so many of the arts it appears to have taken its rise in the Valley of the Nile.

The canon of proportion (pl. lxxix. 3) shows the strict rules which governed the religious art of Egypt, but the sketches on papyrus

* It is becoming the fashion to speak of these paintings as "Alexandrian" in order to emphasise their probable origin. But as the great majority have been found in the Fayum the proper appellation of them is Fayumi.

(pl. lxxix. 1, 2, 4) and on limestone (pls. lxxxi. 1; lxxxii. 1, 4) show the artists in lighter mood. The architect's drawing of a door (pl. lxxx) is interesting as having with it enlarged drawings of the detail. The little sketches of daily life (pls. lxxxi. 2; lxxxii. 2, 3) and the finely differentiated heads of the four foreigners (pl. lxxix. 5) are more vivid examples of the artist's capacity than many of the more conventional drawings.

HANDICRAFTS

The Egyptians were supreme in metal-working, whether for large or small objects. The first metal to be used was copper, which was imported as early as the Badarian period.★ Such copper was pure, without any intentional admixture of any kind, for the mixed metal, bronze, was not known till a comparatively late date. In the xviii-th dynasty tin was used for hardening copper, thus making bronze; the source of the tin is not known.

In more than one scene in the tomb-chapels of the Old Kingdom the working of copper is shown. It was melted in a crucible over a fire which was kept at a fierce heat by men with blowpipes made of reed tipped with clay. The explanatory words above the picture are: "Causing metal to swim." After the molten metal had been poured out and had cooled sufficiently, it was beaten out with smooth stones into sheets of the required thickness, and then cut to shape. But the Egyptians were also expert casters, casting either solid or by the waste-wax (*cire-perdue*) method. This process was known as early as the ii-nd dynasty, when it was used for casting double spouts to fix on bowls of beaten copper. Ewers and basins of hammered copper were made in the i-st dynasty, and were at first for the use of the Pharaoh only. In the iii-rd dynasty they are recorded as belonging to great nobles; lesser people used pottery for their ablutions. Copper was little used for personal adornment except in the shape of beads, and even then it was covered with a thin sheet of gold to hide the baser metal. All tools were cast solid, and the open moulds for such casting are found in town sites. The large bronze doors which figure so extensively in descriptions of temples in the xviii-th dynasty were cast.

In the realm of Art, the great copper statue of Pepy I of the vi-th dynasty (pl. lii. 1) shows that the Egyptian artists were as much at home in metal-work as in stone. The groups consist of the standing figure of the king, followed by his son; the king's figure is life-size (the height of the figure is 5ft. 9½in.). In both figures the body and

★ See p. 2 for the earliest known smelting furnace.

limbs were made by hammering sheets of copper over a wooden core, but the heads were cast by the *cire-perdue* process. The figure of the king was finished with a crown of some other material, probably gold, held in position by plaster; the loin-cloth was also probably of gold for on the retaining plaster are traces of sheet gold. The eyes of both figures are of stone, held in place by plaster (fig. 18). For the gold falcon of Hierakonpolis see p. 165.

Small copper and bronze statuettes are found at all periods, but are most common after the xviii-th dynasty, when they were always of bronze. They vary greatly in artistic merit, especially those of Osiris, which in the Late Period often degenerate to such an extent as to be almost unrecognisable. Portrait statuettes in bronze are rare; the over-whelming majority of these figures represent deities. Some are cast solid, but to save metal the greater number were cast by the *cire-perdue* process. It is in these small figures that the skill of the craftsman can be studied. In many instances the thickness of the metal is about the thickness of a sheet of good notepaper; and it is remarkable that there is no visible support for the core over which the wax was originally spread, nor is there any sign of the escape hole for the molten wax; and there are no vent holes. In the xviii-th dynasty a form of decora-tion was used on some of the bronze statuettes, particularly on the figures of Amon, which suggests that it was a Theban art. This was to hammer fine gold wire into lines which had been made for the purpose when casting; the necklace, the folds of the loin-cloth, bracelets, and other small details were thus emphasised. The effect is very delicate and beautiful. The *cire-perdue* process continued in use until Roman times (pl. lxxxv. 4, 5).

The finest Egyptian metal-work was in gold. No country ancient or modern (with the possible exception of the Renaissance jewellers of Italy) ever reached the Egyptian standard of beauty of design or delicacy of craftsmanship. Jewellers' work began when the dynastic people took possession of the Nile Valley. The four bracelets from the tomb of King Zer are the first to show the skill of the Egyptian jeweller; they are thus of the utmost importance in the history of jewellery and the working of gold. The fastening of the rosette bracelet is of the "hook-and-eye" type. Each end of the bracelet is formed of gold wire twisted together with the thick hair of a cow's tail; at one end is a gold ball made by beating hollow, "leaving about a quarter open; inside it a hook of gold wire is soldered in without leaving the smallest trace of solder visible".★ At the other end the twist of gold wire is turned back on itself and lashed tight to form the

★ Petrie, *Arts and Crafts*, p. 86.

loop. The rosette was made by pressing thick sheet gold into a mould to make the upper half; the lower half was possibly also pressed into a plain mould, then the two halves were soldered together with the same skill that is seen in the soldering of the hook. The date of these bracelets is, at the lowest computation, 3500 B.C., but may well be considerably earlier.

The next great period for gold work is the xii-th dynasty, when the finds at Dahshur and Lahun show what the royal jewellery of that splendid period was like.

The Dahshur jewellery consisted of three pectorals, two crowns, bracelets with inlaid clasps, belts of gold cowries and lion-heads, bead necklaces, and a great number of small objects. The pectorals show the most consummate craftsmanship; each one is different in design as they belong to different periods, and are only alike in the fact that each has as the central motif the name of the Pharaoh in whose reign it was made. The pectoral, which is second in date, is of the time of Senusert III and has a peculiarly interesting design. It is made, like the two others, of a thick plate of gold on which the design has been cut out; the design has been so arranged that though at first sight it appears to have greatly weakened the ornament, the points of contact of the various parts make it thoroughly strong; the bending lotus, for example, is attached to the wing of the vulture and the tail of the lion. When the plate of gold had been cut out, a fine gold wire was soldered round every outline and round every detail, thus leaving a series of hollows which were filled up with lapis lazuli, turquoise, and carnelian cut to fit. The whole surface was then gone over with a burnisher so that the gold wire should key the minute stones firmly into their places. The effect when finished is that of cloisonné enamel. The back of the ornament is engraved with the same design as the front. The two crowns (pl. lxxxiv. 1, 2) are entirely different from one another in design; the most beautiful is made to resemble a wreath of forget-me-nots. This was done by making small five-petalled flowers of turquoise with a tiny centre of red carnelian; the flowers are threaded on gold wires which are caught at intervals by an ornament of four lotus flowers set like a cross. The numerous little ornaments, the bracelet clasps and necklace terminals are made in the same way as the pectorals and give the same effect of cloisonné enamel.

The Lahun jewellery is of the same type, with the exception of the crown (pl. lxxxiv. 3). This is a circular band of gold to fit round the head, ornamented at intervals with rosettes inlaid with coloured stones like the Dahshur pectorals. At the back is a lotus in gold, from which spring two gold feathers, the emblem of Amon; three long streamers hang down, one on each side of the face and one at the back. The interesting part of the workmanship, apart from the beauty of the object itself, is that the crown takes to pieces and could be packed into a small compass for travelling. The streamers are merely hooked on, the feathers and the lotus fit into sockets and can be slipped out; the rosettes also can be slipped out, and the band round the head can be unhooked and laid out flat. The rest of the jewellery was in beauty and workmanship equal to the royal find at Dahshur (pl. lxxxiii).

A style of jewellery characteristic of the xii-th dynasty is of small flat pieces of gold mixed with spirals in gold wire to form a design. The spiral, round or hooked, was at this period a favourite motif for decorating small objects, especially scarabs, where some of the spiral designs are of great beauty.

Granulated gold was another form of decoration which is found at this time. It consists of soldering minute globules of gold in a pattern on the surface of sheet gold, the sheet gold having been previously cut to the desired shape. It seems to have been introduced into Egypt during the xii-th dynasty, and though it is found at later periods, notably in the tomb of Tut-ankh-Amon, the later work is comparatively coarse. The Etruscans at a very much later date practised the same technique. In really good work, such as is found in the xii-th dynasty, the globules of gold are so small and so evenly applied that the decoration looks like a frosted surface. Inlaying in cloisons also remained in use till the end of the New Kingdom; the finest examples after the xii-th dynasty are in the tomb of Tut-ankh-Amon.

Queen Aah-hotep of the xvii-th dynasty possessed, among other lovely pieces of the jeweller's craft, a "cuff-bracelet". This is a plain band of gold decorated with raised figures in gold on a background of dark blue. At first sight the background looks like enamel, but it is actually composed of minute pieces of lapis lazuli cut to fit into the intricacies of the elaborate design. The New Kingdom, however, does not exhibit the same delicacy of workmanship as the earlier work. All the same "there is shown by the Theban jewellers excellent skill in execution, a marked decorative sense, and much inventiveness in symbolical device. Their craft included that of the lapidary and the glass-cutter, inlaying, chasing, repoussé work, embossing, twisted gold-wire filigree-work, and granulated gold work".*

The mass of gold found in the tomb of Tut-ankh-Amon disclosed every variety of jewellers' work. The personal ornaments of the king, his rings and bracelets, call for little remark as they are not as fine as those of the xii-th dynasty, and much of the work appears to have been made for the display of wealth. But the most remarkable

* Carter, *Tomb of Tutankhamen*, iii. 71.

object in the tomb is the gold and jewelled coffin (Frontispiece). It is one of the world's masterpieces; for the proportions are so satisfying, the design which mingles sacred symbols with enfolding wings is so suitable, the colouring of the gold and stones is so enchanting and the craftsmanship so perfect, that it remains the most exquisite piece of Egyptian work. The lid of the coffin, which is the highly decorated part, was fastened to the lower part by eight gold tenons held in place by gold pins. The lid is mummiform, the face carved in the likeness of the young king. The gold mask which covered the face of the mummy is also carved in the king's likeness, and is inlaid with the same exquisite result; but being smaller it is not so striking as the coffin. An interesting point about some of the gold work in the tomb is that the jewellers of the period used "a brilliant scarlet-tinted gold produced by a method which is at present unknown".★ When used with bright yellow granulated gold and black resin, the effect is unusual but very fine.

The jewellery of the xix-th dynasty is in general merely heavier and coarser copies of the beautiful work of the xii-th dynasty. Queen Ta-usert, however, who reigned towards the end of the dynasty, possessed a lovely crown like a wreath of buttercups, of which the gold of the flowers varies from bright yellow to crimson, coloured possibly by the same process as was used for Tut-ankh-Amon's jewels.

All the later jewellery tends to be coarse and heavy, and shows little real craftsmanship (pl. lxxxv. 1), until the Ptolemaic period, when chains of various designs became fashionable. Some of the Ptolemaic bracelets also are good in design.

Silver was little used in the early periods owing to its rarity, but for the same reason it was more valuable than gold. It was not until the expansion of Egypt in the xviii-th dynasty that it was imported in such quantities that it became comparatively cheap. But even then it was not popular for personal ornaments in the dynastic period, the Egyptian taste preferring something more colourful. It was in favour for dishes and bowls, and for the decoration of the floors of the sanctuaries in the temples. It was also used for ornaments which were not worn on the person, such as Tut-ankh-Amon's gold perfume-box, which was set on a silver stand. And the gold hands which were sewn on the bandages of the mummy of Tut-ankh-Amon held a crook and flail of which the cores of the shafts were of silver.

Silver bowls are often fine in decoration though the actual workmanship is not of the best. The greater number have been found in the

---

★ See Lucas in Carter's *Tomb of Tutankhamen*, ii. 170, for a full account of the gold and jewels used in the ornaments and coffin of the king. Gold sequins covered with a rose-purple film were also found. See *J.E.A.*, xx. 62.

Delta and are usually late in date. One, however, which is dated to the xxii-nd dynasty, is of special interest; it has a turned-in rim, like the anti-splash basin of a railway or steamer wash-stand. It came from Bubastis, and is probably part of the Pharaoh's travelling equipment.

It was not until Egypt became poor under Roman domination that silver was much used for personal ornament, most of the gold having been drained out of the country by taxation. In the Coptic period the jewellery shows the poverty of the people, the bracelets and necklets being of silver or even of base metal.

The use of iron in Egypt is peculiarly interesting for it is found there sporadically at various times long before it came into general use. The iron beads of the Gerzean period (p. 8) are the earliest worked iron known; a piece of sheet iron was found between the stones of the Great Pyramid and contemporary with that structure; a wedge-shaped lump of iron was found with copper axes of the vi-th dynasty in the foundations of a temple at Abydos; iron was found in a pyramid of the xii-th dynasty at Dahshur; a dagger of Tut-ankh-Amon was of steel; a scimitar of the time of Rameses II was of iron.★ It was in the xxvi-th dynasty that iron began to be common, but it did not entirely supersede bronze as the material for tools until the Roman period. The earliest iron was certainly meteoric, but the later examples were probably native iron obtained from Sinai. The artificial reduction of iron ore was not an Egyptian discovery, but came perhaps from some country farther east.

Though the inhabitants of the Nile Valley were from the earliest times masters of the art of glazing, they never made glass until late in their history (xviii-th dynasty), and even then the art never became one of the industries of the country.

Stone beads—usually steatite or schist—glazed with a copper blue in imitation of turquoise, were not uncommon in Badarian times. This type of glazing continued all through the prehistoric and historic periods. In the late prehistoric age and until the xii-th dynasty quartz was glazed, chiefly as beads; clear quartz covered with a translucent blue glaze has a beautiful effect and was greatly appreciated. For the glazed quartz boat of the Gerzean period, see p. 9. Early in their history the Egyptians invented a special material for glazing, which is not porcelain, faience or pottery; as it has no parallel elsewhere it goes by the name of *glazed ware* (pl. lxxxvii). The colours of glazes used from the earliest times were blue or green, the colour of turquoise or lapis

---

★ The Biblical record shows that as late as the reign of Saul iron was still a rarity in Palestine, for Goliath's armour was of bronze and only his spear-head was of iron. (1 Sam. xvii. 5–7.)

lazuli; in the xviii-th dynasty other colours were introduced. The kilns of Deir el Bahri produced blues of a depth and richness which have never been surpassed; and at Tell el Amarna much of the wall decoration of the temples and palaces as well as small objects and ornaments for personal use were made in glazed ware of different colours. Akhenaten's craftsmen reintroduced a technique of glazing which had not been practised in Egypt since the i-st dynasty; this was the inlaying of one colour on another. Kohltubes were made with an inlay of dark blue on a white ground, or a dark blue ground with inlay of turquoise blue. From the beginning of the xviii-th dynasty until the Ptolemaic period funerary ushabti figures were commonly made in glazed ware; they vary greatly in technique and colour. During the New Kingdom they are often of the magnificent Deir el Bahri blue, with details and inscriptions in black (pl. lxxxviii. 1); later they are often of a dull blue or green. In the xxvi-th dynasty a different style of glazing came into vogue. The minute and delicate work of this period required and received a thin glaze which did not obliterate the underlying detail (pl. lxxxviii. 3); the colour is always a pale clear blue or a soft greyish-green. As glazed ware was always the cheapest material for amulets and other religious objects great quantities of these were made at all periods; few of them have any artistic merit. The limitations of the Egyptian glazer are seen not merely in his inability to make glass, but in the fact that he never glazed metal to make what is now known as enamel; he also never glazed earthenware.

Glass occurs so rarely until the xviii-th dynasty that it is obvious it must have been an importation from some country with which there was little contact. A glass pendant of the Gerzean period is the earliest piece known; a bead of blue glass imitating lapis lazuli is of the i-st dynasty from Abydos; an ebony tray inlaid with glass is also from Abydos, the wood suggesting an Indian or African origin (pl. lxxxvi. 2). Then there is a blank until the xii-th dynasty when there is one example of a kohl pot of turquoise-blue glass in the characteristic shape of the period. The great conquests of Thothmes III brought into Egypt many craftsmen from foreign countries, and among others there seem to have been glass-makers. Glass beads, black, white, and blue, became increasingly common, but it was not until a century later that other colours were used in glass-making. The range of colours both in glass and glazing that was produced in the reigns of Amonhotep III and his son Akhenaten was never surpassed in Egypt for variety, brilliancy, and beauty.* Glass was largely used to imitate

* For a complete account of glass-making at Tell el Amarna, see Petrie, *Arts and Crafts*, pp. 123–5, and *Wisdom of the Egyptians*, p. 110.

precious stones for inlaying in gold, as in the coffin of Tut-ankh-Amon. A little glass is known in the xxvi-th dynasty, otherwise glass-making died out entirely after the New Kingdom.

Spinning and weaving were practised from the Badarian period, and by the time of the i-st dynasty the Egyptians were producing the finest linen of the ancient world. All through the historic period Egyptian linen was extremely good, and when the Greeks came in contact with Egypt the best linen, called byssus, was brought from Egypt. All the weaving in early dynastic times was of vegetable fibre, and not of wool, against which there seems to have been some prejudice. Usually the fibre was flax, but until the xii-th dynasty other fibres were used occasionally. Both spinning and weaving were done by women (pl. xv).★ The spinning was entirely by the spindle; there is no trace of the spinning-wheel. The weaving loom was sometimes upright, sometimes horizontal, the weave being either the cloth weave or the tabby weave. Shuttles were unknown until the late Roman times, the weft being made by passing a ball of thread by hand through the warp. There was therefore no limit as to the width of a piece of cloth, while in hand-woven cloth where the shuttle is used, it is limited by the distance that the shuttle can be thrown. Sheets of the xii-th dynasty measured 2·859 × 1·242 m. and 2·516 × 1·309 m.; they were remarkable as having a selvedge all round.† In the xii-th dynasty also there was a certain amount of striped cloth made, but as a rule all materials were plain for ordinary people; it was only the Pharaohs who had patterned robes. To make the pattern a ball of thread of the necessary colour was passed to and fro over the part required, thus making a selvedge on each side and leaving a slit between the pattern and the main part of the fabric; when finished, the slit was sewn together with a needle and thread.

The Egyptian was not highly skilled in dyeing; he could dye a fabric in one colour successfully, but he never seems to have attempted the variations in colour which are found in the representations of the dresses of foreigners. He understood the use of mordants, and many of the dyed stuffs still retain their colour, but there are also some colours which were not fast. The colours given in the scenes of the Old Kingdom show that the women of all classes were dressed in red

---

★ In modern Egypt a great deal of the spinning is done by the shepherds, who spin with the spindle as they walk with their flocks. They spin wool; cotton and flax are sometimes spun in private houses by the women. All the weaving is done by men, usually on horizontal looms. The setting of the warp threads is still done as in the xii-th dynasty on pegs against a wall, the operator moving first forward, then backwards.

† Murray, *Tomb of Two Brothers*, pp. 57, 58.

or dark blue, rarely in yellow. The red was an iron dye, the blue was probably indigo, the yellow was saffron during the xii-th dynasty.* The linen found in early tombs shows no trace of colour. Silk seems to have been introduced by the Persians, but never became popular as it did in more northern countries.

Coptic textiles (pl. lxxxix) are almost the only objects of that period which have received any attention from archæologists. Much is known as to the materials, the weaving, the designs of the decorations, and the garments which were worn. Many of these garments were priestly vestments and show the type of vestment in use in the Early Church; others, however, were the ordinary dress of the ordinary people, and as many of the burial garments had been worn by the owner there are interesting examples of darns and of thin places carefully "run". The darning, though coarse, is often very good and even. Hemming is not common, the hem being held down by a kind of buttonhole stitch. The needles were large and thick, therefore the sewing is never fine, except when it occurs as embroidery on the coloured panels of a garment; this is often in white thread on a dark background, and is worked in stem-stitch.†

SCIENCE

The sciences in which the Egyptians excelled were applied mathematics and medicine.‡ Unfortunately their knowledge of applied mathematics was not committed to writing, and there is no record of how they reached the conclusions at which their actions show they must have arrived.

The physical condition of Egypt made engineering a necessity, irrigation being of vital importance in a country where the rainfall is negligible for purposes of agriculture. The annual inundation supplies the necessary moisture in the soil for one harvest only, but the land is so fertile that with even a small amount of irrigation the crops more than repay the outlay. The inundation, though regular as to time, is

* It is possible that saffron dye was used, not for its colour, but as a preventive of lice, which according to Pliny was its use in later periods of the world's history.

† The Coptic period is an almost untouched field of research. The textiles, the language, and the liturgy have been partially studied, but the effect of the new religion on the old paganism, the reason for the collapse of the old order of things, the lives of the people and how these changes affected them, are matters which have been utterly neglected. Even a good history of the Coptic period is wanting.

‡ Though there is no record of any knowledge of chemistry it is perhaps significant that the name of that science and of its predecessor, Alchemy, is simply the ancient name of Egypt, Kemi in the Southern dialect, Khemi in the Northern. Chemistry, then, is the "Egyptian science".

extremely variable in quantity, and also in the pace at which it rises. The primitive Egyptians had no means of knowing what to expect; all they knew was that too high or too sudden a rise meant sweeping away whole villages, and too low a flood meant famine. Of the two evils the latter was the worse, and some means must have been devised in early times to get water to the fields in a year of a low Nile; this could have been done only by water-channels dug to a level which would bring even a low inundation across the land. The water-channel would have a dam at its junction with the river, to act as a road when the river was not in flood; the dam would be cut through when the river rose and so allow the water to pour into the channel and reach the fields. The cutting of the dam at the capital city was a royal ceremony from prehistoric times. On the carved mace-head of the Scorpion-King, the monarch is shown with a hoe in his hand; he has cut the dam, and is watching the water as it flows through the channels round the fields. This ceremony continued annually for century after century; on the day of High Nile the Pharaohs, the Ptolemies, the Roman governors, the Moslem rulers, each in their turn, performed the ceremony, which came to an end only at the beginning of this century. The primitive prehistoric Egyptians must have been sufficiently advanced in engineering knowledge to execute canal-work, for as early as the first historic king, Menes, they successfully carried out the gigantic enterprise of turning the course of the Nile in order to build the city of Memphis on the site where the great river had run.

In dealing with Egypt it is impossible to overstate the importance of the Nile, for the river is the only source of water in the whole country. Waterworks therefore always engaged the attention of the engineers. The great problem was how to conserve the excess water of the inundation and store it up for use in the dry season. The problem was solved in the xii-th dynasty, when that great system of dykes, canals, and sluices was instituted in the Fayum, a system which remained in use till the Roman occupation. Irrigation canals were made in other parts of Egypt, but nothing on the scale of Amonemhat III's work in the Fayum. Canalisation was carried out successfully at various times for purposes of trade or war. In the xii-th dynasty Senusert III cleared and canalised the cataract to make an easy passage for his troopships on their way to the conquest of Nubia. The passage was kept clear by later warrior-kings of Egypt who fought in Nubia. There was a waterway from the Nile to the Red Sea, partly natural, partly artificial. There is no record as to when it was made, but Queen Hatshepsut's trading expedition passed along it, and the record treats it as being as natural a highway as the Nile itself, showing that it had been made so long before that it was in no sense a novelty. Setekhy I of the xix-th dynasty crossed a large canal on the frontier of Egypt on his way to the re-conquest of Palestine. It seems probable that this canal was neglected and was silted up in the reigns of the degenerate Pharaohs who followed, for in the xxvi-th dynasty Necho began a waterway from the Delta to the Red Sea, perhaps the same that Hatshepsut's ships used more than a thousand years previously, or the one which Setekhy mentions. "Its length is a voyage of four days, and in width it was dug so that two triremes might sail rowed abreast. Necho stopped digging it in the middle of the work, the following oracle having caused an impediment, 'that he was working for a barbarian'." The real reason for the stoppage of the work was probably the great mortality among the workmen. The canal was finished under Darius the Great when the Persians ruled Egypt.

In spite of their engineering knowledge the ancient Egyptians never built bridges. The river was always crossed, as it is now, by a ferry, the boat being large enough to take animals and freight as well as human passengers. A full canal was probably crossed on a raft; shallow water was waded through.

Astronomy again was one of the sciences which the Egyptians studied. In a country where clouds are the exception and not the rule, the study of the heavens is comparatively easy. The positions of the constellations and the courses of the planets were known. The two most important constellations were the seven stars of the Great Bear, which were known as the Imperishable Stars, and Orion (Sahu), which was regarded as a deity. The Dog-star, Sirius or Sothis, was the chief of all stars, for it was the herald of the inundation, and its reappearance at dawn at the summer solstice was celebrated as a religious festival. It was dedicated to Isis and there was a legend that the tears she shed at the annual death of Osiris caused the inundation.

In Gerzean times the astronomers had discarded the lunar year of three hundred and sixty days; they retained the division of the year into twelve months of thirty days each, but added five extra days to the year to bring it into accordance with astronomical facts. The change, though drastic, was still not sufficient, but no further alteration was made till Ptolemaic times when an extra day was incorporated into the calendar every four years. Under the Pharaohs two calendars were in operation: the official calendar, in which the year consisted of 365 days and therefore lost a day every four years, but kept the date by the days of the month; and the solar calendar of $365\frac{1}{4}$ days, by which all agricultural festivals were kept and by which the dates of astronomical value were calculated. There is no record of any fear of eclipses for there are no religious services and no charms for averting the danger to the sun or moon. It would seem that the date of an eclipse was so accurately calculated that the populace knew what to expect. Actual observations of the stars are recorded in the tomb of Rameses VI of the xx-th dynasty. This is a kind of star-map drawn as the figure of a seated man, the position of each star as it moved being marked on the figure. In this way the culminations of stars are shown at each hour of the night for every fortnight in the year.

The year was divided into twelve months, and each month into three ten-day weeks. The beginning of each week was indicated by the rising of the *decan*-star; the names of the decans are often given in the lists. The star-maps and *decan*-lists were intended probably for astrological rather than for astronomical purposes, for the ancient Egyptians practised astrology and cast horoscopes. Recognisable horoscopes are not found till the xii-th dynasty. In that period ivory batons engraved with astronomical signs and figures of the deities of birth show that these were nativity horoscopes. In these some of the signs of the Zodiac and most of the planets can be identified, and the end of life is indicated by the head of Anubis the jackal-god of death.

One of the most interesting results of the mathematical knowledge of the ancient Egyptians was the invention of water-clocks. The division of time into years, months, and weeks was comparatively easy; the sun and the moon were time-indicators. But to divide the day and night into hours was a more difficult task, for even at the latitude of Memphis or Thebes the length of the day differs according to the season of the year. The division of the day and night into twelve hours each was early; perhaps the division into this arbitrary number was to correspond with the twelve months of the year. But as the time between sunrise and sunset is different in summer and winter, the length of the hours had to vary also; in summer the day, and therefore the hours, would be longer than in winter. The difficulty would then be to devise some means of showing the hours according to the season. This was triumphantly achieved as early as the xi-th dynasty (more than two thousand years B.C.) by an adaptation of the system of water flowing into or out of a vessel. In the primitive system of measuring time the water flows in or out of the vessel at a given rate, as is still done in some parts of Africa for measuring the time of allowing water to irrigate a field, when the water-channel is shared by more than one cultivator. But it was one of the glories of Egyptian science that an instrument was invented which showed the variation in the length of the hours. Whether Sen-Irui was the actual inventor is not certain, probably not, but at least he gives the information in the inscription in which he describes his knowledge of Art and Science: "I know what belongs to the sinking waters, and the weighings of exact calculation." The sinking waters refer to the Egyptian water-clock which was of the outflow variety. The earliest actual specimen known is of the reign of Amonhotep III (about 1400 B.C.). It is of alabaster "shaped like a flower-pot, provided with one small aperture at the side near the bottom. The pot was filled with water, which *flowed out* gradually through the opening, and by noting the water level against a scale of markings on the inner surface an estimate of the intervals of time was obtained."* This example was in all probability a royal piece, for it is highly decorated with inlay of coloured stones and glass. Fragments of other clepsydræ of the same type are known, on one of which is the inscription, "To fix the hours of the night if the decan stars are not visible, so that in this way the correct time of the sacrifice will be observed."† There is an inscription of a slightly earlier date in the tomb of Amonemhat at Thebes, who lived in the reign of Amonhotep I; he was evidently the chief scientific authority of his time. Although the inscription is greatly damaged there is sufficient remaining to show that he had studied the division of time and made a clepsydra: "I found that the winter night was 14 hours long. . . . I found an increase in the length of the nights from month to month, and a decrease month by month. I made a *merkhyt*‡ reckoned from the zero of the year. It was for the King. Never was one made like it since the beginning of time. Every hour lies to its time. The water runs out through one outlet only." Though such water-clocks are rare it is clear that they were first invented in Egypt; they were introduced into Greece from Egypt, and under their Greek name were spread throughout Europe.

The method of working out the measurements of the clocks is referred to by Sen-Irui when he says that he knows "the weighings of exact calculation". A very considerable amount of mathematical knowledge would be required to make a water-clock of the kind at any period, more particularly when mathematical instruments of precision were not known. The maker of such a clock would need to calculate the volume of water, and to work out the scales for the difference in the length of the hours in summer and winter and for the difference in the speed of the water-flow according to the seasonal temperature. The "weighings of exact calculation" seem to be connected with the "sinking waters" of the outflow type of water-clock, and can be explained by the fact that "the determination of a volume of water is very conveniently carried out by weighings, since the volume is proportional to the mass".‖ Besides the actual vessels, there

---

* R. W. Sloley, "Ancient Clepsydræ", *Ancient Egypt* (1924), p. 43.
† Ibid., p. 44.   ‡ *Merkhyt* is a noun formed from the verb *rekh*, "to know".
‖ "The Stele of the Artist", *Ancient Egypt* (1925), p. 33 *seq.*

are extant a certain number of cubit-measures, on which the fractions have the names of the months marked against them, and are called "hours filled with water", showing that they applied to water-clocks.* It is therefore clear that as early as the xi-th dynasty Egyptian physicists could make an instrument capable of recording accurately the small divisions of time at the different seasons of the year.

That the Egyptians should have an accurate knowledge of anatomy after the introduction of embalming is not surprising, but the truly surprising thing is that King Atothis (Zer) of the i-st dynasty should be credited with having written a treatise on the subject. It is unlikely that any real knowledge of anatomy existed at that date, but the Egyptians had a custom of referring knowledge of any kind to as early a date as possible if it could not be stated to be divine. After mummification became customary, the embalmers must have acquired a considerable amount of information as to the internal organs, and it is possible that they learned to distinguish the effects of certain diseases; but any such observations were not recorded in writing. There is, however, some reason to believe that they were aware of the importance of the heart, though it is uncertain if they realised the circulation of the blood. They undoubtedly knew a great deal of the properties of drugs, and many medical papyri are extant giving the names and uses of medicinal plants. Their medical knowledge was far in advance of medieval Europe, and their anatomical knowledge and treatises were the foundation of the Greek writings on the subject.

* Borchardt, *Geschichte des Zeitmesserung*, pp. 60–3.

VI

LANGUAGE AND LITERATURE

THE WRITING

THE knowledge of hieroglyphs was lost for more than thirteen centuries; then after the great revival of learning in Europe a Jesuit, Athanasius Kircher, in 1636 wrote a treatise on the Coptic language and roused the interest of European scholars. The event, however, which had most effect on the study was the discovery in 1799 (by French soldiers digging the foundations of a fort at Rosetta) of an inscribed slab of stone, the inscription being (as was surmised at the time) in three languages. This was the famous Rosetta Stone, which is actually inscribed in two languages—Egyptian and Greek—but in three scripts, hieroglyphic, demotic, and Greek. The Greek was of course quickly translated, and many scholars tried unsuccessfully to read the two other scripts. By 1816 Sir Thomas Young, to whom the world owes the wave theory of light, had established the fact that the hieroglyphic and demotic scripts were but two different forms of writing, not two languages; he also proved that different signs could be used for the same sound; and that the "royal rings" (now called "cartouches") contained royal names. Eight years later in 1822 Jean François Champollion (1790–1832) published his celebrated *Lettres à M. Dacier*, in which he showed the right method of decipherment. His *Précis du système hiéroglyphique* published in 1824 revolutionised the whole subject and laid the foundation of the true reading of this dead and forgotten language. It is a pity, for his own reputation, that he completely ignored the work of his predecessors, without which he could not have made his final discoveries. Since then so much work has been done in the identification and meaning of words and phrases as well as in the discovery of the grammatical rules which govern the language that ancient Egyptian can now be learned, like any other language, by means of grammars, dictionaries, and texts with commentaries.

Ancient Egyptian is related to both the Semitic group of languages and to the Hamitic group. So far it is the Semitic connection of Egyptian which has received attention, while the Hamitic side of the language still awaits the same scientific investigation. The language was never static; it altered in the course of time, when new words and new constructions were introduced and old forms died out and old words either became obsolete or changed their meaning. The last phase of the language, Coptic, is as much like the language of the Old Kingdom as French or Spanish are like Latin.

The historic period in any country begins with the written record; in Egypt this was about four thousand years before Christ, when the spoken language was reduced to a readable script. Before that time there had been a system of signs scratched on pottery vessels which seem to have been, like our trade-marks, an indication to the purchaser what the contents of the vessel were and their quality; some of the signs were also undoubtedly the owner's marks. There are as well a few which are recognisably the same as the later hieroglyphs, but it is uncertain whether they had the same phonetic value or the same meaning as in the later written language.

The dynastic Egyptians either introduced a complete system of writing or developed what had already begun, for in the 1-st dynasty both hieroglyphic and hieratic writing are found, so also is a decimal system of numeration up to a million.

The origin of the writing was the same as among all primitive nations, namely pictures; unlike other nations the picture forms were never discarded or simplified but remained in use until the end for all sculptured records and for written religious documents. For ordinary secular purposes there was another script, known to the Greeks as hieratic, which was a running hand in which the picture signs were so abbreviated and altered that almost all likeness to the originals is lost. This was in common use until about 700 B.C. It bore the same relation to the hieroglyphs that handwriting does to print. It developed into a more rapid, but at the same time a more illegible, script called demotic by the Greeks, which remained in use until within the Christian era. Whether because of the difficulty of reading so complicated a script or for some other reason, demotic was discarded and the Egyptian language was then written in a Greek script with a few extra letters derived from the hieroglyphs to represent sounds which could not be expressed in the Greek. This combination is known as Coptic, which survived as a spoken language until the seventeenth century. It is still used in the liturgy of the Coptic Church, and has been revived to a certain extent as a spoken language among the priests.

The Greeks are responsible for many of the modern ideas concerning the Egyptian system of writing. With their genius for misunderstanding anything outside the narrow limits of their own small country, they ascribed mystical meanings to a script they could not read, and gazed with awe at the strange signs sculptured on temples and tombstones. The Egyptian guides, like guides in every country, exploited this weakness of the Greek tourists, with the consequence that a farrago of absurdity has been handed down through the centuries and is still current.

The hieroglyphs (*i.e.* sacred signs) were called by the Egyptians "the words of God", and thus recorded the belief that they were of divine origin.* The knowledge of them was jealously guarded by the priests and scribes, though the reading and writing of hieratic was not uncommon. The decorative value of the hieroglyphs appealed to an artistic people, and the signs were used with beautiful effect on sculptured walls and stelæ. For sheer beauty no other script has ever approached the Egyptian hieroglyphs. This is the real reason why they were never discarded until the whole of that great civilisation died under the heavy heel of Rome. Even at their worst, when under the Ptolemies the forms of the signs were bungled and crowded together, the effect of an inscribed wall has a richness and beauty which is never seen with any other script.

The desire to retain the beauty of their script led the Egyptians into strange methods of writing. One of these was so important that it was followed, though not so rigorously, in hieratic and demotic; this was the arrangement of the signs, which had to be written as far as possible in square groups. In order to effect this, many of the hieroglyphic signs can be written either vertically or horizontally, or there are alternative signs with similar sounds. Another method applies to hieroglyphs only; the normal method of writing any of the three scripts is from right to left, as in modern Arabic, but when a decorative effect was required, the writing could be in either direction. A royal inscription on a wall or a stela can begin in the centre and be duplicated to right and left. On a coffin there is often a band of inscription round the upper part, in which are written the prayers for the dead; on one side the prayer to Osiris, on the other the prayer to Anubis. The prayers invariably begin at the head and are carried round till they meet at the foot; one prayer therefore reads from left to right, the other from right to left. Any other hieroglyphs on the sides of the coffin will follow the direction of those on the band. In an ordinary inscription the direction in which it is to be read is determined by the figures of the living creatures, which face towards the beginning.

Hieroglyphs were usually painted,† and each had its own appropriate colour (pls. xcv; xcvi). The birds are particularly beautiful as many of them are coloured as nearly like life as was possible with the

* In Jewish legend the alphabet was written with a pen of flame round the august and terrible crown on the head of God.

† In long inscriptions, such as the Pyramid Texts, the hieroglyphs were often incised and painted in monochrome, usually green or blue.

few pigments at the disposal of the artists. Owing to the fewness of the pigments there is a certain convention as to the colours of some of the objects: copper is painted blue, gold yellow, wood either green or red, water blue with black lines, textiles red.

Hieroglyphic signs are conveniently divided into four classes:

1. Alphabetic.
2. Syllabic.
3. Word-signs.
4. Determinatives.

1. Alphabetic (uniliteral) signs represent a single sound; there are twenty-four (pl. xcv).

2. Syllabic signs (pl. xcvi. 1, 6, 8, 9, 10) may be either biliteral or triliteral, that is to say, they may represent a combination of two or three consonants; the position of the vowels is never indicated. The main difficulty in learning to read Egyptian lies in the number and use of the syllabic signs, for many are used entirely for their sound value in spelling out words without any reference to their original meaning. Another difficulty for the beginner is the custom of writing the principal letter, usually the last, of the syllable after the sign; it is not to be pronounced but is an indication to the reader as to how the syllable ends. Syllabic signs originated as pictures of objects but lost their meaning early.

3. Word-signs (pl. xcvi. 4, 7) are pictures of objects used as the words for those objects. They are not common, on account of the fact that many of them became merely syllabic signs. When, however, they are used they are generally followed by an upright stroke, the numeral 1, to indicate to the reader that the word is complete in one sign.

4. A determinative is a picture of the object which has already been written out in alphabetic and syllabic signs (pl. xcvi. 2, 3, 11, 12). The Egyptians never attempted to simplify their beautiful writing, but as it grew more complicated they added more helps to the reader. Some of the determinatives are simple, as a pair of walking legs for any verb of motion (pl. xcvi. 12), as walking, running, dancing, coming, etc. But when the word expressed something abstract which could not be represented in a picture, they used the picture of a roll of papyrus tied up and sealed (pl. xcvi. 5), showing that the meaning of the word could be expressed in writing though not pictorially.

In transliterating Egyptian words one is faced with the same difficulty that arises in transcribing any other foreign language, for there are sounds in every language that do not occur elsewhere and for which no combination of letters is adequate. In examining the

Egyptian alphabet (pl. xcv) it will be seen that many of the alphabetic signs express sounds which in English have to be indicated by two letters, sh, th, kh. Then again there are two forms of H, two of Kh, and two of S. And it will be noticed that there are no vowels, except the two semi-vowels W and Y, and that there are two letters, *aleph* and *ayin*, which have no equivalents in English. Unless one adopts the scientific method of using dots and dashes, with "comma bacilli" for aleph and ayin, there is no possibility of making a correct transliteration, and one is reduced to compromise. The Egyptian letter now called aleph was probably the same as the modern Arabic *hamza* or glottal stop, a sound often found in European languages though never indicated in them by a letter. The ayin is a special sound, and in languages where it occurs it is a strong consonant; it has no equivalent in any European language. In the scientific transliteration aleph is represented by the smooth breathing of the Greek, and ayin by the rough breathing, but these signs do not necessarily convey any indication of the actual pronunciation.

The vowels and their position in a group of consonants present a problem which is far from being solved. The earlier Egyptologists were consistent in using the Greek forms of Egyptian names; or if there were no Greek equivalents, a compromise was effected, for it would be impossible to pronounce a group of consonants like Mrnpth or Nfrhtp. But the sound values which the Greeks attached to certain letters were used, and aleph (fig. 20) was called A because it occurs twice with that value in the name of Cleopatra; Y (fig. 21) was also A for it is the initial of the name Amon; ayin (fig. 22) was a third A

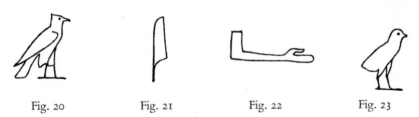

Fig. 20   Fig. 21   Fig. 22   Fig. 23

for it is a component of the name of Rameses; and W (fig. 23) became U because it has that value in many Coptic words. But there are hundreds of words in which none of these four signs occur. For some of these Coptic furnished the vowels; htp could then be pronounced hotep; and for those for which there was no equivalent in any known language a short ĕ was conventionally inserted so as to make a group of consonants pronounceable, e.g. nzm becomes nĕzĕm. Certain well-known words such as Pharaoh, Rameses, Isis, Osiris, Anubis, were too firmly established to admit of any change in the spelling.

Modern Egyptologists are now making great efforts to establish a system of transliterating Egyptian names which is supposed to combine scientific accuracy with the actual pronunciation of the period when the name was used. This method has been imported from Germany, and is a curious hybrid evolved partly from the Greek, partly from the Coptic, and partly (like the camel) from the German inner consciousness; contemporary transliterations being disregarded. The name of the Sun-god, which occurs in the official title of every Pharaoh from the iv-th dynasty onward, is spelt in Egyptian with two consonants (fig. 24), R and ayin; and in the contemporary cuneiform of the

Fig. 24

xviii-th and xix-th dynasties it was clearly pronounced as two syllables, ri-ya. The official names of Rameses were (when in readable transliteration) User-maot-Rê setep-en-Rê Rameses-mery-Amon; in the cuneiform transliteration they were: Was-mua-Ria satep-na-Ria Ria-masesa-mai-Amana.* The Greeks, however, seem to have heard the ayin as a nasalised sound, for they transliterated Khaf-Rê as Khephren, and Men-kau-Rê as Mykerinos (the os being the Greek termination). The Coptic has PH for R-ayin, and it is from the Coptic that the modernist pronunciation is taken. Khefren and Mykerinos are taken from the Greek, but so far English scholars have fought shy of the Greek form of Khufu, Cheops, on account of the slightly comic effect of the name both in writing and sound. Senusert, however, is now given the Greek form of Sesostris. Amonemhat is Ammenemes, Paseb-khanu is Psusennes. But in the most illogical way Aahmes, which in Greek is Amasis, is now Ahmose; Amon-hotep, in the Greek Amenophis, has become Amenhotpe; and Thoth, which is θωθ in Greek, is now Dhout in some combinations, and Tuth in others. In short, there is at present no authoritative, or even conventional, transliteration of Egyptian names.

LITERATURE

The early poetry of most countries seems to be bound by the same forms, repetitions of a phrase, parallelism, and alliteration. All these are found in our own early poetry as well as in the early poetry of Egypt. One great essential in early poetry is rhythm; this is very

* Sayce, *Ancient Egypt* (1922), p. 68.

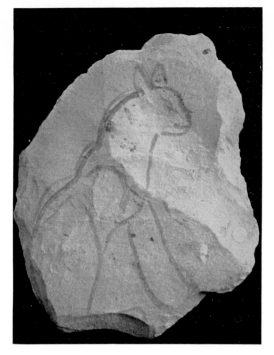

Photograph by Dr. S. Pritchard

Gayer-Anderson Coll.
Fitzwilliam Museum

1. Outline sketch of cat.   On limestone

Photograph by Dr. S. Pritchard

Gayer-Anderson Coll.   Fitzwilliam Museum

2. Coloured sketch of man driving a bull.   On limestone

PLATE LXXXI

2.

Gayer-Anderson Coll.

3.

4.

Photograph by Dr. S. Pritchard   *Gayer-Anderson C*
Fitzwilliam Mu.

Artists' sketches on limestone

PLATE LXXXII

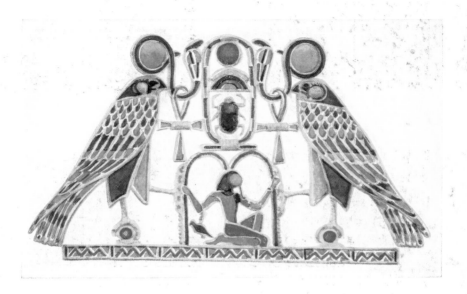

Gold and jewelled pectoral.   Dynasty xii.
Found at Lahun

PLATE LXXXIII

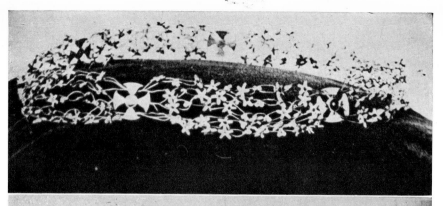

1. Forget-me-not crown.   Dahshur

2. Second crown.   Dahshur

3. Princess's crown.   Lahun

PLATE LXXXIV

Photograph by Dr. S. Pritchard   *Fitzwilliam Museum*

Photograph by Dr. S. Pritchard   *Fitzwilliam Museum*

1 (top). Gold work.   Late period
2 (above). Scarabs
3 (below). Eyes for inserting in statues
4, 5 (right). Bronze castings for furniture

Photo M.A.M.   *Petrie Coll.*

Photograph by Dr. S. Pritchard   *Fitzwilliam Museum*   Photo M.A.M.   *Petrie Coll.*

PLATE LXXXV

Photograph by Dr. S. Pritchard
Fitzwilliam Museum

1. Ripple-chipped flint knife.   Amratean

Ashmolean Museum

2. Part of ebony tray inlaid with glass.   i-st dynasty

Petrie Coll.   Photograph by Dr. S. Pritchard   *Fitzwilliam Museum*

3. Kohl vase.   Alabaster   4, 5. Kohl vases.   Variegated glass

PLATE LXXXVI

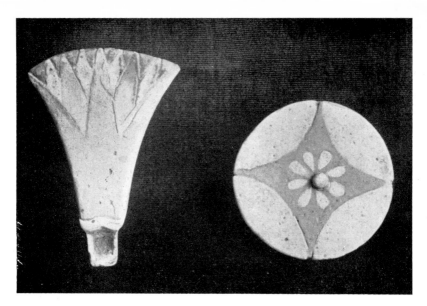

Photograph by Dr. S. Pritchard *Fitzwilliam Museum*

1. Inlay.   Glazed ware

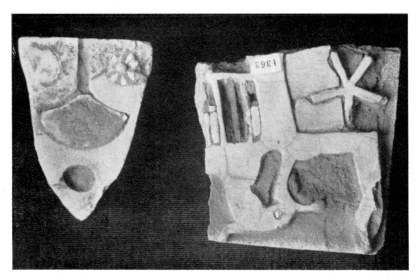

Photograph by Dr. S. Pritchard *Fitzwilliam Museum*

2. Glazed ware inlaid in stone

PLATE LXXXVII

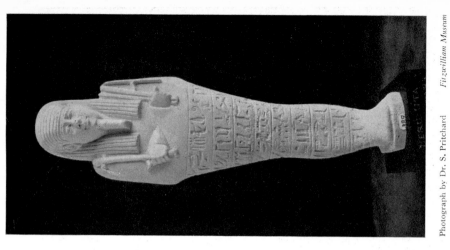

Photograph by Dr. S. Pritchard   *Fitzwilliam Museum*

3. Ushabti figure. Pale green glaze.
Dynasty xxvi

2. Ushabti figure. With soul as
a bird clinging to its breast

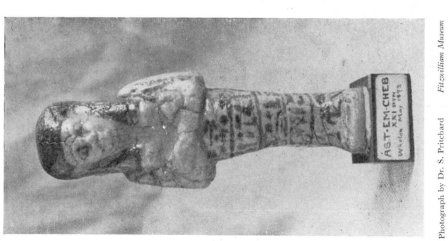

Photograph by Dr. S. Pritchard   *Fitzwilliam Museum*

1. Ushabti figure. Blue glaze.
Dynasty xxi

PLATE LXXXVIII

Photograph by Dr. S. Pritchard   *Fitzwilliam Museum*

Photograph by Dr. S. Pritchard   *Fitzwilliam Museum*

Coptic textiles

PLATE LXXXIX

1. Foreign envoy introduced to Pharaoh by Vizier

2. Lady using sistrum and menyt

3. The god 'Ash in Egypt

4. The God 'Ash in
Europe

PLATE XC

Flinders Petrie when he became the Edwards Professor

PLATE XCI

Flinders Petrie when he retired from the
Edwards Professorship

1. Christ in glory. Pottery handle. Coptic.

2. St. George. Pottery handle. Coptic.

3. St. Menas and his camels.   Ivory reliquary

PLATE XCIII

markedly the case in Egypt wherever it is possible to test the phrasing. But as the vowels were not written it is not always certain where the accent should fall. Rhyme was never used, metre was everything. Alliteration was not uncommon, but was never carried through a whole poem, it occurs only for a few lines. Repetition was constantly used as a mode in the earlier poems, but was discarded to a great extent in and after the xix-th dynasty, though of course retained for choruses. Parallelism was much favoured, and is found in many of the official hymns and religious texts. Seeing that it was also in favour among the Hebrews for their religious poetry, it can only be supposed that they obtained it, as they did so much of their civilisation and even their literature, from Egypt. The monotonous effect of repetition and parallelism was perhaps required for religious chants as producing a more solemn result on the minds of the worshippers.

RELIGIOUS

Religious literature predominates in Egypt. This is always the case when the priests are the only persons who can write and make the records, and it is only rarely that any secular literature survives from an early period. In Egypt the earliest body of texts that can be called literature is entirely religious, and comprises a series of hymns and spells sculptured on the walls of the burial chambers in the pyramids of five kings of the vi-th dynasty (c. 2800 B.C. or perhaps earlier). These are now known as the Pyramid Texts. The content and the language of these Texts show that they are of greater age than the time when they were thus committed to writing; they have clearly been copied and re-copied so many times that often the language is too corrupt to be comprehensible. It is, however, possible to translate the greater part of the inscriptions, though many of the allusions are baffling. The Pyramid Texts consist of hymns and spells for the benefit of the dead king, and as they are the earliest liturgy and exposition of religion in the world, they throw a great light on primitive beliefs and official creeds. The knowledge of them was handed on, undoubtedly by word of mouth, till the time of the xii-th dynasty, when many of the Texts appear on the painted and sculptured coffins of that period. So much of Egypt's past perished under the rule of the Hyksos that it is not surprising to find no survival of the Texts until the xviii-th dynasty. Then a few of the early spells occur in that interesting compilation to which the misleading title of "Book of the Dead" was given by early Egyptologists.

The Book of the Dead is a series of chapters (literally, divisions) written on papyrus and often illustrated with miniature painting,

H

which are found in graves. The chapters are not necessarily connected with one another, for they are not consecutive; and there is no reason why they should be regarded as part of a "book". For convenience' sake the name "Book of the Dead" is retained, so also is the numbering of the so-called chapters.

The earliest of the hymns in the Pyramid Texts is the so-called "Cannibal Hymn" of Wenis (Unas). It is uncertain whether it was chanted to the king during his life to show him what a splendid future awaited him, or whether it was sung at his funeral. It is totally unlike anything which occurs later and reflects perhaps some of those customs of primitive Egypt from which Osiris is said to have converted his subjects.

The sky pours water, the stars darken;
The Bows rush about, the bones of the Earth-god tremble.
They are still, the Pleiades,
When they see Wenis appearing, animated . . .
Wenis is the Bull of the sky, who conquers according to his desire,
Who lives on the being of every god,
Who eats their entrails, who comes when their belly is filled with magic
From the Island of Fire. . . .
It is Wenis who judges with Him whose name is hidden
On this day of Slaying the Oldest One.
Wenis is the Lord of Food-offerings, who knots the cord,
Who himself prepares his meal.
It is Wenis who eats men and lives on the gods.
It is the "Grasper-of-Horns" who is in Kehau, who lassoes them for Wenis,
It is "He-who-is-upon the Willows" who binds them for Wenis,
It is "The Wanderer who slaughters the Lords", who strangles them for Wenis,
He cuts out their intestines for him.
It is "He-of-the-Winepress" who cuts them up for Wenis,
Cooking for him a portion of them in his evening cooking pots.
It is Wenis who eats their magic and swallows their spirits;
Their great ones are for his morning portion,
Their middle-sized ones are for his evening portion,
Their little ones are for high night portion,
Their old ones are for his incense burning . . .
Wenis is a god, older than the oldest. . . .
He has taken the hearts of the Gods,
He has eaten the Red Crown, he has swallowed the Green One,
Wenis rejoices that he devours the *absu* which are in the Red Crown;
Wenis flourishes, their magic is in his belly.
He has swallowed the intelligence of every god.
Lo, their soul is in the belly of Wenis, their spirits are with Wenis.*

★ *J.E.A.*, x. 97.

This hymn shows Wenis as the great God of all, devouring the gods of old, he himself being older than the oldest. But to anyone not blinded by religious fervour it would be evident that when the next king or god arrived Wenis would suffer the fate that he had meted out to his predecessors. This may be the reason that the hymn is omitted in later tombs.

The interest of the next extract is that the king is regarded as a messenger from Geb, the earth god, to Osiris, the god of fertility, to report on the harvest. It begins with the sensation in Heaven caused by the arrival of the king: "There is strife in Heaven and we see a new thing, say the Primordial Gods. The Ennead is dazzled, the Lords of Forms are in terror of him. The Double Ennead serves him as he sits on the throne of the Lord of the Universe. The gods are afraid of him, for he is older than the Great Ones. He seizes Command, and Eternity is brought to him. Cry aloud to him in joy for he has captured the horizon. O Ferryman of the Field of Offerings, bring me there! It is he! Hasten! It is he! Come! He, the son of the Boat of the Morning, to whom she gave birth above the earth, that immaculate birth whereby the Two Lands live! He is the herald of the year, O Osiris! See, he comes with a message from thy father Geb. Is the year's yield fortunate? Very fortunate is the year's yield. Is the year's yield good? Very good is the yield of the year!"

In the Old Kingdom, though the king became Osiris at death, he was still filled with energy and activity, but in the xii-th dynasty there was a change and Osiris was regarded as almost entirely passive, depending on other deities for reverence and even protection.

A characteristic piece of devotional literature is the hymn to Osiris, which begins as a hymn and ends as a prayer. Only a few lines of this lengthy poem are quoted here:

Hail to thee, King of kings! Lord of lords! Prince of princes! Possessor of the Two Lands even from the womb of his mother Nut! Ruler of all the lands of Agert! Gold are his limbs, lapis lazuli is his head, and turquoise is in his hands. Pillar of millions! Beautiful of face in the Sacred Land! Grant me splendour in heaven, power on earth, and acquittal in the Nether World; and a sailing downstream as a living soul to Busiris, and a sailing upstream to Abydos as a *bennu*-bird, and a going in and a coming out.

Besides hymns and spells for the dead there is another type of religious literature also connected with the dead. These are the good wishes of the relatives, which when recited in the correct chant and with the correct gestures were believed to secure the happiness of the dead man. A typical example is from the tomb of the scribe Amonemhat, who lived in the reign of Thothmes III (*c.* 1490 B.C.):

Recitation: O steward, who reckonest the grain, the scribe, Amonemhat, justified; mayest thou enter into and go forth from the West, mayest thou stride through the gate of the Nether World, mayest thou adore Rê when he arises from the mountain, mayest thou be satisfied with repasts from the table of the Lord of Eternity. *Recitation:* O steward who reckonest the fields, the scribe, Amonemhat, justified; mayest thou wander as thou listest in the beautiful margin of thy garden-pond, may thy heart have pleasure in thy plantation, mayest thou have refreshment under thy trees, may thy desire be appeased with water from the well which thou didst make, for ever.*

A hymn to the Sun-god, which forms part of the Book of the Dead, is typical of this kind of literature in the New Kingdom:

Hail to thee, Rê, in thy rising! O Atum-Harakhti! Mine eyes adore thee. When thou crossest in peace in the Boat of the Evening, thy rays rest upon my body. Thy heart is gladdened by the wind when in the Boat of the Morning. The Never-Resting Stars chant to thee, the Imperishable Stars praise thee, when thou settest in the horizon of Manu. Beautiful art thou at the two limits of the heavens. O Living Lord, thou art established as my Lord. Hail to thee, Rê at thy rising! Hail to thee, Atum at thy setting in beauty! Hail to thee, Harakhti-Khepri, who created himself!

Akhenaten's great Hymn to the Sun is so well known that it is purposely omitted here, for there are other lesser hymns of the same period which show the same fervour (real or simulated) for the new form of religion as the celebrated one. Even before Akhenaten changed his name and broke away from the old religion and the old capital city, there were hymns to the Sun in the name which was afterwards given to the Aten. Here is a hymn to Rê-Harakhti (the horizon-Horus) from a tomb at Thebes:

Hail to thee! When thou dawnest on the horizon thou illuminest the orbit of the Sun-globe [the Aten]. Thy beauty is on all lands, and men see only by means of thee. They awake when thy light arises, and their arms are raised in welcome to thy *ka*. Thou art God who created their bodies so that they may live. They sing chants when thy rays fall on the earth, even as I give praise to thy fair face, O child of *Him-who-rejoices-in-the-horizon*.

A prayer for the king in one of the tombs at Tell el Amarna begins as a hymn of praise of the Aten:

Beautiful is thine arising, O *Harakhti-who-rejoices-in-the-Horizon-in-his-name-Shu-who-is-in-the-Sun*,† thou living Sun, beside whom there is none else; who strengthenest the eyes with thy rays, who hast created all that exists. Thou risest in the horizon of heaven to give life to all that thou hast made, to all men, to all beasts, to all that flies and flutters, to all reptiles that are in the earth. They live when they behold thee, they sleep when thou settest. Make thou thy son, the King Nefer-khepru-Rê Akhenaten,

---

* Gardiner, *Tomb of Amenemhet*, p. 102.
† This is one of the official names of the Aten.

to live with thee for ever, to do what thy heart desireth, and to behold what thou doest every day, for he rejoices when he beholds thy beauty. Give him joy and gladness, so that all that thou encirclest may lie under his feet, while he offers it to thy ka—he, thy son, whom thou thyself hast begotten. The South and the North, the East and the West, and the Isles in the midst of the sea, shout for joy to thy ka. The southern boundary is as far as the wind blows, the northern as far as the sun shines. All their princes are overthrown and made weak by his power, that splendid vital force that animates the Two Lands and creates what the whole earth needs. Let him be for ever with thee, for he loves to look on thee. Give to him many Sed-Festivals and years of peace. Give to him of all that thy heart desires as much as there is sand on the shore, as scales upon fishes, and as hair upon cattle. Let him sojourn here until the white bird turns black, until the black bird turns white, until the hills rise to depart, until water flows upstream, the while may I continue in attendance upon him, the good God, until he assigns me the burial that he has granted.*

One of the heresies which Akhenaten flaunted in the face of the Amon-worshippers was the statement that light as well as heat emanated from the sun. The two official names of the Aten emphasise this heresy: the one is "Heat which is in the Aten", the other is "Light [Shu] which is in the Aten". Any scientific discovery which alters the preconceived religious ideas concerning the universe is bound to be strongly opposed by the priesthood, as was the case with Galileo and Darwin. Being the king, Akhenaten could not be touched, but the opposition was too strong for him to remain in the capital; it is possible that his exile from Thebes was not purely voluntary. His despotic insistence on his position as a god, his fanatical adherence to the tenets of his new religion, his utter disregard for his duties as a king while stressing his royal rights, make him a strange, though hardly a pleasing, figure in the history of his country and the history of religion.

Besides the great and splendid prayers and hymns which are engraved on the walls of temples and tombs or written on papyrus buried with the wealthy, there are a few little hymns of the common people which are sometimes worth attention; a little hymn to the setting sun shows a more intimate feeling towards the god than the more elaborate literary efforts in the great temples:

I give praise when I see thy beauty;
I hymn Rê when he sets.
O august, beloved, and merciful God,
Who hearest him that prays,
Who hearest the entreaties of him who calls upon thee,
Who comest at the voice of him who utters thy name.†

* Davies, *Rock-tombs of El Amarneh*, iii. pl. xxix, p. 31.
† *J.E.A.*, iii. 91.

A strange little hymn to Thoth was written by King Haremheb, when he was only a scribe, and therefore a devotee of Thoth:

Praise to Thoth, the son of Rê, the Moon, beautiful in his rising, Lord of bright appearings, who illumines the gods! Hail to thee, Moon, Thoth, Bull in Hermopolis, who spreads out the seat of the gods, who knows the mysteries, he who sifts the evidence, who makes the evil deed rise up against the doer, who judges all men. Let us praise Thoth, the exact plummet in the midst of the balance, from whom evil flees, who accepts him who avoids evil, the Vizier who gives judgment, who vanquishes crimes, who recalls all that is forgotten, the remembrancer of time and of eternity, who proclaims the hours of the night, whose words abide for ever.*

It seems probable that the court poets produced ecstatic verse on the accession of every king, as has been the custom in all countries and periods, but few of such poems have survived in Egypt. Of these one of the best is the poem by an unknown author on the accession of Rameses IV. There is only one copy of it known, written on a limestone ostrakon:

Happy, happy day! Joy in earth and heaven! Lo, the Lord of Egypt has appeared! They who fled have come back to their homes; they who hid can now return again; they who suffered hunger eat their bread in peace; thirsty ones are satisfied with drink;† naked and unclean are clad in robes of white; captives are set free throughout the land, casting off their fetters gleefully; reconciled are brothers heretofore at strife. From his sources comes the River brimming high, bringing joy and gladness to all hearts. Mourning widows now set wide their doors again; maidens chant once more their songs of happy love.‡

DRAMATIC

Egyptian drama, as it has come down to us, was entirely a religious rite; like the Art of Egypt it never broke free from the fetters of religion. But within the limits imposed upon it, it has dramatic force and movement. The best-known of the plays are the *Creation Play*, the *Coronation Play*, and *Horus and Setekh*. Of these the last is in some ways the finest. It was acted yearly on the 21st of the month Mechir, in the temple of Edfu, in honour of the local god, Horus; the action took place within the temple precincts partly on the sacred lake and partly on its banks. The actors were probably some of the temple personnel, but if the Pharaoh were present he would take the part of Horus, and the Queen would probably be Isis. The translators§ suggest that the spectators became so excited at certain incidents that they shouted with the chorus.

The play was in commemoration of the wars between Horus and

---

* *J.E.A.*, x. 3.   † Lit.: are drunken.   ‡ *Recueil des Travaux*, ii. 116.
§ Blackman and Fairman, *J.E.A.*, xxviii (1942)–xxx (1944).

Setekh, the final victory of Horus, "his coronation as king of a united Egypt, the dismemberment of his foe, and his 'triumph' or 'justification' before the tribunal of gods in the 'Broad Hall' ". The play consists of a prologue, three acts divided into scenes, and an epilogue. It was actually a narrative, "recited by a reader, linking together a number of dramatic performances in which the players by short set speeches, gestures, and actions gave life and reality to the reader's story". To make the action clear the translators give, in square brackets, the name of the character who is speaking.

It is interesting to note that in the introductory words to the first scene there is a confusion between the two Horuses, a confusion which is found in many of the religious texts. The description of the boat and the comparison of its different parts with rather unexpected objects and persons is in the true Egyptian style, which was evidently much admired. Setekh himself is usually called a hippopotamus in the text but is represented as a pig in the illustrations which accompany the words.

I give here scenes 1 and 2 of Act 2, from Blackman and Fairman's translation.

Scene 1

Come, let us hasten to the Pool of Horus, that we may see the Falcon in his ship, that we may see the son of Isis in his war-galley, like Rê in the Bark of the Morning. His harpoon is held firmly in his grip, as [in that of] Horus of the Mighty Arm. He casteth and draggeth, that he may bring captive the Hippopotamus and slay the Lower-Egyptian Bull. Rejoice, ye inhabitants of Retribution Town! Alack, alack, in Kenmet!*

[CHORUS] Seize thy baldric, come down and stand fast, having thine adornments which belong to Hedjhotpe,† thy net which belongeth to Min, which was woven for thee and spun for thee by Hathor, mistress of the th-plant.‡ A meal of forelegs is assigned thee, and thou eatest it eagerly. The gods of the sky are in terror of Horus! Hear ye the cry of Nēhes! Steady, Horus! Flee not because of them that are in the water, fear not them that are in the stream. Hearken not when he (Seth) pleadeth with thee.

[CHORUS AND ONLOOKERS] Hold fast, Horus, hold fast!

[ISIS] Take to thy war-galley, my son Horus, whom I love, the nurse which dandleth Horus upon the water, hiding him beneath her timbers, the deep gloom of pines. There is no fear when backing to moor, for the goodly rudder turneth upon its post like Horus on the lap of his mother Isis. The mast standeth firmly on the footstep, like Horus when he became ruler over this land. That beauteous sail of dazzling brightness is like Nut the great,§ when she was pregnant with the gods. The two lifts, one is Isis,

* Kenmet is the Oasis of Khargeh, where Setekh was worshipped.
† A god of weaving.   ‡ The translators suggest "coriander".
§ Nut was the sky-goddess, mother of the five great deities.

the other Nephthys, each of them holding what appertaineth to them upon the yard-arms, like brothers of one mother mated in wedlock. The row-locks are fixed upon the gunwale like the ornaments of princes. The oars beat on either side of her [*i.e.* the ship] like heralds when they proclaim the joust. The planks adhere closely and are not parted the one from the other. The deck is like a writing-board filled with images of goddesses. The baulks in the hold are like pillars standing firmly in a temple. The belaying-pins in the bulwarks are like a noble whose back is concealed. The scoop of real lapis lazuli baleth out the water as fine unguent, while *iyh*-weed★ scurries in front of her like a great snake into its hole. The hawser is beside the post like a chick beside its mother.

[CHORUS AND ONLOOKERS.] Hold fast, Horus, hold fast!

[ISIS.] Assault the foe, slay ye him in his lair, slaughter ye him in his [destined] moment, here and now! Plunge your knives into [him] again and again!

The gods of the sky are in terror of Horus. Hear ye the cry of Nēhes. [Steady, Horus!] Flee not because of them that are in the water, fear not them that are in the stream. Hearken not when he [Seth] pleadeth with thee.

Lay hold, Horus, lay hold on the harpoon shaft. I, yea, I, am the Lady of the shaft. I am the beautiful one, the mistress of the loud screamer† which cometh forth upon the banks and gleameth after the robber-beast, which rippeth open his skin, breaketh open his ribs, and entereth his [heart].‡ I forget not the night of the flood, the hour of turmoil.

[CHORUS AND ONLOOKERS.] Hold fast, Horus, hold fast!"

Scene 2

"[QUEEN.] Rejoice, ye women of Busiris and ye townsfolk beside Andjet! Come and see [Horus] who hath pierced the Lower-Egyptian Bull! He walloweth in the blood of the foe, his harpoon-shaft achieving a swift capture. He maketh the river to flow blood-stained,§ like Sekhmet in a blighted year.

[CHORUS OF WOMEN OF BUSIRIS.] Thy weapons plunge in mid-stream like a wild goose among her young ones.

[CHORUS AND ONLOOKERS.] Hold fast, Horus, hold fast!

[QUEEN.] Rejoice, ye women of Pe and Dep, ye townsfolk beside the marshes! Come and see Horus at the prow of his ship. like Rê when he shineth in the horizon, arrayed in green cloth, in red cloth, decked in his

★ This seems to be the trailing water-weed so often depicted in boating scenes.

† The "loud screamer" is the harpoon, so called from the whistling noise it makes as it flies through the air.

‡ I have ventured to insert the word "heart" here, though the translators have left a blank as in the original.

§ The belief that the annual change in colour of the water of the Nile was due to the blood of the god Setekh is identical with the legend of the god Adonis; in both legends the god is killed and his blood falls into the water. Setekh was slain in a fight, and it is very possible that in the primitive drama, where a living man acted the part, he was disguised in a mask, as seems to have been the case with the Minotaur. The mask would so hamper the victim that his death was assured.

ornaments, the White Crown and the Red Crown firmly set on his head, the two uræi between his brows. He hath received the crook and the whip, being crowned with the Double Diadem while Sekhmet abideth in front of him and Thoth protecteth him.

[CHORUS OF WOMEN OF PE AND DEP.] It is Ptah who has shaped thy shaft, Soker who hath forged thy weapons. It is Hedjhotpe in the Beauteous Place, who hath made thy rope from yarn. Thy harpoon-blade is of sheet-copper, thy shaft of *nbs*-wood from abroad.

[HORUS.] I have hurled with my right hand, I have swung with my left hand, as doth a bold fen-man.

[CHORUS AND ONLOOKERS.] Hold fast, Horus, hold fast!"

It is clear that, though Horus has little to say, he had the most important rôle in the drama. The continual shouts of "Steady, Horus!" "Hold fast, Horus!" show that he was in action all the time, raising the excitement and enthusiasm of the spectators.

TRIUMPH-SONGS

The Triumph-Songs are in a class by themselves, they recount the conquests and glorious victories of the Egyptians, and are extra-ordinarily interesting as showing both the development of the poetry and the change in sentiment. They undoubtedly existed from the earliest times, but none are recorded until writing had become common. One of the earliest, and at the same time of the most primitive in style and in sentiment, is of the vi-th dynasty. It is the type of song which has prevailed in Egypt from time immemorial, a line of solo and a line of chorus, the chorus-words being repetitive.

> This army returned in safety,
>> It had hacked up the land of the Sand-dwellers.
> This army returned in safety,
>> It had destroyed the land of the Sand-dwellers.
> This army returned in safety,
>> It had overturned their strongholds,
> This army returned in safety,
>> It had cut down their figs and vines.
> This army returned in safety,
>> It had thrown fire on all their troops.
> This army returned in safety,
>> It had slain tens of thousands of soldiers.
> This army returned in safety,
>> It had seized multitudes of living captives.★

As the Pharaohs were only tributary princes for a long period after the vi-th dynasty there are no Triumph-Songs till the warrior-kings

★ Sethe, *Urkunden*, i. 98–110.

of the splendid xii-th dynasty went into battle. As is so often the case, the outburst of literature did not occur until nearly a century after the times of war and trouble. The earlier kings of the xii-th dynasty have left no songs extolling their victories; there is nothing till the reign of Senusert III whose Triumph-Song is of the same form as the earlier example, but is considerably longer and more sophisticated. Only a few lines are quoted here:

> Twice joyful are thy ancestors before thee,
>> Thou hast increased their portions.
> Twice joyful is Egypt at thy strong arm,
>> Thou hast guarded the ancient order.
> Twice great are the Lords of his city,
>> For he is a shelter shielding the timid from the enemy.
> Twice great are the Lords of his city,
>> For he is a rock shielding from the blast on a day of storm.
> He has come, he has made Egypt to live,
>> He has destroyed afflictions.
> He has come, he has protected the Two Lands,
>> He has given peace to the Two Regions.★

Amonhotep III appears to have copied the Triumph-Song of Thothmes III in putting the words into the mouth of the god Amon:

> When I turn my face to the South I work a wonder for thee.
> I cause the chiefs of the miserable Kush to turn to thee,
> Bearing all their tribute on their backs.
> When I turn my face to the North I work a wonder for thee,
> I cause the countries of the ends of Asia to come to thee,
> Bearing all their tribute on their backs;
> They present themselves to thee with their children
> In order that thou mayest give to them the Breath of Life
> When I turn my face to the West I work a wonder for thee.
> I cause thee to capture the Tehennu, none are left.
> They are building this fortress in the name of my Majesty,
> Surrounded with a great wall reaching to heaven,
> Settled with the children of the chiefs of the Nubian Yunu-folk.
> When I turn my face to the Sunrise I work a wonder for thee.
> I cause to come to thee all the countries of Punt
> Bearing all the sweet woods of their countries,
> To crave peace with thee and the Breath of Life.†

In all the early Triumph-Songs until the end of the xviii-th dynasty the poets never broke away from the stilted archaic form of making every stanza, and often every alternate line, begin with a special phrase. The Songs were also merely a glorification of the victorious Pharaoh, and are general epithets of praise and laudation. There is

★ Griffith, *Hieratic Papyri*, pp. 2, 3.
† Petrie, *Six Temples at Thebes*, pls. xi, xii, p. 25.

no indication of what had actually happened, and no description of any battle. In the xix-th dynasty the poets had abandoned the stiffness of the earlier work, the Triumph-Songs had become descriptive but without lessening the splendour of the Pharaoh. In the two great Triumph-Songs of this period their beauty lies not so much in the epithets applied to the king as in the descriptive power of the poet. In the Triumph-Song of Rameses II, it is the rush of the actual battle that is described; in the Song of Mer-en-Ptah it is the feeling of the people after the danger is over that is the finest part of the poem.

Pentaur's poem on the Battle of Kadesh, when Rameses single-handed charged the Hittite chariotry and drove them back into the river, is very long. I quote here only the salient portions:

> Then like Mentu rose the King, took his arrows and his bow
> Like to Baal in his hour with his panoply of war.
> When he turned to look behind, chariots closed the outward way;
> Kheta, Kadesh and Arvád, in their thousands ringed him round.

Here the poem changes to the account given by the king in the first person; he describes how he was left alone to face the enemy, all his soldiers having fled. In this desperate situation he prayed to Amon for help:

> At the cry of my despair swiftly came the god to me,
> Took my hand and gave me strength!
> Till my might was as the might of a hundred thousand men.
> With the rapid onward sweep of a fierce consuming flame
> I destroyed their serried ranks.
> Like a hawk among the birds, striking down on either hand,
> Slew and wearied not to slay.
> In terror did they flee, to the water's edge they fled,
> Deep like crocodiles they plunged.
> Rotted were their hearts with fear as they tasted of my hand,
> And amazed they shrieked aloud,
> "Lo, no mortal man is he! This is Sutekh in his wrath,
> This is Baal's very self."

The anonymous poet of King Mer-en-Ptah is at his best when giving an account of the country after the defeat of the invaders, although his description of the defeat has some fine passages:

To Egypt has come great joy, and the towns of Ta-mery* rejoice. The people speak of the victories which King Merenptah has won against the Tahenu: "How beloved is he, our victorious Ruler! How magnified is he among the gods! How fortunate is he, the commanding Lord! Sit down

* Ta-mery is one of the many names of Egypt. It means the cultivated land in contra-distinction from the uncultivable desert.

happily and talk, or walk far out on the roads, for now there is no fear in the hearts of the people." The fortresses are abandoned, the wells are reopened; the messengers loiter under the battlements, cool from the sun; the soldiers lie asleep, even the border-scouts go in the fields as they list. The herds of the field need no herdsmen when crossing the fulness of the stream. No more is there the raising of a shout in the night, "Stop! Someone is coming! Someone is coming speaking a foreign language!" Everyone comes and goes with singing, and no longer is heard the sighing lament of men. The towns are settled anew, and the husbandman eats of the harvest that he himself sowed. God has turned again towards Egypt, for King Merenptah was born, destined to be her protector.*

Piankhy's Triumph-Song is totally different from anything which had gone before, for it has the very human touch of the mention of the Pharaoh's mother and her pride in her son:

> Happy is the mother, who bore thee, O great Conqueror,
> Happy is the breast on which thy head once lay,
> Happy are the arms which cradled thee in infancy,
> Happy now is she whose son we hail today.

LOVE SONGS

The love poems of ancient Egypt are in many ways like those of any other country, and therefore run easily into English verse. Thus the lover likens the maiden to all the flowers in the garden:

> Come through the garden, Love, to me.
> My love is like each flower that blows;
> Tall and straight as a young palm-tree,
> And in each cheek a sweet blush-rose.

Then there is the lover who falls ill with longing to see his beloved:

> When in the house I lie all day
> In pain that will not pass away,
> The neighbours come and go.
> Ah, if my darling to me came,
> The doctors she would put to shame,
> *She* understands my woe.†

Bridal songs were sung as they still are in the villages of Egypt, the theme always being the surpassing beauty of the bride. One of the most charming is the bridal song of the princess Mutardis; it has a refrain which may have been chanted by a chorus:

---

* Petrie, *Six Temples at Thebes*, p. 26.
† Weigall, *A Short History of Egypt*, p. 166.

Sweet of love is the daughter of the King!
Black are her tresses as the blackness of the night,
 Black as the wine-grape are the clusters of her hair.
The hearts of the women turn towards her with delight,
 Gazing on her beauty with which none can compare.

Sweet of love is the daughter of the King!
Fair are her arms in the softly swaying dance,
 Fairer by far is her bosom's rounded swell!
The hearts of the men are as water at her glance,
 Fairer is her beauty than mortal tongue can tell.

Sweet of love is the daughter of the King!
Rosy are her cheeks as the jasper's ruddy hue,
 Rosy as the henna which stains her slender hands!
The heart of the King is filled with love anew,
 When in all her beauty before his throne she stands.

The lament of the forsaken maiden whose lover has proved faithless
has been the theme of many poets in all countries, but the Egyptian
poem is perhaps the earliest of its kind:

Lost! Lost! Lost! O lost my love to me!
 He passes by my house, nor turns his head,
I deck myself with care; he does not see.
 He loves me not. Would God that I were dead!

God! God! God! O Amon, great of might!
 My sacrifice and prayers, are they in vain?
I offer to thee all that can delight,
 Hear thou my cry and bring my love again.

Sweet, sweet, sweet as honey in the mouth,
 His kisses on my lips, my breast, my hair;
But now my heart is as the sun-scorched South,
 Where lie the fields deserted, grey and bare.

Come! Come! Come! And kiss me when I die,
 For Life—compelling Life—is in thy breath;
And at that kiss, though in the tomb I lie,
 I will arise and break the bands of Death.

STORIES

As Egyptian literature is the earliest in the world, it is interesting to
know how certain forms of it arose. There are many stories of the
Middle Kingdom which almost amount to novels, but they are so
condensed as to be bald and dull in translation. This appears to have
been due to their being merely notes for the guidance of a professional

story-teller, who, like the bard of our own early history, travelled about the country and made his living by narrating interesting or amusing stories to an illiterate audience. For such a man, especially for a beginner, notes would be useful, if not essential. The story could be lengthened or abridged at will, conversations could be interpolated where necessary, and the tale enlivened by appropriate gestures.

The early stories are more in the nature of fairy tales in which magic plays a large part, but the *Story of Sinuhé* is the precursor of the modern novel, especially the novel of adventure. Sinuhé, the hero of the romance, was a near relative of the queen; for some un-explained reason he took fright when he heard of the death of the old king, and fled out of Egypt. In crossing the desert of Sinai he nearly died of thirst, but was rescued in the nick of time by a tribe of Bedawin, whose chief was so pleased with him that before long Sinuhé found himself married to the chief's eldest daughter and in possession of a fine country and of the headship of a tribe. After various adventures, including a successful combat with an overbearing bully who terrorised the whole country, he grew old and was apparently lonely, for all his children were grown up, and a great longing came over him to return once more to his native land. He therefore wrote a humble petition to the Pharaoh begging for permission to return. The Pharaoh replied in gracious terms, and when the letter arrived Sinuhé was wildly excited: "The letter reached me as I stood in the midst of my tribe; it was read to me, and I threw myself on my belly, I touched the dust and strewed it on my hair. I strode about the camp, rejoicing and saying, 'How can such things be done to a servant whose heart led him astray to barbarous lands? Verily, good indeed is the Benevolent One who has delivered me from death, who has permitted me to end my life in the Residence.' " He at once settled all his affairs and travelled to Egypt. On arriving at the Residence (*i.e.* royal palace), he was received with honour, "ten men coming [behind] ten men going [in front] to conduct me to the palace, and the royal children stood in the gate to receive me". The interview with the Pharaoh being very satisfactory, Sinuhé was given a "house such as might have belonged to a Councillor, and meals were brought to me from the palace three and four times a day, besides what the royal children continually brought me. There was made for me a pyramid of stone among the pyramids. The chief architect undertook the building of it, the chief draughtsman designed it, the chief sculptor carved it, the chief builders of the ceme-tery busied themselves with it. All the splendid things, which are necessary, were placed in it. Chantry priests were given to me, and there was made for me a mortuary estate with fields near the tomb as is done for a Chief Councillor. It was his Majesty who had all this done.

And so I live, rewarded by the King, until the coming of the day of death." Sinuhé ends his account of his life with a little poem in which he contrasts the misery of his life at the beginning and the pleasantness of its close.

> Once a fugitive fled in his terror,
>   Now I am known in the palace of Pharaoh.
> Once a weary one fainted from hunger,
>   Now I have bread to give to my neighbour.
> Once a man fled from Egypt all naked,
>   Now I am clothed in white linen garments.
> Once a man ran to take his own message,
>   Now I have slaves and servants in plenty.
> Fair is my house and wide is my dwelling,
>   For I am known in the palace of Pharaoh.*

Another adventure story is of a man who went to sea "in a ship which was one hundred and twenty cubits long and forty cubits wide and in it were one hundred and twenty sailors of the very pick of Egypt. They scanned the sky, they looked at the land, their hearts were braver than lions, and they could foretell a storm before it arose and a tempest before it came into being." In spite of their skill the ship foundered in a storm and all on board perished except the hero of the story. He was cast on a magic island which was inhabited by a gigantic serpent who was kind to the shipwrecked man, and told him that in four months a ship would arrive and take him away. When that happy event occurred, the serpent gave him a cargo of "myrrh, eye-paint, giraffes' tails, a great mass of incense, elephants' tusks, grey-hounds, monkeys, apes, and all kinds of costly things.

"I went down to the shore where the ship lay. I hailed the crew, and gave praise on the shore to the lord of the island, and they who were on board did the same. Then we voyaged northwards to the Residence of the King, and we reached it in two months as he had said. I entered before the King, and presented to him all the treasures that I had brought from the island. And his Majesty thanked me before all the officers of the whole land, and I was appointed to be a hench-man, and was presented with some of his serfs."

A later story, which is perhaps again fiction founded on fact, re-counts the taking of Joppa during the first campaign of Thothmes III. The "club" was probably the king's sacrificial mace, a blow from which, even if not delivered with full strength, would render a man senseless. The story shows that a stratagem for surreptitiously intro-ducing armed troops by the enemy into a besieged town was not the

* Gardiner, *Notes on the Story of Sinuhé.*

invention of the Greeks, but was practised by the Egyptians. The first part of the story has been destroyed, but it is evident that Thothmes III's principal general, Tehuti, was conducting the siege of Joppa, that he had invited the prince of Joppa to a meeting, possibly to discuss terms, and that there had been a feast with plenty of wine. "Now after an hour, when they were drunken, Tehuti said to the prince of Joppa, 'I will come to thee with my wife and child into the city. Let the grooms bring fodder for the horses and give them fodder. Or let an Aper [an Egyptian mercenary] come.' Then they laid hold of the horses and gave them fodder. Then the prince of Joppa wished to see the club of King Thothmes, and this was told to Tehuti. And the prince of Joppa himself came and said to Tehuti, 'My desire is to see the great club of King Thothmes. By King Thothmes, hast thou it with thee today? Then be so good as to bring it to me!' Tehuti stood before him and said, 'Look at me, O Prince of Joppa! Here is the club of King Thothmes, the fierce-eyed lion, the son of Sekhmet! His father Amon has given him strength to slay his enemies!' And he hit the prince of Joppa on the head, and he fell down senseless before him. Then he bound him with leather thongs, and put copper chains with four rings on his feet.

"Then Tehuti caused to be brought five hundred sacks which he had made, and caused two hundred soldiers to get into them, and their arms were filled with fetters and chains, and they were fastened up. And brave soldiers were assigned to carry them—five hundred in number*—and it was told them, 'When ye come into the town, let your comrades out, and catch hold of all the people of the town and put the fetters on them.' Then one of them went out and said to the charioteer of the prince of Joppa, 'Thy lord says, Go and say to thy mistress: Be glad of heart, for Sutekh has given to us Tehuti and his wife and his children. Lo, here is the tribute', meaning thereby the two hundred sacks full of men and all the chains and fetters. So he went ahead of them to gladden the heart of his mistress, saying, 'We have Tehuti.' So they opened the closed gates of the town for the soldiers. Then they entered into the town and let out their comrades. And they caught hold of the townspeople, both small and great, and put the fetters and chains on them. The strong arm of Pharaoh had captured the city."

The Story of the Doomed Prince is one of those charming tales which have delighted children for many centuries; it is the earliest

* The five hundred soldiers carrying the sacks could not enter the town armed. Their weapons and those of the two hundred men in the sacks were put with the fetters in the extra three hundred sacks. If all the sacks were made up to look alike, the human freight would pass unnoticed in the joyous excitement.

1 (above). Modern Coptic church showing cedar-wood iconostasis inlaid with ivory and ebony

2, 3 (right). Chalice in wooden case, as is related in the legend of the Grail

4 (below). Coptic priest in vestments of purple and gold brocade

PLATE XCIV

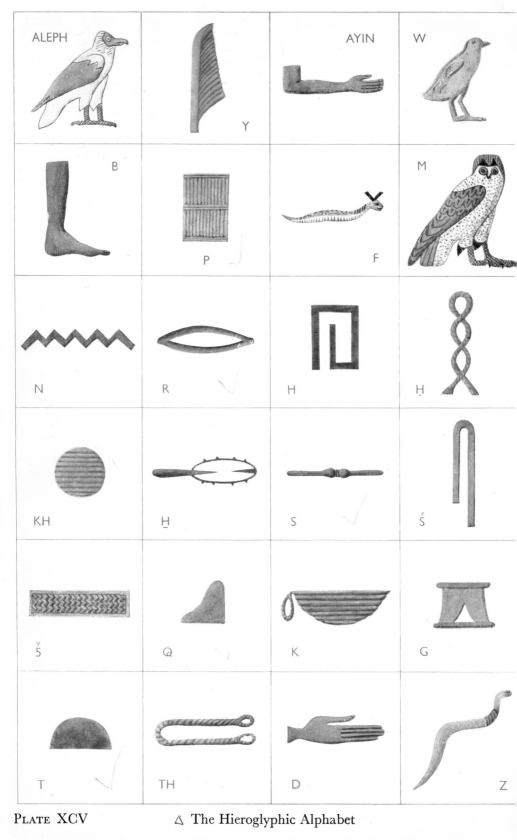

PLATE XCV △ The Hieroglyphic Alphabet

Syllables, Word-signs and Determinatives

1. Sign of life.
2. Sign for writing.
3. Sign for speaking.
4. Foreign country.
5. Sign for abstract words.
6. White or light.
7. Man.
8. Syllable ta.
9.   „   sha.
10. „   tha.
11. Boat.
12. Determinative for motion.

PLATE XCVI

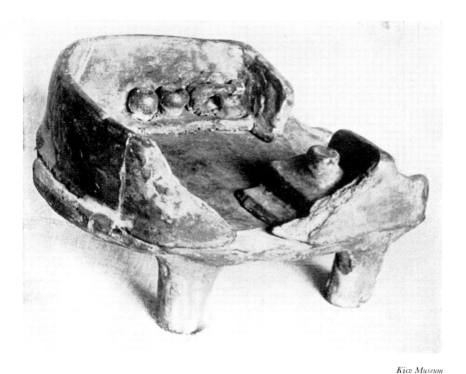

1. Soul-house from Tripolye.   Pottery

2. Female figure from Tripolye.   Pottery

PLATE XCVII

known example of its kind. It begins with a childless royal couple who at last have their heart's desire fulfilled, and a boy is born to them. The Hathors, prototypes of the fairy godmothers, come to foretell the fate of the baby, and in the usual manner foretell disaster, for they say that his death will be by a dog, a serpent or a crocodile. To avoid the danger, the boy is sent to live in a house away in the desert, but one day he sees a man walking with a dog behind him. On asking what that creature is, he is told it is a dog. He then so desires to possess a dog that the fond parents give way, and he is allowed to have a puppy. When the boy is grown up he remonstrates with his parents for keeping him shut up, saying, "Inasmuch as I am fated to three evil fates, let me follow my heart's desire, and let God do what is in His heart". The parents again give way, and the prince sets off with his dog, and travels as far as Naharina. The prince of Naharina has only one daughter, and in the customary manner of royal parents in fairy tales he had shut her up in a tower. This tower had seventy windows which were seventy cubits from the ground; and the princess's hand in marriage was promised to any suitor of royal rank who could climb up to the princess's window. The hero of the story makes friends with the suitors, whom he informs that he is the son of an official driven from home by a jealous step-mother. No reason is given for this perversion of the truth. Of course he is successful in reaching the window and the princess falls in love with him and he with her; but the prince of Naharina will not let her marry a man of such low rank, and orders him to be killed; but when the princess declares that if her lover is killed she will kill herself, her father relents, and they are married. The young prince tells his wife about his three dooms, and she suggests killing the dog, at which the prince is horrified, and says, "I am not going to kill my dog which I have had since it was a little one." Then the story suddenly shifts to a mysterious Mighty Man living in the same town as the prince and princess, who binds a crocodile with cords. Then the story returns to the prince, who falls asleep, and his wife sets a bowl of milk beside him. A serpent comes and drinks the milk, drinks till it is drunk, and lies upside down; the wife kills it with her dagger, and says to her husband, "Behold, thy God has given one of thy dooms into thy hand; He will also give thee the others". The prince goes for a walk with his dog, which chases game, and the prince follows on foot; the dog enters the river with the prince after him. There the prince meets the crocodile who takes him to the Mighty Man, saying, "I am thy doom following after thee." Here the story ends abruptly as the papyrus is incomplete.

Another story of travel, which appears to be either fiction founded on fact or a skit on travellers' tales, belongs to the xxi-st dynasty. It relates the adventures of a certain Wen-Amon, who was sent to Syria by the High-priest of Amon to buy cedar wood for making the Boat of Amon. For his own protection and to impress the people with whom he was likely to come in contact he took with him an image of Amon, known as Amon-of-the-Road.* This tale shows a great advance on the earlier stories; conversations are recorded, the incidents are such as might happen to a stranger in a strange land, there is a certain amount of character-drawing, and even an attempt at descriptive writing. Wen-Amon began his foreign adventures by having a large sum of money stolen from him, and he spent many days trying to get the prince of Byblos to find the thief. At last the prince sent for him: "I found the prince sitting in his upper chamber with his back against the window, while the waves of the great Syrian Sea broke behind him." Wen-Amon had a stormy interview with the prince, who tried to bargain with him about the cedar wood and infuriated him by saying, "What are these childish journeys that they have caused thee to make?" Wen-Amon replied indignantly, "Fie! These are not childish journeys at all. There is no ship on the sea that does not belong to Amon. The sea is his and his is the Lebanon, of which thou sayest it belongs to thee, whereas it is merely a plantation for the Boat of Amon. And now thou hast made this great god spend nine-and-twenty days after he had landed here. He is still the same that ever he was, and yet thou wilt stand there and bargain about the Lebanon with its lord." The prince was rather frightened and consented to provide the wood, for Wen-Amon pointed out that Amon himself had come in the person of Amon-of-the-Road. But even when Wen-Amon had obtained the ship and stowed the wood on board his troubles were not over, for eleven ships from Zakar were standing in to the port to capture him. The prince, however, said to the men of Zakar, "I cannot take the messenger of Amon prisoner in my land. Let me send him away and then you can pursue him and take him prisoner." This was done, but Wen-Amon's ship was swifter than those of Zakar, and he got safely away and reached Cyprus. There he fell into further trouble, and met the Queen of Cyprus, but the papyrus breaks off at this point, and the story of his adventures in Cyprus are unknown.

A demotic story, probably Ptolemaic, begins with a childless couple —the son and daughter-in-law of Pharaoh—who long for a child. The wife eats a magic fruit and in due course bears a son, whom she calls Si-Osiri (Son of Osiris). The child proves to be the most mar-

---

* Temples had sometimes more than one figure of the god; in which case each image had a separate function. Amon-of-the-Road was clearly the helper of travellers and could be taken out of Egypt, so also could Khonsu-Expeller-of-Demons, who was taken to Bekhten to cure the little princess.

vellous of children, for he has in him all the wisdom and knowledge of the whole world. One day, when he was five years old, he stood with his father looking out of the window of the palace, watching two funerals on their way to the desert. The first was that of a rich man, and the funeral was of the grandest; many priests and mourning women, and the funeral offerings were lavish and numerous. Behind this magnificent cortège came the funeral of a very poor man with no followers and no funeral offerings. His father said to Si-Osiri, "I hope to have the fate of the rich man when I die". Si-Osiri replied, "I wish for you the fate of the poor man." At which the father was hurt, but Si-Osiri offered to take him where he could see for himself. The two went out to the desert cemetery and arrived at the Other World. Unfortunately the papyrus is incomplete at this crucial point, the method of getting to the Other World being on the missing portion. The Other World consisted of a series of vast halls, where various strange sights were seen. As the two advanced, the halls were filled with the cries and screams of a man lying in a doorway with the pivot of the door turning in his right eye. Passing through the doorway, they entered into the presence of Osiris himself. The god sat enthroned, surrounded by a multitude of magnificent personages; among them was a man, richly clad, to whom everyone paid great reverence. In front of Osiris was the great Balance, and Si-Osiri explained to his father that it was here that the dead came for judgment. Their deeds were placed in the scale-pans, the good deeds in one, the bad in the other. If the bad deeds outweighed the good, the sinner was punished; if the good deeds outweighed the bad, the doer was rewarded. Si-Osiri was careful to explain that in every case regard was had as to the opportunities the dead man had had in life to do good or evil. For this reason the rich man was being punished because he had had many chances of doing good and had not taken them, therefore he was now that wretched creature lying in the doorway being tortured by the pivot turning in his right eye. But the poor man had always done good according as he had had opportunity, therefore he was now one of the blessed in the presence of Osiris, and was the richly clad man to whom all paid reverence, and all the funerary equipment of the rich man had been given to him, and he was now enjoying it. "And that," said Si-Osiri triumphantly, "is why I wished for you the fate of the poor man and not of the rich man."*

* Griffith, *Stories of the High-priests.*

VII

FLINDERS PETRIE

(Pls. xci; xcii)

No book on Egypt can be regarded as complete without some reference, however slight, to the man whose work on the glorious past of that ancient country is the foundation of all modern archæology. As his fellow-worker for many years at University College, London, I may perhaps be forgiven for considering myself specially qualified to write of that work as I saw it.

In 1877 there appeared a little book of rather more than a hundred and fifty pages called *Inductive Metrology*. The author was a young man of four and twenty, who signed himself W. M. Flinders Petrie. The publication of that modest volume transformed the whole of the study of the Past, and brought its author with a rush to the forefront of the learned world. Until Petrie's appearance in the field there had been no archæology, only antiquarianism, with collections of "curios" or "relics of the past". And it was the hobby of a few learned men, whose horizon was bounded by Biblical or classical history. They were the slaves of the written word, and believed nothing that was not vouched for by documentary evidence. But even documents were not always above suspicion if they did not agree with preconceived ideas, and Herodotus's accounts of Egypt were treated with scorn. It was considered clever to say of Herodotus, "Father of History, indeed! Father of Lies more likely!" To these people Greek Art was a sacred thing, which had come into the world full-blown. Greek literature also had had no beginning. They were not quite separate and special creations of God, but were very nearly so, and it was almost blasphemy to suggest that when the Greeks themselves said how much they owed to Egypt they might have been speaking the truth.

Into this milieu came Petrie's bombshell. *Inductive Metrology* intimated to the learned world that a new method of investigation had come into existence, a method in which the written word had no part and which proved that there was a form of culture and civilisation before the time of the Greeks. For Petrie, without any written word to assist him, had discovered the unit of measurement used by the builders of Stonehenge and other stone circles in England. Facts and not words were now to be the order of the day. His next work was the measurement of the pyramids and temples of Gizeh, undertaken to prove the truth of Piozzi Smyth's theories concerning the Great Pyramid, and there never was anyone who more conclusively disproved that theory than Flinders Petrie. Then came excavation, when he evolved a technique which has been followed by every archæologist ever since. It was in his first year of excavating that the learned world suffered its second bombshell, for he discovered the Pelusian Daphnai of Herodotus, thus vindicating that historian's veracity, and—horror of horrors—proving that there were Greek artistic remains before the time of Pheidias. The shock was severe, and some of the older classicists could not bring themselves to believe the facts. Then Petrie found the lost site of Naukratis, and in his excavations in the Fayum he discovered Greek papyri including some fragments of the Iliad.

Petrie's find of foreign polychrome pottery at Kahun raised a storm of indignation and incredulity when he proved that it was Ægean in origin and xii-th dynasty in date. It seems almost incredible that so little time ago he was able to write as follows: "The question rests thus: the external evidence is clear for the dating of the pottery to the xii-th dynasty; the foreigners of the Mediterranean were already known to the Egyptians and were actually living in this town; and this pottery is distinctly foreign or Ægean. The only difficulty lies in the Greek archæologists objecting to any such early date for such pottery. . . . No one as yet has found anything to date before the Mykenæan period in Greece. What state the Ægean was in at an earlier date we do not know. It has nothing to do with the historic civilisation of Greece; it is a branch of the bronze age of Europe, as much as Hallstatt or Etruris. . . . We have here a prepossession to deal with as to what is likely in a period as yet totally unknown, the pre-Mykenæan age."* Petrie's contention that the pottery was Ægean in origin was triumphantly justified when Evans found the Kamares ware in Crete, and now the modern Greek archæologists point to it as proof of the extreme antiquity of Greek civilisation.

The excavations at Tell el Amarna brought to light the whole of the essential facts of Akhenaten's reign. Little new information has been forthcoming from that site since Petrie brought both the site and its founder into prominence.

It was at this time that Petrie became the Edwards Professor of Egyptology in the University of London. The Chair was founded by Miss Amelia B. Edwards, who herself had done a certain amount of excavating in Egypt, and it was designed for the teaching of Egyptian archæology and the training in scientific excavation.

Naqada was the next great discovery, when the prehistoric civilisa-

* Petrie, *Illahun, Kahun, and Gurob*, p. 11.

tions of Egypt were first brought to light. Even Petrie did not dare
to suggest so subversive an explanation as prehistory for the strange
pottery and other objects and the peculiar burials that he found, and
contented himself with calling these people a New Race. This one
mistake was never forgiven him, and even after his death it was cast
up against his memory that he had failed to recognise, as prehistoric,
objects the like of which had never been seen before.

By his finds at Diospolis Parva and at Abydos Petrie settled the
sequence of the prehistoric periods and the order of the kings of the
i-st and ii-nd dynasties. His system of Sequence-dating has made it
possible to bring order into the archæology of any country, and it has
been applied successfully in other places besides Egypt.

Petrie's main work was in Egypt, but his excavations at Tell el Hesy
in Palestine settled the sequence of pottery in that country. In his old
age he returned to work in Palestine in an attempt to find the origin
of the Hyksos, and to fill in the blanks of their occupation of Egypt.
Palestine, however, offers little of interest to any but the Biblical
student, and though his work has thrown light on the early history of
that country it has not the glow of human interest which Egypt
always has.

When Petrie began his career, Herodotus was our only guide to the
history of Egypt; when he ended that career, the whole of Egyptian
prehistory and history had been mapped out and settled. Since then a
few details have been found to fill in small gaps in knowledge, but no
fundamental changes have been made, and little new knowledge has
been added to that vast amount which he laid bare to the world.

Petrie's two limitations were his want of knowledge of the ancient
Egyptian language and his rather unsympathetic attitude towards the
Egyptian religion. Over the first of these the learned philological
pundits shook their grave heads and said his work was "unscholarly",*
yet he was able to translate the inscriptions on objects of the i-st
dynasty, inscriptions which made even F. Ll. Griffith pause; he could
tell the date of any inscription by the form of the hieroglyphs; and he
could pick out almost at a glance personal and place names in a long
inscription. For instance, he recognised the name of Israel on the
Mer-en-Ptah stela before the great scholar who was translating the
inscription had realised it. Though he had little real sympathy with the
ancient religion, he was the only person who reduced to order that
apparently bewildering and chaotic mass of deities.

His zest for work was amazing. Even in those last long months
when he lay in the hospital in Jerusalem waiting for death, he spent

* "When an author collects together the opinions of as many others as he can and
fills half of every page with footnotes, this is known as 'scholarship.'"

his time in putting down on paper some of his vast accumulations of knowledge for the benefit of those who shall come after.

It is very certain that if one has been associated in one's work with a genius, one's estimate of lesser intellects is necessarily affected. I have worked with many men; it has been my favoured lot to know more than one genius, each in his own line; the rest, however, were only highly intellectual. The difference between the genius and the clever man cannot be expressed in words, for between talent and genius there is a great gulf fixed. There is in the genius a divine spark, a vitality, a living force, a driving power, which can never be found in the lesser intellect. The genius goes straight to the goal without apparent effort, and his goal is the truth as he sees it and which in time others are forced to see also. He has that foresight which is insight, which is the gift of God, and cannot be acquired by anyone who is not so endowed. To those who can appreciate the greatness of the gift, it is an inspiration to work with a genius, as all Petrie's students have found. Every archæologist owes to Petrie that systematic arrangement of knowledge which lays bare the history of the peoples of the past in every country. Without Petrie there would have been no archæology, we should still have been bound by the written word and the dry-as-dust philologists and antiquarians.

So I end my book, as I have begun it, with the name of Flinders Petrie, the man who made known to the world so much of the Splendour that was Egypt.

APPENDIX I

FOREIGN CONNECTIONS

THE foreign connections of Egypt have not yet received sufficient attention. The trade with the Ægean is now a commonplace of the archæology of the eastern Mediterranean; the trade with Palestine and Syria is obvious. But so little serious work has been done on the connections with places farther afield, especially the trade with the East, that I venture to make a few suggestions.

I have pointed out that there was probably trade with India, Persia, and other Eastern countries; these being grouped together by the Egyptians under the name of the Land of Punt.

The importance of the cobra and of the lotus in both Egypt and India suggests some connection from the religious point of view. This, however, is merely a conjecture, without proof so far. But there are facts which prove that there was trade with the Middle East from the earliest times. Lapis lazuli is known among the Badarians, and was commonly used in the later prehistoric and the Pharaonic periods. It is a stone which comes from Asia, and was probably imported through Persia. India is the home of sweet-scented woods, notably sandalwood; and it is remarkable that the Egyptians could not obtain sweet woods except from the East. In the xviii-th dynasty a sketch of a barndoor cock shows that there was so much communication with India that an indigenous Indian bird could be so well known in Egypt as to be sketched. Thothmes III clearly had hens, for it is recorded that he had two birds which laid eggs every day. The cheetah or hunting leopard, which appears to be peculiar to India, is among the products of Punt brought to Hatshepsut.

In the xxvi-th dynasty, when the circumnavigation of Africa was an accomplished fact, there must surely have been many sailors sufficiently daring to venture the voyage to India. This is proved by the fact that some of the flowers in the wreaths found at Hawara are indigenous to India. And there is no doubt that Indians visited, perhaps lived in, Egypt during the Persian and Ptolemaic periods, for unmistakable Indian figures were among the pottery votive-figures in the temple of Ptah at Memphis.

Under the Ptolemies there is some evidence that Buddhist missionaries, sent out by King Asoka, reached Egypt and there introduced that system of monasticism which had so great an effect on European religion.

In the Mediterranean area little or no research has been made as to trade with Egypt outside Crete and the Ægean. Yet there are traces of the connections in the xii-th dynasty with Malta and even farther west. The connections with Russia I give below, and an important though unexpected connection with England in early Christian times is found in the legend of the coming of the Holy Grail* (pl. xciv; 2, 3).

CONNECTIONS BETWEEN EGYPT AND RUSSIA

(Reprinted from *Antiquity*, xv (1941), p. 384. By kind permission of the Editor.)

Some years ago Sir Flinders Petrie claimed that there were definite connections between ancient Egypt and southern Russia, more particularly with the Caucasus; but as his opinion was based entirely on literary and philological evidence archæologists have been averse from accepting it. Archæological evidence in support of that claim is, however, coming in by slow degrees, and it seems probable that in time the evidence will prove that the Founder of the science of Archæology was right in his conjecture.

I bring forward now two pieces of evidence in support of his claim; the first is literary and pictorial, the second is purely archæological.

(1) As I have already published the first in full detail (*Ancient Egypt* (1934), p. 115), I merely give a summary here. The name of the god 'Ash occurs five times in the inscriptions of Egypt, and in four of the five it is evident that he is of foreign origin. He appears first on the sealings of wine-jars of the ii-nd dynasty (Petrie, *Royal Tombs*, Plate. xxii, 178, 179; Plate xxiii, 199, 200), where he is shown in connection with vineyards. In the v-th dynasty he is called "Lord of Tehennu", *i.e.* the Land of the Olive-tree (Borchardt, *Sahuré*, p. 17). In the vi-th dynasty he is mentioned in an unintelligible passage in the Pyramid Texts of King Pepy. In the xviii-th dynasty (*c.* 1500 B.C.) his name occurs in chapter xcv of the Book of the Dead in a rain-charm, "I am the Terrible One in the thunderstorm. I am refreshed by this 'Ash". The connections with the vine, the olive, and with rain, give plain indication that this is not an indigenous god in Egypt, but his actual provenance can be demonstrated with some certainty. A representation of him in the xxvi-th dynasty (*c.* 600 B.C.) depicts him with three heads (pl. xc. 3), a lion, a snake, and a vulture; his name is written beside him, "'Ash of many faces". Here again he is obviously foreign for no indigenous Egyptian god is multiple-headed. In Sebastian Münster's *Cosmographia Universalis*, published in 1545, there occurs the picture of a three-headed god which must surely be the same as the god 'Ash, for the heads are those of a lion, a snake, and a vulture (pl. xc. 4). Though Münster calls them the heads of a lion, a toad, and an eagle, a comparison of the two representations shows that they are as similar as it is possible to be, allowing for two different styles of art. The "eagle" has the feathering down the back of the neck, a characteristic of the Egyptian vulture; the "toad" is copied from the snake's head; in both examples the band showing the edge of the mask worn by the human impersonator of the god is clearly indicated; and in Münster's

* Murray, *Ancient Egypt*, 1916.

picture the figure wears a loin-cloth, a unique feature in a European representation of a "demon". My point here is that Münster states in so many words that this deity was called up to advise Marcomir, King of the Franks, when that monarch and his tribe were still in the land of Scythia.

(2) My second piece of evidence is entirely archæological, and again points to a connection between southern Russia and ancient Egypt. Among the finds of the Tripolye culture found on a site on the Dnieper are the objects illustrated here. The first is of a pottery tray (pl. xcv. 1), which in many ways so closely resembles the soul-houses of the xii-th dynasty (pl. ix) that there seems no reasonable doubt as to the relation between them. In the Russian example the tray has a surrounding wall with an opening in front, at the side are water-jars and the figure of a woman kneeling to grind corn at a saddle-quern; all these features are the same in both Egypt and Russia.* Petrie has shown that in Egypt the soul-house developed from the simple tray to the complexity of a two-storied dwelling with furniture; from which it is clear that soul-houses of that type either arose or were elaborated in Egypt. But the Russian examples show that the type had been long enough in Russia to evolve an essential feature of Russian life—the big stove at the entrance. Yet even this may be a modification, possibly a misunderstanding, of the miniature granaries found in the later Egyptian types. A fragment of another soul-house found on the same site indicates that the complete example was not unique.

Pl. xcvii. 2 shows a seated female figure in pottery, found on the same site as the soul-houses. This should be compared with the figures in Petrie's *Prehistoric Egypt*, Plates iv, 9; v, 4, 5; vii, 15, for figures leaning backwards; and Plate vii, 16, for a figure leaning forward. In both the Egyptian and Russian examples there is the same attitude with outstretched legs, the same beak-like face, the same treatment of the breasts, and where the arms occur in the Egyptian figures the position is the same as in the Russian. In the forward-leaning figure (Petrie, op. cit., Plate vii, 16) there is the same extension of the buttocks, a detail which was probably necessary to keep the balance of the backward-leaning figure but quite unnecessary in the Egyptian example. The dating of this Egyptian figure is interesting. Petrie dates it tentatively only by the shape of the boat in which it was found, but at the same time he says of a similar, though much rougher, figure on the same plate that he would date it to the xii-th dynasty by the pottery.

In the Russian figure the flattening of the back of the head, and the flattened excrescences pierced with holes at the sides of the head, representing ears pierced for earrings, are reminiscent of the pottery figurines of women —usually called dolls—found in Egypt and dated to the xii-th dynasty, which are known to have a foreign origin.†

* Petrie, *Gizeh and Rifeh*, for wall with front opening, pls. xiv, xxii. 60; for water-jars, pl. xxii. 60, 57; for woman grinding corn, pl. xviii. 118, xxii, central on right; for granaries, pl. xxii, centre on left.

† Capart, *Recueil de Monuments Egyptiens*, pl. 66, on extreme left.

Judging by the archæological evidence Professor Gordon Childe considers that "on a short chronology the whole Tripolye development would lie within the limits of the periods ii to iv". This would coincide with the xii-th dynasty of Egypt, a period to which soul-houses and certain types of female figurines belong. It was a time when Egyptian connections were with the North. At present those connections are known as being almost exclusively with Crete, probably because Crete has been well and scientifically excavated and other countries are still unexplored. The archæological riches of ancient Russia are as yet almost untouched.

APPENDIX 2

MARRIAGES AND MATRILINEAL DESCENT

The marriages of the Pharaohs of the xvii-th and xviii-th dynasties, wherever they can be traced, show that marriage with the heiress-queen was the main factor in succeeding to the throne. The marriages were therefore contracted in every degree of consanguinity. The titles of the queens indicate their position and their relationships to the Pharaohs whom they married. The "Lady of the Two Lands" was the heiress, who became the "Great Wife of the King". She was at the same time very often the "King's Sister", and either the "King's Mother" or the "King's Daughter". Such titles relate of course to the living King; "Wife of the God" refers to the previous King, who being dead has become the god Osiris.

In the case of Hatshepsut there is some difficulty as her titles are not the same as those of an ordinary Queen, for she claimed to be the actual Pharaoh. But her marriages can be inferred. She was the daughter of Thothmes I and Queen Aahmes the heiress-queen, and the action of Thothmes I in associating her with him on the throne suggests that she was married to him, her mother being then presumably dead. What her connection was with Thothmes II does not appear; but in view of the vital importance of marriage with the heiress, Thothmes II could not have obtained the kingdom without marrying her. Thothmes III was about twenty when he was chosen by Amon, therefore of an age to marry; and Hatshepsut's two daughters, Nefru-Rê and Hatshepset, are called the daughters of Thothmes III, indicating her marriage with that Pharaoh. Nefru-Rê died young, but Thothmes married Hatshepset his daughter by Hatshepsut,* and she became his Great Wife.

* Though the names of these two queens are confusingly alike, the meanings are different; Hat-shepsut means Chief of Noble Women; Hat-shepset means Noble Chieftainess.

The genealogies of small officials show the same custom of consanguineous marriages.

Genealogy of Har-her-nekht. Held no office.

This is a complicated genealogy. Har-her-nekht had two brothers and a sister, born of different mothers, showing that the relationship was through the father. The complication comes in by the fact that the father, Sebek-Iam,

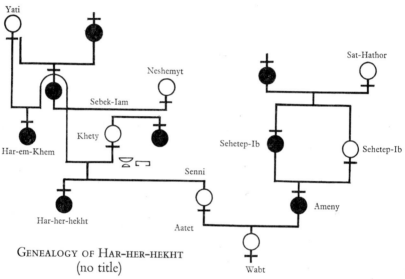

GENEALOGY OF HAR-HER-HEKHT
(no title)

His father Sebek-Iam born of Yati
His mother Khety born of Neshemyt
His brother Har-em-Khem born of Yati
His brother Senni born of Neshemyt
His sister Aatet born of Khety
Her daughter Wabt born of Amony
His mother Sehetep-Ib born of Sat-Hathor
His father Sehetep-Ib born of Sat-Hathor

whose mother was Yati, had a son by Yati, and a daughter by his daughter Khety. There is then a mother-son marriage and a father-daughter marriage.

By the position of the names on the stela there is also a short genealogy of Amony the husband of Aatet. He was the child of a brother-sister marriage.

Genealogy of Pa-unt. Scribe of the cemetery.

In this genealogy the parentage of Nefer-hotep shows very clearly a mother-son marriage. The marriage with Kanes, his wife's mother, suggests that Snebtisi might have been also his daughter as well as his wife.

In early Egypt the Pharaoh, *i.e.* the man who had married the heiress-queen, appointed one of his sons to be his successor, that son would in his turn marry the heiress and become Pharaoh. That son might be the son of the heiress or of a non-royal mother; it was by marriage, and not by birth, that a man became king. In the xviii-th dynasty, though marriage was still all-important, the choice of the new Pharaoh had fallen into the hands of the priests of Amon, who appointed Thothmes III by stopping the image of the god before him. Thothmes III's mother was not the great

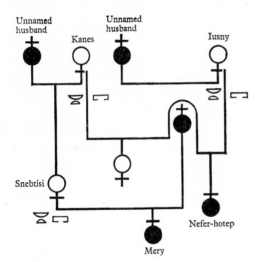

Pa-unt born of Iusny

His wife Snebtisi born of Kanes

His son Mery born of Snebtisi

His son Nefer-hotep born of Iusny

His daughter . . . born of Kanes

heiress, though probably in the line of succession. In the xix-th dynasty the eldest son of the heiress-queen appears to have been the acknowledged heir. These customs can be traced in the Judean kingship, which also shows the growth of patrilineal rights with survivals of matrilineal customs.

Saul and David were both appointed by God, *i.e.* by the man who united in himself the offices of High-priest and ruler of the land. Saul was of royal descent, for his great-grandfather was Jehiel, "the father of Gibeon" whose wife, Saul's great-grandmother, was Maachah, which being the name of a tribe shows that she was royal. It was not uncommon to call a ruler by the name of his or her country. David secured his position by marrying two royal ladies, Michal and Maachah.★ In this connection it is worth noting that

★ Is it possible that Ahinoam, daughter of Ahimaaz and wife of Saul, was the same as Ahinoam the Jezreelite, whom David "took"? Saul's otherwise insensate fury against David can be understood if David held both heiresses, Ahinoam as well as her daughter, Michal.

Jonathan, Saul's eldest son, had no claim to the throne, in spite of his immense popularity. Yet it seems clear that, among the Benjamites at least, there was growing up the idea of inheritance in the male line, for Abner succeeded in maintaining Saul's surviving son, Ishbosheth, for two years as king over Benjamin. The war between Ishbosheth and David went on for a considerable time, and only came to an end by Abner's defection to David. David refused to make peace with him, "except thou first bring Michal, Saul's daughter, when thou comest to see my face".*

Owing to the bitter quarrel between David and Michal, "Michal Saul's daughter had no child unto the day of her death",† therefore the succession in the female line went to the children of the other royal lady, Maachah of Geshur, whose children were Absalom and Tamar. The episode of Amnon and Tamar was perhaps an attempt on the part of the man to capture the heiress; it failed for she fled to her brother Absalom, who according to Josephus married her. Amnon was David's eldest son, and as the custom of primogeniture in the male line was then beginning, Absalom, having made sure of the heiress, slew his elder brother. Absalom seems to have bided his time till there was no heiress-queen in David's harem, then as the husband of the heiress he made war on his father. The daughter of Absalom and Tamar was Maachah, who carried the kingdom because she was the daughter of the heiress. She became the chief wife of Rehoboam, who was not of royal birth on the mother's side. Rehoboam was succeeded by his son Abijam, "three years he reigned in Jerusalem, and his mother's name was Maachah the daughter of Abishalom".‡ After Abijam's death his son Asa came to the throne: "Forty and one years he reigned in Jerusalem and his mother's name was Maachah the daughter of Abishalom."§ The only way that both Abijam and Asa could have had the same mother was by the marriage of Abijam with his own mother.

(An asterisk denotes women's names.)

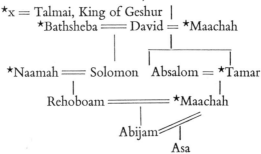

The position of Abishag in connection with David, Solomon, and Adonijah is worth consideration. The extreme care that was taken to find the right woman for a ceremonial marriage with David; the request by the

* 2 Sam. iii. 13.　　　　† 2 Sam. vi. 23.
‡ 1 Kings xv. 2.　　　　§ 1 Kings xv. 10.

ambitious Adonijah that he might have her to wife, and the consequent breaking of Solomon's most solemn oath to spare Adonijah's life, all point to the fact that Abishag was not only in the direct line of descent but was actually the heiress-queen whose husband could claim the throne by right of marriage with her.*

Among the Claudian Emperors of Rome matrilineal descent and its consequent marriages in every degree of consanguinity were still practised though those customs were obsolete among the people. Messalina's descent in the female line is very clear, and there are several noteworthy facts to be observed in that genealogy.

Julia and her daughter Atia both married men of humble birth, yet it was Atia's son who became Emperor, and it would seem that Atia's daughter Octavia may have been regarded as the heiress, which would account for her husband, Antony, attempting to seize the throne. In the matrilineal system of descent, Antony had the prior right to the throne as the husband of the heiress. Messalina certainly seems to have regarded herself as the heiress, for she publicly divorced Claudius and married Silius; and it is evident that Claudius was well aware of what that action involved, when he asked, "Is Silius the Roman Emperor, and am I a private citizen?" The murder of Messalina left her daughter Octavia as the heiress. This was made clear when Claudius died, for his son Britannicus, though of an age to reign, was passed over in favour of the heiress's husband Nero.

(An asterisk denotes women's names.)

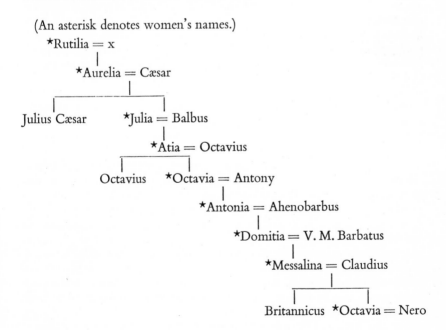

* 1 Kings i. 3, 4; ii. 13–25.

APPENDIX 3

SCARABS

(Pl. lxxxv. 2)

Among the many amulets and ornaments worn by the ancient Egyptians during the historic period, the most important are the scarabs. These little objects are made of stone or glazed ware and are in the form of the scarabæus-beetle (hence the modern name of *scarab*). The actual beetles appear to have been sacred in the prehistoric times, for they have been found, carefully preserved, in many of the early graves.

The scarabæus is a dung beetle; it lays its egg in the droppings of animals, then rolls the dung into a ball and pushes the ball with its hind-legs into a hole in the ground. These beetles can be seen in full activity in any part of Upper Egypt in a sunny place over which animals have passed. But the beetles will also lay their eggs in the dead body of one of their companions, and this is perhaps the reason why the scarab was taken by the ancient Egyptians as the emblem of the resurrection, for they saw life coming out of death as the young beetles emerged.

The Egyptian word for the beetle is Kheper,* and the deity who takes his name from the creature and is represented as a beetle is Khepri, He of the Beetle. Kheper, however, means also To be, to exist; therefore Khepri can also mean the Existent One. In the theology of the Egyptians he was Existence itself and could therefore give existence to others; as a beetle he pushes the ball of the Sun into the Other World in the evening; as a beetle he waits in the Other World to revivify the dead Sun, when the soul of Rê and the soul of Khepri are united; and in the morning he as a beetle pushes the ball of the sun over the horizon of the earth. Khepri the god appears to be merely a theological abstraction, but the beetle was a popular form which conveyed to the common people the idea of external existence.

Scarabs begin as early as the i-st dynasty, become increasingly common throughout the historic period, and disappear under the Ptolemies. These little objects are carefully carved in the shape of a beetle, but the underside, where the legs should occur, is left flat and engraved with a name or with some magical design. The earliest scarabs have royal names only and were possibly used for a double purpose, to protect the wearer by the power of a divine name and to show that he held some office under the royal god. In the Middle Kingdom (*c.* 3000–2780 B.C.) design scarabs become frequent, the designs are often spirals arranged in intricate and beautiful patterns. In the New Kingdom (*c.* 1590–1370 B.C.) designs and the names of gods and goddesses are common, so common in fact that one is forced to believe that many of the scarabs were sold as souvenir-charms at various shrines. In the Late period scarabs are merely charms.

Scarabs were at first made of stone—steatite or schist—glazed blue or

* Is there a possible connection between this word and the Indo-European Kafer?

green. In the Middle Kingdom carnelian and amethyst scarabs were made; as these stones were very hard and difficult to engrave, the base was covered with a gold plate on which the appropriate signs were cut. Cheap scarabs were made in glazed ware, not in stone.

Scarabs used as amulets for the dead are differently made from those for the living. Instead of the flat base with engraved signs, the legs of the insect are carved, showing that it was the actual beetle that was represented. In the late New Kingdom and succeeding dynasties it was customary to make large scarabs with wings to be laid across the breast of the mummy, as signifying the belief in eternal existence. Large scarabs in dark stones, chiefly basalt, were also made for the dead. These have a flat base on which was engraved the Chapter of the Heart from the Book of the Dead.

Scarabs were so popular that in countries adjacent to Egypt they were copied locally. The most important of these are the scarabs made in Palestine by the Hyksos long before they invaded Egypt. Such scarabs are distinctive, the hieroglyphs are clearly copied by people who could not read them, and the backs of the beetles show no division of the wing-cases as do the Egyptian examples. In the xxvi-th dynasty the Greeks of Naukratis had a regular trade in scarabs for export to the Ægean.

APPENDIX 4

THE NEW YEAR OF GOD

(Reprinted by kind permission of the Editor from the
Cornhill Magazine, 1934.)

Three o'clock and a still starlight night in mid-September in Upper Egypt. At this hour the village is usually asleep, but to-night it is astir for this is Nauruz Allah, the New Year of God, and the narrow streets are full of the soft sound of bare feet moving towards the Nile. The village lies on a strip of ground; one one side is the river, now swollen to its height, on the other are the floods of the inundation spread in a vast sheet of water to the edge of the desert. On a windy night the lapping of wavelets is audible on every hand; but to-night the air is calm and still, there is no sound but the muffled tread of unshod feet in the dust and the murmur of voices subdued in the silence of the night.

In ancient times throughout the whole of Egypt the night of High Nile was a night of prayer and thanksgiving to the great god, the Ruler of the river, Osiris himself. Now it is only in this Coptic village that the ancient rite is preserved, and here the festival is still one of prayer and thanksgiving. In the great cities the New Year is a time of feasting and processions, as blatant and uninteresting as a Lord Mayor's Show, with that additional note of piercing vulgarity peculiar to the East. In this village, far from all great cities, and—as a Coptic community—isolated from and therefore uninfluenced either by its Moslem neighbours or by foreigners, the festival is one of simplicity and piety. The people pray as of old to the Ruler of the river, no longer Osiris, but Christ; and as of old they pray for a blessing upon their children and their homes.

There are four appointed places on the river bank to which the village women go daily to fill their water-jars and to water their animals. To these four places the villagers are now making their way, there to keep the New Year of God.

The river gleams coldly pale and grey; Sirius blazing in the eastern sky casts a narrow path of light across the mile-wide waters. A faint glow low on the horizon shows where the moon will rise, a dying moon on the last day of the last quarter. The glow gradually spreads and brightens till the thin crescent, like a fine silver wire, rises above the distant palms. Even in that attenuated form the moonlight eclipses the stars and the glory of Sirius is dimmed. The water turns to the colour of tarnished silver, smooth and glassy; the palm-trees close at hand stand black against the sky, and the distant shore is faintly visible. The river runs silently and without a ripple in the windless calm; the palm fronds, so sensitive to the least movement of the air, hang motionless and still; all Nature seems to rest upon this holy night.

The women enter the river and stand knee-deep in the running stream praying; they drink nine times, wash the face and hands, and dip themselves in the water. Here is a mother carrying a tiny wailing baby; she enters the river and gently pours the water nine times over the little head. The wailing ceases as the water cools the little hot face. Two anxious women hasten down the steep bank, a young boy between them; they hurriedly enter the water and the boy squats down in the river up to his neck, while the mother pours the water nine times with her hands over his face and shaven head. There is the sound of a little gasp at the first shock of coolness, and the mother laughs, a little tender laugh, and the grandmother says something under her breath, at which they all laugh softly together. After the ninth washing the boy stands up, then squats down again and is again washed nine times, and yet a third nine times; then the grandmother takes her turn, and she also washes him nine times. Evidently he is very precious to the hearts of those two women, perhaps the mother's last surviving child. Another sturdy urchin refuses to sit down in the water, frightened perhaps, for a woman's voice speaks encouragingly, and presently a faint splashing and a little gurgle of childish laughter shows that he too is receiving the blessing of the Nauruz of God.

A woman stands alone, her slim young figure in its wet clinging garments silhouetted against the steel-grey water. Solitary she stands, apart from the happy groups of parents and children; then, stooping, she drinks from her hand once, pauses and drinks again; and so drinks nine times with a short pause between every drink and a longer pause between every three. Except for the movement of her hand as she lifts the water to her lips, she stands absolutely still, her body tense with the earnestness of her prayer, the very atmosphere round her charged with the agony of her supplication. Throughout the whole world there is only one thing which causes a woman to pray with such intensity, and that one thing is children. This may be a childless woman praying for a child, or it may be that, in this land where Nature is as careless and wasteful of infant life as of all else, this is a mother praying for the last of her little brood, feeling assured that on this festival of mothers and children her prayers must perforce be heard. At last she straightens herself, beats the water nine times with the corner of her garment, goes softly up the bank, and disappears in the darkness.

Little family parties come down to the river, a small child usually riding proudly on her father's shoulder. The men often affect to despise the festival as a women's affair, but with memories in their hearts of their own mothers and their own childhood they sit quietly by the river and drink nine times. A few of the rougher young men fling themselves into the water and swim boisterously past, but public feeling is against them, for the atmosphere is one of peace and prayer enhanced by the calm and silence of the night.

For thousands of years on the night of High Nile the mothers of Egypt have stood in the great river to implore from the God of the Nile a blessing upon their children; formerly from a god who demanded a human life as his price, now from a God who Himself has memories of childhood and a Mother. Now, as then, the stream bears on its broad surface the echo of countless prayers, the hopes and fears of human hearts; and in my memory remains a vision of the darkly flowing river, the soft murmur of prayer, the peace and calm of the New Year of God. *Abu Nauruz hallal.*

LIST OF KINGS

The dates of the early dynasties are given according to two authorities, P stands for Petrie, B for Breasted. In and after the New Kingdom the dates are those of Petrie only. The words in brackets give the number of kings and the length of each dynasty as recorded by Manetho (Africanus and Syncellus). The mythical ten kings of Thinis are now included under Dynasty O. For purposes of calculation of the dates, see p. 12.

After the iv-th dynasty the Pharaohs, with few exceptions, took an official name on coming to the throne. This name was an epithet, compounded with the name of the Sun-god Rê; and, like the personal name, was enclosed in a cartouche.

PROTO-DYNASTIC
  Dyn. i. 4777–4514 B.C. (P).
            3400– B.C. (B).
Narmer-Menes
Aha
Zer
Zet
Udy-mu
Merpaba
Semerkhet
Qa
(8 kings. 253 years.)
  Dyn. ii. 4514–4212 B.C. (P).
            — 2980 B.C. (B).
Hotep-ahaui
Ra-neb
Neteri-mu
Perabsen
Kha-sekhem
Ka-ra
Kha-sekhemui
(9 kings. 302 years.)
  Dyn. iii. 4212–3998 B.C. (P).
            2980–2900 B.C. (B).
Sa-nekht
Zoser-Neterkhet
Snefru
(9 kings. 214 years.)

OLD KINGDOM
  Dyn. iv. 3998–3721 B.C. (P).
            2900–2750 B.C. (B).
Shaaru

Khufu
Khafra
Men-kau-Rê
Dadef-Rê
Shepses-kaf
Sebek-ka-Rê
(8 kings. 284 years.)
  Dyn. v. 3721–3503 B.C. (P).
            2750–2625 B.C. (B).
Userkaf
Sahu-Rê
Shepses-ka-Rê
Neferf-Rê
Ni-user-Rê
Men-kau-Hor
Dad-ka-Rê-Ysesi
Wenis
(9 kings. 248 years.)
  Dyn. vi. 3503–3335 B.C. (P).
            2625–2475 B.C. (B).
Tety
User-ka-Rê
Pepy I
Meren-Rê
Pepy II
Mehti-em-saf
Neter-ka-Rê
Queen Neith-aqert
(6 kings. 203 years.)

FIRST INTERMEDIATE PERIOD
  Dyn. vii. 3335– B.C. (P).
            2475– B.C. (B).

(70 Memphite kings who reigned 70
    days.)
Dyn. viii.
(27 Memphite kings. 146 years.)
Dyn. ix.
(19 kings. 409 years.)
Dyn. x. –3005 B.C. (P).
          –2160 B.C. (B).
(10 kings. 185 years.)

MIDDLE KINGDOM

Dyn. xi. 3005–2778 B.C. (P).
Yntef I
Yntef II
Mentu-hotep I
Mentu-hotep II
Mentu-hotep III
Mentu-hotep IV
(16 kings. 43 years. The whole
    number of the above mentioned
    kings is 192, who reigned during
    the space of 2,300 years and 70
    days.)
Dyn. xii. 2778–2565 B.C. (P).
          2000–1788 B.C. (B).
Amonemhat I
Senusert I
Amonemhat II
Senusert II
Senusert III
Amonemhat III
Amonemhat IV
Queen Sebek-nefru
(7 kings. 160 years.)
Dyn. xiii. 2565–2112 B.C. (P).
          1788–   B.C. (B).

SECOND INTERMEDIATE PERIOD

Dyn. xiv. 2112–1928 B.C. (P).
(76 kings. 184 years.)
Dyn. xv. 1928–   B.C. (P).
(Of the Shepherds. 6 foreign Phœni-
    cian kings. 284 years.)
Dyn. xvi. –1738 B.C. (P).
(32 Hellenic Shepherd kings. 518
    years.)

NEW KINGDOM
Dyn. xvii. 1738–1587 B.C. (P).
          –1580 B.C. (B).
Seqenen-Rê I
Seqenen Rê II
Seqenen-Rê III
Kames
(43 Shepherd kings and 43 Theban
    Diospolites. The Shepherds and
    Thebans reigned altogether 151
    years.)
Dyn. xviii. 1587–1375 B.C.
Aahmes I
Amonhotep I
Thothmes I
Thothmes II
Queen Hatshepsut
Thothmes III Men-Kheper-Rê
Amonhotep II
Thothmes IV
Amonhotep III
Amonhotep IV Akhenaten
Smenkh-ka-Rê
Tut-ankh-Amon
Ay
Haremheb
(16 kings. 263 years.)
Dyn. xix. 1375–1202 B.C.
Rameses I
Setekhy I
Rameses II
Mer-en-Ptah
Setekhy II
Amon-mes
Si-Ptah
Setekh-nekht
(7 kings. 209 years.)
(In this second book of Manetho are
    contained 96 kings and 2,121
    years.)
Dyn. xx. 1202–1102 B.C.
Rameses III
Rameses IV
Rameses V
Rameses VI
Rameses VII
Rameses VIII

Rameses IX
Rameses X
(12 kings. 135 years.)

LATE PERIOD
Dyn. xxi. 1102–952 B.C.

Upper Egypt	Lower Egypt
Herihor.	Smendes
Piankhy.	Paseb-khanu I
Pinezem I.	Amonemypt
Masaharta.	Si-Amon
Pinezem II.	Paseb-khanu II

(7 kings. 130 years.)
Dyn. xxii. 952–749 B.C.
Sheshank I
Osorkon I
Takeloth I
Osorkon II
Sheshank II
Takeloth II
Sheshank III
Pamay
Sheshank IV
(9 kings. 126 years.)
Dyn. xxiii. 749–721 B.C.
Piankhy I
Pedubast
Osorkon III
Takeloth III
(4 kings. 28 years.)
Dyn. xxiv. 721–715 B.C.
Bocchoris
(6 years.)
Dyn. xxv. 715–667 B.C.
Shabaka
Piankhy II
Shabataka
Taharka
Tanutamon
(3 kings. 40 years.)
Assyrian Invasion 667 B.C.
Dyn. xxvi 672–525 B.C.
Necho I
Psamtek I
Necho II

Psamtek II
Psamtek III
Apries (Hophra)
Amasis II
Psamtek IV
(9 kings. 150 years and 6 months.)
Persian conquest 525 B.C.

PERSIAN PERIOD
Dyn. xxvii. 525–332 B.C.
(8 Persian kings. 124 years and 4 months.)
Dyn. xxviii.
Amyrteus the Saïte
(6 years.)
Dyn. xxix.
(4 kings. 20 years and 4 months.)
Dyn. xxx. 379–342 B.C.
Nectanebo I
Zeher
Nectanebo II
(3 kings. 38 years.)
(The whole number of years in the third book 1,050 years.)
Conquest by Alexander, 332 B.C.

PTOLEMAIC PERIOD, 332–30 B.C.
Ptolemy I Soter I
Ptolemy II Philadelphus
Ptolemy III Euergetes I
Ptolemy IV Philopator
Ptolemy V Epiphanes
Ptolemy VI Philometor
Ptolemy VII Euergetes II
Ptolemy VIII Eupator
Ptolemy IX Neos Philopator
Ptolemy X Soter II
Ptolemy XI Alexander I
Ptolemy XII Alexander II
Ptolemy XIII Philopator
Ptolemy XIV Philopator
Ptolemy XV Philopator
Cleopatra
Conquest by Octavius, 30 B.C.

BIBLIOGRAPHY

It is impossible to give an exhaustive bibliography of Egyptian Archæo-logy. I have therefore given only a few works of each author mentioned in this list, and the student is advised to refer to the publications of the learned Societies for the Archæology and to the specialist Journals for the language and literature.

BLACKMAN, A. M.   Luxor and its Temples.
—— Les Temples immergés de la Nubie.
BORCHARDT, L.   Das Grabdenkmal des Koenigs Ne-user-Rê.
—— Das Grabdenkmal des Koenigs Sahu-Rê.
BREASTED, J. H.   Ancient Records of Egypt.
—— Development of Religion and Thought in Ancient Egypt.
—— History of Egypt.
BRUNTON, G.   Mostagedda and the Tasian Culture.
BUDGE, E. A. W.   Book of the Dead.
—— The Mummy.
—— The Rosetta Stone.
CAPART, J.   Primitive Art in Egypt.
—— Thebes, the glory of a great Past.
—— Une rue de Tombeaux à Saqqarah.
CARTER, H.   The Tomb of Tutankhamen.
CHAMPOLLION, J.   Monuments de l'Egypte et de la Nubie.
DAVIES, NINA.   Ancient Egyptian Paintings.
DAVIES, N. DE G.   Tomb of Antefoker.
—— Tomb of the Vizier Ramose.
DEVAUD.   Les Maximes de Ptahhotep.
EMERY, W. B.   Archaic Egypt, A Funerary Repast.
ENGELBACH, R.   Ancient Egyptian Masonry.
—— The Problem of the Obelisks.
ERMAN, A.   Aegyptische Grammatik.
—— Handbook of Egyptian Religion.
—— Life in Ancient Egypt.
—— Literature of the Ancient Egyptians.
GARDINER, A. H.   Admonitions of an Egyptian Sage.
—— Attitude of the Ancient Egyptians to Death.
—— Egyptian Hieratic Texts.
—— Egyptian Grammar.
—— Tomb of Amenemhet.
GRIFFITH, F. Ll.   London and Leyden Magical Papyrus.
—— Petrie Papyri.
—— Stories of the High-priests of Memphis.
—— Studies presented to F. Ll. Griffith.

LEPSIUS, R.   Denkmaeler aus Aegypten und Aethiopien.
MARIETTE, A.   Les Mastaba de l'ancien Empire.
—— Le Sérapéum de Memphis.
—— Monuments divers.
MASPERO, G.   Dawn of Civilisation.
—— Egyptian Archæology.
—— Hymne au Nil.
—— Passing of the Empires.
—— Struggle of the Nations.
MURRAY, M. A.   Ancient Egyptian Legends.
—— Egyptian Sculpture.
—— Egyptian Temples.
—— Elementary Egyptian Grammar.
—— Tomb of Two Brothers.
PENDLEBURY, J. D. S.   City of Akhenaten.
—— Tell el Amarna.
PETRIE, W. M. F.   Arts and Crafts of Ancient Egypt.
—— Egypt and Israel.
—— Egyptian Decorative Art.
—— Egyptian Tales.
—— History of Egypt.
—— Illahun, Kahun, and Hawara.
—— Kahun, Gurob, and Hawara.
—— Koptos.
—— Making of Egypt.
—— Medum.
—— Methods and Aims in Archæology.
—— Pyramids and Temples of Gizeh.
—— Religion and Conscience in Ancient Egypt.
—— Revolutions of Civilisation.
—— Tell el Amarna.
—— Tools and Weapons.
—— Wisdom of the Egyptians.
REISNER, G. A.   Mycerinus.
—— Development of the Tombs.
ROSELLINI, N.   I Monumenti dell' Egitto e della Nubia.
SETHE, K.   Das aegyptische Verbum.
SMITH, W. S.   History of Sculpture and Painting in the Old Kingdom.
WAINWRIGHT, G. A.   The Sky Religion in Egypt.
WEIGALL, A. E. P. B.   Guide to the Antiquities of Upper Egypt.
WOOLLEY, C. L.   Digging up the Past.
WRESZINSKI, W.   Atlas zur Altægyptischen Kulturgeschichte.

Journals.

Ancient Egypt.
Annales du Service des Antiquités de l'Egypte.

Journal of Egyptian Archæology.
Proceedings of the Society of Biblical Archæology.
Recueil de Travaux relatives à la philologie et à l'archéologie Egyptiennes et Assyriennes.
Sphinx.
Zeitschrift für Aegyptische Sprache.

Publications of Societies and Museums

British School of Archæology in Egypt.
Catalogue général des antiquités égyptiennes du Musée du Caire.
Cambridge Ancient History.
Description de l'Egypte.
Egypt Exploration Society.
Egyptian Research Account.
Fondation Egyptologique Reine Elisabeth.
Metropolitan Museum of Art.   Egyptian Expedition Publications.
Metropolitan Museum of Art.   Papers.
Mission Archéologique francaise du Caire.

INDEX

INDEX 243

Book of the Dead, 112, 128, 131, 132, 178, 199, 202
Books for the Young, 75
of Thoth, 97
Boomerang, 90
Boy-kings, 18, 39
Bracelets, 5, 180, 182
Brazier, 85
Bread, 2, 86, 87
made by women, 85
Break-bond, 151
Breath of Life, 132
Breccia, 8
Bribery a capital crime, 135
Bricks, Burnt, 151
Sun-dried, 5, 149, 151
Wide spacing of, 150
Bronze, Black, 132, 133, 134
Statuettes, 165, 180
Broome, Miss Myrtle, xiii
Brunton, Mrs. Winifred, xiii
Bubastis, 48
Buddhist missionaries, 222
Building in brick, 150
in stone, 151, 153
in unbonded sections, 150
materials, 146
methods, 150-51, 153
Bull amulets, 5, 9
gods, 98, 99
worship, 98
Bureaucracy under the Ptolemies, 61
Burial customs, 2, 5, 10, 121-25
Burnt offerings, 88
Business letter, 76
Busiris, Centre of Osiris worship, 104
Buto, see Wazt
Buttercup crown, 83, 183
Byblos, Prince of, 67, 216

Cæsarion, son of Cleopatra, 71
Cakes, 86
Calendar, 12, 189
Cambyses the Persian, 53
Canalising of the Cataract, 24, 188
Canals, 26, 52, 54, 60, 61, 284, 285
Candles, 88
Cannibal hymn, 200
Cannibalism, Ceremonial, 5, 104
Canon of proportion, 178
Canopic jars, 122, 123
Canopy, 81
Cape sleeves, 88
Capitals, Coptic, 148
Foliage, 148
Hathor-head, 117, 148
Lotus-bud, 148

Capitals, Rose lotus, 148
Palm-leaf, 148
Capital punishment
by suicide, 47
for bribery, 135
for high treason, 47, 62
for perjury, 62
Career of an architect, 76
of a priest, 77
Carnelian, 181, 231
Cartonnage, 124, 171
Casting by *cire-per due* process, 179, 180
Castor oil, 84, 88
Cataract, 24, 188
Categories of deities, 93
Cats, 96
Cattle breeding, 79-80
Caucasus, 66, 223
Causes of changes in religion, 92
Cedar wood, 67, 132, 133
Celestial river, 128
Cenotaphs, 160, 163
Census of farm animals, 57, 60
Centaurea, 83
Chains, 183
Chairs, 81
Princess's, 82
Changes in religion, 92
of form of government, 22
of names of culprits, 47
Character of Akhenaten, 38
of Hatshepsut, 33
of Hyksos, 27
of Kings of xix-th dynasty, 40-41
of Sahu-Rê, 17
of Thothmes I, 32
of Thothmes III, 36
Charcoal, 85
Chariot, 36, 42, 44, 45, 48, 85-86
Charioteer, 85-86
Cheese, 87
Chequer-board, 9, 91
Children of Horus, 123
Circumnavigation of Africa, 68
Civil service, 61
war, 20, 32, 45, 53, 68
Clapping, 142
Clay, 2, 6, 146
Foreign, 2
mortar, 149, 151
statuettes, 10
used in buildings, 140
Cleopatra, 38, 56, 70-71
Fate of children of, 71
Marriages of, 70-71
Cleopatra, Death of, 113
Clepsydræ, xvii, 190-92